Women Escaping Violence

Women Escaping Violence

E M P O W E R M E N T

T H R O U G H

N A R R A T I V E

Elaine J. Lawless

University of Missouri Press
Columbia and London

Copyright © 2001 by Elaine J. Lawless
University of Missouri Press, Columbia, Missouri 65201
Printed and bound in the United States of America
All rights reserved
5 4 3 2 1   05 04 03 02 01

Library of Congress Cataloging-in-Publication Data

Lawless, Elaine J.
　Women escaping violence : empowerment through narrative / Elaine J. Lawless.
　　p.   cm.
　Includes bibliographical references and index.
　ISBN 0-8262-1314-6 (alk. paper)—ISBN 0-8262-1319-7 (alk. paper)
　1. Abused women—United States.　I. Title.
HV6626.2 .L39 2001
362.82'92'0973—dc21   00-050795

⊗™ This paper meets the requirements of the
American National Standard for Permanence of Paper
for Printed Library Materials, Z39.48, 1984.

Text design: Stephanie Foley
Jacket design: Vickie Kersey DuBois
Typesetter: BOOKCOMP, Inc.
Printer and binder: Thomson-Shore, Inc.
Typefaces: Crackhouse, GilSans, and Minion

Two of the chapters in this book have appeared in different form as "Transformative Stories: Women Doing Things with Words," in *Journal of Applied Folklore* 4, no. 1 (1999): 61–77, and as "Transformative Re-membering: De-scribing the Unspeakable in Battered Women's Narratives," in *Southern Folklore* 57, no. 1 (1999): 65–79.

I dedicate this book to all the women

who daily endure violence in their lives,

to those who have escaped,

and to those who have died

at the hands of men who say they loved them

and in memory of my grandmothers,

Erma Helvey Dunlap and Mary Cole Lawless,

whose lives I have only begun to imagine

through the writing of this book,

and for my mother, Angie Mae Dunlap Lawless,

who now has time to savor a cup of tea

A wife isn't a jug...
She won't crack if you hit her ten times.

RUSSIAN PROVERB

Because of the angels—

I commend you because you remember me in everything and maintain the traditions just as I handed them on to you. But I want you to understand that Christ is the head of every man, and the husband is the head of his wife, and God is the head of Christ. Any man who prays or prophesies with something on his head disgraces his head, but any woman who prays or prophesies with her head unveiled disgraces her head—it is one and the same thing as having her head shaved. For if a woman will not veil herself, then she should cut off her hair; but if it is disgraceful for a woman to have her hair cut off or to be shaved, she should wear a veil. For a man ought not to have his head veiled, since he is the image and reflection of God; but woman is the reflection of man. Indeed, man was not made from woman, but woman from man. Neither was man created for the sake of woman, but woman for the sake of man. For this reason a woman ought to have a symbol of authority on her head, because of the angels.

I Corinthians 11:2–10

MY BIRTHDAY

I went to hell this week
   alone.

I watched a man with gaping mouth
   scream with no sound.
Bent above the body of his dead wife,
he'd been screaming, thusly, for a million
   years
knife in hand.

Below another knife I saw
a man and woman tear asunder
   a child
who had trusted both without question
but finally questioned both the same.

And, then, a mirror image of myself
showed me the door and handed me
   a bloody key.

I escaped
   wounded, but free.

ELAINE J. LAWLESS
SEPTEMBER 29, 1978

Contents

Acknowledgments

MOST IMPORTANT, I MUST thank all the women who made the writing of this book possible. Sadly, I cannot name them here, but I thank them all, in my heart, and name them silently.

I thank my family for nourishing my soul and providing for me a safe and loving space in which to live and work. Sandy Rikoon, Jessie, and Kate helped me survive the writing of this book, listening, encouraging, and holding me sometimes when I simply needed to cry. I am blessed by their presence in my life. And from a distance, my son, Alex, continues to help me to learn how to be a mom as I also work at teaching and writing.

I thank all the women in the domestic violence movement who welcomed me into their work spaces and taught me so much. Especially, I am grateful to the warmth and acceptance of Victoria Godino Constance, Pat Glasier, Karen Johnson, Betty Acree, Wanda Thatcher, Sandy Lillard, Jan Parentau, and so many others I came to know working in the close quarters of the office of the local shelter. They taught me how to continue the work that needs to be done, even while my heart was breaking. And my deepest gratitude to Pat and Karen, who read every word of this book and helped make the work as reciprocal as possible, given the unusual and difficult circumstances. I also thank Lisa Montgomery and Sharon Farquhar, who helped me complete the tedious job of transcribing the tapes of the women in this study, and sometimes added at no charge their own perceptions of what they were hearing.

I thank all my students at the University of Missouri, who convince me daily that I chose the right career. I especially thank my graduate students (and co-teachers), who challenge me daily and make me think about the enterprise we call ethnographic writing. Their intelligence and profound sense of ethics inspire me always to try harder. In this light, I especially thank Janet Alsup, Carolyn Bening, Kenn DeShane, Deb Forsman, Kristen Harmon, Lisa Higgins, Heather Hignite, Reinhold Hill, Yolanda Hood, Jamilia Jones, Todd Lawrence, Jackie McGrath, Ginny Muller, Lucia Pawlawski, Anthony Phillips, and Lucy Stanovich, all of whom have talked with me about this book, read parts of it, and helped me through the rough spots. My gratitude also goes to Amy Wilson, the artist who created the powerful painting that graces the front of this book.

And I thank my dear friends and colleagues in Columbia and at the University of Missouri—Gertrude Lindener-Stawski, Kim Ryan, Sharon Welch, Win Horner, and Mary Lago—who listened to me as I worked my way through the writing of this book and heard perhaps far more than they ever wanted to hear about the lives of women living in violence. And I thank Beverly Jarrett at the University of Missouri Press, who encouraged me to let Missouri publish this book and made me feel special in the process.

Finally, I wish to thank the University of Missouri Research Council for funding this research.

Prelude   REFLECTIONS ON A MONDAY MORNING AT THE SHELTER

MONDAY MORNINGS ARE DIFFICULT. I come into the shelter office and read the staff log and the "action cards" that have been filled out over the weekend. Weekends are always bad. Fridays, people get their paychecks and go drinking or worse. Some start Friday afternoon and drink or shoot their way through the entire weekend, pausing only late Sunday night in a futile attempt to face a bleak Monday morning. At the same rate, it seems, the vibes in the shelter begin to change late Friday afternoon and the place is even busier over the weekend. We are the official place to obtain ex partes or orders of protection when the courthouse office is closed, which ironically enough is usually after lunch on Friday until Monday morning. It's like a conspiracy; they close up shop when women most often face the rages of their abusers, and when their kids are home from school. Everything is intensified. And in the winter, the kids are underfoot—bored, forced to be indoors; the television is blasting; the smaller ones scream because they are hungry, or wet, or they are exhausted from no sleep during the loud and abusive nights. They search the apartment for their mother, who may by now be crouched below a table in a far closet or sitting in the cold on a back step, stealing a quick cigarette, a beer, a quiet minute to nurse a black eye, her broken or bruised ribs, the ripping pain in her head from his grip on her hair.

Her hand unconsciously moves to the worst of the pain on her head and notes with very little effort and no surprise that she can feel her scalp—that place on her head actually has no hair anymore at all. Her fingers absently caress the tender spot. She wonders if it will grow back, not really caring anymore one way or another; her fingers urge the hair from the edges, though, to cover the gaping hole. Maybe a bow or a comb will help; a different hairdo, a hat? From there her mind's eye moves down onto her face, wondering how bad it looks. She wonders if anything is broken. Maybe her nose . . . she tries to gently move the muscles in her face, exploring the possibilities. The cigarette smoke makes her eyes water and her nose burn. She can move it a bit. Hard to tell. It's been broken before. She really cannot recall what it once looked like; was it pert? Turned up? Long and aristocratic? She cannot remember. She doesn't think she has any pictures anymore from her teen years. Somehow that might help her figure how she got to where she is now—

xv

a picture from the past, before all the boyfriends, before the babies, before the abuse and the fights began, before the money got so scarce and the drinking got so bad.

She can hear the little ones calling her, crying. She tries not to respond, but she feels her breasts swell and the milk begin to drip onto her naked stomach. She is as still as a mouse, unaware that the misty rain has begun to sting her face, rest gently on her eyelashes, caress the aching bald space. She shivers involuntarily, trying to hug herself, but knowing her wrenched arm and fragile bones cannot comfort her this morning. The wind gently blows the folds of her thin nightgown. She pulls the edges in between her knees and bends over as far as she can without falling forward off the unstable wooden step, which is already at a slant, and without mashing her aching breasts too much. The cries from inside grow more insistent. Her breasts are unbearable; they embody a pain that is greater even than that of her arm, her nose, her head. She needs to go back inside, she knows; yet she remains still on the step, praying for—what? She doesn't have a clue. Perhaps to die. Right there in the cold rain on the step, to freeze until there is no pain left, until she can feel nothing, until she cannot hear the children's cries, until she cannot feel the fear, the aches, the broken bones, her bare head. Death seems like such a promise and a blessing. Could she just sit there for hours and hours and hours until she actually disappeared?

She sits bolt upright when the battered screen door opens suddenly into the small of her back. She yelps as she feels his hand pull painfully hard on her hair, pulling her back into the kitchen. "What do you think you're doing out there, you stupid bitch? Git in here and feed these stupid kids. They're making all this god-awful racket. I can't hear myself think. I can't hear the T.V. And where's my breakfast? Do you think there's a maid or something going to come in and do all your work? I don't think so. This place is a pigsty—you useless whore!"

His hand pulls back. She watches it as though she's in a dream. She has no time to duck or scream before it strikes the side of her face and her own ear begins to scream, ringing and ringing deep in her head. And her eye won't open for a few minutes, even though she's crying and trying to blink as she pulls a dirty pan from the sink to start some eggs. In the same motion, she swoops the smallest child from the floor, creating a quick shelf for her with her right hip and offering her breast, even as she turns on the burner, trying hard not to collapse onto the dirty linoleum floor, trying to ignore the ringing in her ear. Later, she thinks, when he leaves for more beer or passes out on the sofa, she'll call that 1–800 number she wrote down on the back page of the phone book. She will call the women's shelter. Maybe they can help. She just may not make it through another weekend here. She just may not make it.

* * * *

The hot line lights up as the phone rings at the shelter. I dread these calls. I just hope I can ask all the right questions. "This is the shelter," I answer the phone. "Can I help you?" hoping fervently that I can. I reach for the intake sheet even as I begin to speak.

HOT-LINE INTAKE CALLS

Date: *January 28, 1998*
Start time of call: *8:30* A.M.
End time: *8:40* A.M.
Staff/vol initials: *EL*
Victim's Name: *anonymous woman*   City: County:
Caller's Name (if different):   Agency:

IMMEDIATE PROBLEM:

Physical Abuse	*Self*	Chronic/frequent caller:	
Emotional Abuse	*Self*	Ex Parte Info:	
Threat of Abuse	*Self*	Homeless:	
Past Abuse	*Self*	Incest:	
DV Counseling	*Self*	Divorce counseling:	
Rape/Sexual Assault	*Self/Other*	Custody counseling:	
Child Sexual Abuse	*Self/Other*	Suicide counseling:	
Child Abuse	*Self*	Police problems:	
Child Counseling	*Self/Other*	Prosecutor/court problems:	
Abuser Counseling	*Self/Other*	$ Assistance requests:	
Stalking	*Self/Other*	Other: (list)	
Rape	*Self/Other*		

IF CALLER HAS BEEN ABUSED, ASK:
Are you safe? *No*   Are you hurt? *Yes*
Name of abuser/rapist? *Will not give name*
Relationship to victim? *Husband*   Where are you now? *Home*
Can you get to safety? *Probably not*   What do you want to do? *Leave*

IF CALLER WANTS SHELTER OR COUNSELING, ASK:
Have you ever stayed at the shelter? *Yes*   If yes, when, where? *Last year*
Ages and genders of children coming into shelter? *Three girls, 6, 2, 18 months*

Approved for shelter? (Call Supervisor) *Yes*

SAFETY PLANNING:

Do you feel safe where you are? *No*   If not, where can you go? *Nowhere*

What are your safe places? *Only the shelter*

Will your abuser find you in these "safe places"? *Not at the shelter*

Do you have a way to get to the safe place? *No, cab*

Can you arrange for transportation and a safe place in case you need them?
Cab?

DESCRIBE THE CALLER'S SITUATION:

Anonymous woman called in around 8:30 A.M. Husband has left house for
a few minutes. She seems pretty terrified. She has been beaten several times
this week, possibly broken nose, wrenched arm, hair pulled out. He's drinking
a lot and gets more abusive when he's drinking. He's not working and just
hanging around the house. She hasn't been to work in 2 1/2 weeks, thinks she's
probably lost her job. No money. The heat has been turned off and the kids
are getting hungry. She's nursing the youngest still. She doesn't have a car. She
would like to come into shelter and she'll call a cab to get here. She's really
afraid of him and thinks the violence will escalate in the next few days. She's
afraid he'll put her in the hospital or maybe even kill her.

DESCRIBE YOUR ACTIONS:

Asked her what she wanted to do. Called the director to see if she could get
approval to come in. I am frustrated because we are basically full and there's
really no room for a woman and three kids. Had to tell her to call back, but
also told her that if it gets worse we will "make room for them." Also told her
we could call other shelters and try to relocate her to a different town if she
wanted to do that. Asked her what his response will be to her leaving; he'll
be very angry, she says. Last year it was only worse after she went into shelter
then went back home. This time, she says, she will not go back. But (she was
crying) she really does not know where she can go. Her mother and her sister
are tired of taking her in and helping her with the kids. She probably doesn't
have a job and things are looking really, really bad for her. I tried to encourage
her to be strong and get her stuff together so she could leave and told her to
be sure and call us back as soon as she could.

I wondered if we'd ever hear from her again.

* This is the form used at the shelter to document every hot-line call we receive.
This is not a record of an actual call, but it could have been.*

Prologue PUTTING THINGS INTO PERSPECTIVE

I SPENT TODAY IN my office at the university. I worked with my deluxe computer, talked with my colleagues, and met with my graduate students, all of whom have been missing me, they say. I've been gone from them. For months, I have been actually only a few blocks away from this academic world, a mere five minutes by car, across Main, over on Butler, but moving without question toward that "other" part of town where there are noticeably fewer streetlights and the projects look dim in the early, winter twilight. There are more bare bulbs on the porches here; people walk more; I lock my doors anxiously. And I am even more anxious as I park in the shelter parking lot and get out of my car, glance around to see that no one is lurking, lock my doors, buzz to enter the building, hear the familiar solid door locking behind me. Safe.

Ironically, I do not feel "safe" in this safe shelter. It is the most unsafe space in my current life, in fact. Lucky for me, I feel I am "safe" in my own home; I am "safe" in my university office; "safe" on the Internet and in my classes. But here I am not safe from the fears and dangers that come through the front door with all of the women who flee violence to hide here. I am not safe from their black eyes, broken noses, their split lips, the eyes of their children. I spent the entire day on campus today because I feel as though I'm losing my self. I forget who I am in other places. I forget that I know how to teach, how to write, how to get grants, how to run committees with finesse. Those skills haven't transferred to this space and to the needs of the women who are in residence here. They ask me real-life questions I cannot answer. I feel very ignorant at the shelter. Someone wants to know about an ex parte hearing, someone else wants to know the AFDC (Aid to Families with Dependent Children) regulations, someone else wants to know about child custody, another about pro bono lawyers, another about the rules concerning their husbands and boyfriends bonding out of jail. Their questions are constant; I'm really proud of myself when I know the answer. Aha, I'm so pleased. I got asked that question last week and now I know the answer, or at least I know who to call to get the answer, or part of the answer, or, no, that answer was particular to that other woman and really wouldn't apply to you because you're from another county, or a different state, or the abuse was a little different, or you've got six kids, not two; well, maybe I don't really know the answer. I guess I really cannot help you. I'm sorry.

These days I've got a knot in my stomach that never really goes away. I'd like to be able to just "turn it off" when I walk out the door and leave the scene, depart the premises, say good-bye until tomorrow. But the faces haunt me now; they go with me in my car, they go home with me, they sleep with me, they live in my dreams. When the women leave and go "back home"—which does not mean they go back to their mothers; it means they go back to their abusive partners and husbands—I want to scream and shout, but I don't. I don't even cry, at least on the outside. Inside, I am often crying, and as I drive away the tears release, spill down my face. But to work here you learn quickly that for every woman who leaves the shelter, there are two more coming in who need your attention—and who do not need to see your tears about the one who wouldn't stay more than three or four days, who just stayed until the pain subsided, and her eye opened up a tiny crack, and the black and purple changed to a garish yellow-green. Then, yes, then, she would think about the consequences and go back home. But someone else was right there, in that mental snapshot, staring at me over the top of the half door, asking me new questions or old ones with a new twist. I don't have time to grieve. And, besides, many of them come back. There she is again. The same face, new questions, new bruises.

I feel completely and absolutely inadequate here. My doctorate, my books, my degrees, my teaching awards, whatever has defined me for the past decade and more, means little. I am identified as a provider of services. I need to get some things done to provide some aid, assistance, safety, shelter, and help to women in need. That's all. There are counselors to hear their stories and try to empower them to sort through tomorrow and the next day, the next week at the most. There are staff people prepared to support them as they apply for food stamps, get on the waiting list for Section 8 housing, get a Medicaid card for them and for their children. There are court advocates who will help them fill out ex partes, go to court hearings to file them, talk with the prosecutor, get a lawyer, get an order of protection. We are a place of resources; if we cannot provide what they need, we will telephone around until we find an advocate or an expert or an administrative official who can perhaps help them do what they need to do. There are people from START (the Sexual Trauma Assault Response Team) to meet them in the emergency room if they have been raped, a helper, and a nurse to make sure they get in immediately.

My tears are for their broken homes and their broken faces, for the hideous and frightening lives of their children, for their nightmares, and for me, because my tears are no help to them at all. Who needs my tears? Get over it, Wilma tells me. You cannot help her that way. Find a way to help her. You find it unfair—well, that's original. You are right: It's not fair that *she* had to leave in the quiet hours of the darkest part of the night to come here, leaving all that she owns and holds dear, with the exception, perhaps, of her children. It's not fair that he beat her to a pulp, and she sees her time here as a chance to "just get away for a while" and let this thing cool down. It's not fair that she's looking at no work, no money, no food, no transportation, no hope, no future, no child care, no family or friends—while maybe, at home, right now, he's stretched out on the sofa watching T.V. It's not fair that she has to come into what feels a bit like a prison, with its lockdown, curfews, and anonymous location—while he runs around "outside" free. Life's not fair, Elaine. Get a grip. And no, you cannot drive her down to the bank to see if her new AFDC card is activated and drop her kids off at school for her because she didn't think to get her car before he bonded out of jail. It's not allowed. You cannot drive her anywhere. And one more thing: don't get too chummy. You seem to be the type to want to be these women's friend. Don't. Build a wall: Build a wall around your emotions, and build a wall between yourself and these women. Don't get attached—don't ask too many questions; don't learn too much; don't start caring more than the necessary, prerequisite amount. Help her do what she needs to do. And Elaine, make certain you are helping her do what *she* wants to do, not what you want her to do, *not what you want her to do*. But it's so clear, I think: Here's what she needs to do. She could go this afternoon; she could get a friend to . . . but, no, she hasn't even thought of that as a possibility. And, no, it wouldn't be appropriate for me to suggest it.

I'm stymied, frustrated, and angry. My stomach hurts sometimes. And today I had to get away—it felt so freeing, so good, to just not go over there—the place can suck you dry. Why is that? Maybe because you feel so helpless. Maybe because there is so little you can actually do that you need to do it more and more and more and more. I've obsessed on this place; I'm over there more than I'm in my university office. Oh, sure, I can say it's because I'm a good ethnographic researcher and I am over there to get the flavor of the place, to know it from the inside out, to be a worker there alongside the other staff, to rub shoulders with the residents, know them by name, know something of their situations, their stories, their plans, their frustrations. I could claim it's about ethnographic immersion in the shelter culture. And there *is* a shelter culture, to be sure. No doubt about that. It's a transient group, bonded by violence and circumstances too dangerous and too insidious, too private, to ever really say aloud outside these walls. These are mothers sharing a kitchen, caring for each other's children, sharing and stealing each other's cigarettes. And it is, like prison, a dangerously volatile situation, rife with petty jealousies, inconsistent stories, lies, fears, abusive behaviors learned and impossible to park at the curb. And I cannot stop myself from going there, week after bloody week.

Women Escaping Violence

Introduction GATHERING STORIES

A murder suspect who was the subject of an intense manhunt this weekend surrendered at 1:50 A.M. today in police headquarters.

Mark Hammett, 34, has been charged with first-degree murder and armed criminal action in the stabbing death of his ex-girlfriend, Christina Kinder. . . .

Police . . . said Kinder was stabbed at least nine times in the upper torso.

[A neighbor of Kinder's mother] described Hammett as "a control freak." . . .

[Kinder] wrote in a request for an order of protection that Hammett held a shotgun to her head and threatened to kill her that night. He also struck her several times, bruising her jaw, chest and shoulder. . . .

. . . Hammett had a history of stalking Kinder. [He] left as many as 29 messages on her answering machine in one day.

[Neighbors] said they had seen Hammett around the trailer park, spying on Kinder. . . . [One] pointed to a sheltered area amid tall weeds where the grass was flattened, saying Hammett lay there concealed to watch Kinder. . . .

Columbia Daily Tribune,
December 7, 1998

THE AUTHOR'S STORY

I WANT TO TELL you about the stories in this book, and about the person who is your guide through this tricky terrain. As the author, I want to serve *not* as an "authority" on domestic violence, but as an educated and spiritually motivated guide. I do not undertake this responsibility lightly. As a researcher and as someone who learns by listening carefully to the voices of women, whether in oral or literary form, I find much in the women's stories gathered for this book to ponder, study, and share with you, the reader. As your guide through this dangerous and frightful landscape, I intend to keep my presence known.

I have been altered by the experience of this work, and like anthropologist Ruth Behar, I believe that no work is worthy of our time and attention unless it "breaks our hearts."[1] This means that I agree to be a living human being guiding the reader through the pages of this book that I have crafted out of my work at the shelter, my experiences answering the hot line, my listening to women's stories in every imaginable space, my community work for justice and safety for women, and my own reconstructing of my mother's and my grandmother's stories as I have attempted to acknowledge the way violence has affected my own life. I acknowledge and embrace both the personal and the political in this work; to do otherwise would be to make the work a farce, to render it ineffective and corrupt. I believe we must accept that our lives must have meaning in order to insure that they *do* have meaning. We cannot merely live; we must work for justice. If we do, then our life will have meaning. This is a work for justice. I will be your guide to help you see what I have seen and, hopefully, to make a difference in how you see and understand the ways violence affects all of our lives.

On a more personal note, I believe I was drawn to this work because I, too, survived an abusive marriage. To write that sentence requires almost more strength than I can muster. In fact, I wrote this entire book without writing that sentence. I have come back now, at the end of this book journey, to admit that I have a story, too. In our time, writing about one's self has become a professional imperative—that is, we are required now to acknowledge our cultural and social "baggage," our biases and our political leanings, to the extent to which we are able to recognize these and admit to them—but such writing may also lead to a dangerous fall into the trap of selfish indulgence. Thus, I have been more than a little reluctant to place myself into the narrative of this book. Yet as the book came full circle, I realized that working on the book and with the women's stories repeatedly invoked my own story, in a kind of narrative imperative that should be honored for the book to become "whole."

The poem entitled "My Birthday" in the front pages is my own poem. I want to claim that moment in my own history. It is my escape poem, and like the stories of the women in this book it bears a conflicted story, ambiguous in its rendering of the child for the sake of the mother's freedom. There are no magical formulas for escape and safety here; these are not fairy tales with happy endings, and tomorrow's story may hold a different ending from the one offered today. But they are real stories, and they are true stories. In fact, the truth to which they bear witness is a truth that I fear reflects the lives of many, if not most, women who live in intimate relationships with men. This may seem harsh, and I am ready for those who will renounce such sweeping judgments. But the evidence is still pouring in; the stories are still accumulating. Women are eager to tell their narratives, and they ask me to "take their stories"—for telling them validates a life, names the abuse, honors the escape. Like me, they have fled, "wounded but free."

To say I have endured and escaped an abusive marriage will, on one level, endorse this work. I know of which I speak. Daily I am reminded in one way or another how the abuse that I left more than twenty years ago still manages to affect my life, my sense of well-being, my self-esteem. But the importance of my own story goes far beyond the effects of that abusive relationship. To ground my life in the reality that binds the stories of the women in this study, I must also go back to my own childhood, to my mother's life, and to her mother's life. It is in the reflection of the truth of those stories that my own takes shape; honoring them with naming is part of the important work to be done as well. Later in this book, I will try to weave those stories into the frame set by the women who tell their stories here.

So, you ask, and I ask myself, how did I come to write this book? I am not currently in an abusive marriage, my life is good and happy and wholesome and supportive. What could possibly have drawn me to write about battered women? Why did I want to locate shelters, enter them, listen to women's stories, find out about their survival in violence and their escapes? I believe we are drawn to life work that bears meaning for us. That is not to say that our research and writing is "merely" therapeutic, in a kind of simplistic formula, but rather in ways that admit to our seeking knowledge and understanding where we most desire and search for it. Yet to study and think and write about ideas or concepts that have no relation to our personal *beings* seems futile and empty. In my past work, I have certainly been drawn to the study of women and religion because of my own sense that something is askew when women's experiences are left out of the narrative that defines what is religious and spiritual. That work has fed me wondrously and generously for years, and I am grateful for work that has true meaning and nurtures my mind as well as my soul. I am presently closer to this work on battered women and cannot articulate quite so profusely how and why I came to this study.

We are all at different stages in the telling of our lives. But the importance of speaking becomes clearer to me by the day. No one said this would be easy. It isn't. And the journey for the reader into this particular house of horrors should be undertaken with caution. Beware: There are horrendous stories ahead, terrors that will chill you and cause you to turn away. This is not a book for the weak. But listening to the stories is an active counterpart to the telling of the stories. The speakers need you to listen, and they will, simply by their bravery and their verbal skills, invite you to "hear" them. And that action will invite you to participate as well. It is in this way that I propose that the book becomes an exercise in dialogue: The women in these pages tell you and me their stories; maybe then, I can tell mine and you can tell yours, or at least acknowledge your own story to yourself. It is the collective story we need to expose, to speak, and to hear, recognizing at the same time that each story in and of itself is significant, different, and personal.

My field research for this book was conducted throughout the state of Missouri; at first, I traveled from shelter to shelter with my friend Victoria, who worked with the Missouri Coalition Against Domestic Violence (MCADV). These visits with Victoria were an attempt to ascertain whether the "community response efforts" that had been established throughout the state (linking the efforts of shelters, police, courts, and communities) were effectively working for the women involved. These were poignant first introductions for me, and a whole range of images lingers in my mind to this day. One shelter fades into another. I don't remember where I heard any given story; individual women's faces merge with other women's faces, although one or two are still crystal clear even years later. Early on, I certainly had no reference for putting these experiences, the stories, the shelters, into any kind of perspective. That first hot summer I was just a "visitor" traveling around, soaking up information, smells, sounds, voices, and viscerally responding to what I heard and saw. I nearly vomited as we fled from one particularly horrendous situation when we realized a young girl's mind had simply escaped into the safety of madness as she tried to tell us how her stalker had over and over managed to push his way into her house, her bedroom, her body, defying the police, orders of protection, bolt locks on the door, alarm systems, until her brain was mush. Vic and I sat in the 107-degree heat on the concrete curb in a small town in southern Missouri and wept together after hearing her story, then tried to leave to our own better worlds, only to find we were locked out of her steaming car and had to suffer there for four more hours, unable to go back into the shelter, for what we feared inside was more dangerous than the heat we had to endure on the outside.

That fall, I signed up to take the requisite forty hours of volunteer training and then began to work at a local shelter, drawn to the work as to a light. What this work had to do with my own life was a mystery to me. I only knew that I wanted to dedicate some of the hours of my work week to helping at the shelter. I had never really done volunteer work before; my life with teaching and writing, caring for a household, and raising three children and some sheep had kept me thoroughly busy and content. It was not out of boredom that I sought to add another, and disturbing, aspect to my life; I loved the work, although it was extraordinarily difficult to work there. And soon I knew something: I was destined to write a book about women living in and escaping violence. At first I had no idea what this book might look like or be "about." But working there was the first step, I knew. I should be at the shelter; I should work there. I should observe, on a regular basis, the life in the shelter, the work of the staff, and listen carefully to the stories of the women residents. For more than a year, I was exposed to life in the shelter as well as the intersections of shelter life and the court system, police, shelter workers, counselors, lawyers, social agencies, and abusers. I heard stories all the time in the shelter, and narratives are something I study. So it was the stories that led to the work for this book.

THE CHAPTERS IN THIS BOOK

Because the stories in this book are solicited stories, they represent, in some ways, narratives that exist apart from the times and places in which the women would normally share parts of their stories. Most of the women who graciously shared their stories on tape for me have never been asked to tell their entire narrative before. Only certain parts of their stories have been told, and honed, and told again, in different contexts. Chapter 1, "Safe and Unsafe Living," is an ethnographic foray into shelter life, a story told from the author's point of view; I retell stories heard in the shelter from women who live there. In Chapter 2, I deal with how the women must tell their stories to acquire shelter in the first place and how they then use these stories to seek and obtain different kinds of services—prosecution against their abusers, orders of protection, custody of their children. And yet there are aspects of violence that the narrators cannot speak; this is the subject of Chapter 3, "Describing the Unspeakable." I am interested in women's language—how they tell what they are able to tell, how they use disclaimers, and how they articulate theories they have about the way the world is put together. I will examine the ways in which they recount violence, and how both language and silence work together to tell what is actually "unspeakable." In Chapters 4 and 5, I explain how the women tell the stories of their childhood memories and how they talk about themselves and their families. I was curious about whether or not they would render themselves as "victims" in their narratives, and how they portray their own subjectivity. In Chapter 6, I explore how they describe their interactions with their abusive and violent partners, and how they convey the terror of the incidences that compelled them to flee and seek the safety of the shelter. In my conclusion, I look back at my own life, and my mother's and my grandmother's lives; in doing so, I draw us all into the collective story of sadness and abuse. Importantly, this book concludes with four life narratives, verbatim and complete as recorded on tape. By including the entire transcriptions, I respect the holistic power of their stories and emphasize the empowerment that comes with the telling of their stories.

TRUTH IN STORYTELLING

One thing I am *not* particularly interested in is trying to determine whether or not the accounts the women gave to me are "accurate" or "truthful" in some historical or "factual" sense. By saying this, I am actually contesting the notion that "truth" exists or that one account might be more "truthful" than another. I honor the stories I receive as gifts of their imagination at that moment in time. I believe the narratives reveal a "truth" about how the women view themselves and their world as reflected in these narratives. How they "see" themselves on that given day clearly directs their narrative. As far as we are concerned, there is no other truth than that one.

"Truth" is relative, although I am cognizant of the dangers of saying that so bluntly. I accept the truth of the telling. I believe most of what these women recount is, in fact, very close to a historical rendering of incidences they have experienced, told from their position and their subjectivity within the experience, as well as in the way they are able to reconstruct and come to terms with it in the later retelling. Certainly, what they tell me are the ways they have framed their lives in order to keep living. They must, it seems, sort out their life experiences in such a way that makes sense, given where they are now living. They have brought a few belongings, and possibly their children; they come broken and broke and vulnerable into a safe shelter. The past must justify and explain this present moment, the "now" of where they are today. And telling their stories, framing their lives for me and my tape recorder, may actually help them frame or reframe how they approach tomorrow. The story each woman tells for me (and for herself) is a story that crafts a "self" that evolves from her earliest memories to this present moment. The telling provides a kind of re-collecting of the parts of her "self," a making sense of the past, a restructuring of what seem to be disparate parts of their being into the construction that is now the "I" of her voiced narrative. Her voice, then, becomes the embodiment of her "self." I see this act of voicing the self as a healthy one for any one of us. For, otherwise, we must carry around in our mind, in our consciousness, in our flesh and our bones, those disembodied, separate encounters. The telling becomes the glue to holding some of our memories together to create a newly constructed holistic self. As Janie asserted when she finished her story, "That's my story and I'm sticking to it." Her story was news to me. I don't know any better than to believe the story I was told. It is, for me, a true and honest telling. But the telling, for her, has made a difference in how she sees herself.

The telling gives her the opportunity to craft a narrative self that has cohesion and meaning, with reference to past and future, one that can rationalize and justify her shortcomings and her bravery alike. "This is who I am. Thanks for asking." She walks out different from when she walked in.

LIFE STORIES RESEARCH

Orally constructed life stories are a special breed of narrative. Unlike literary autobiography or memoir, or the shorter stories told spontaneously in the shelter, life stories have not been self-consciously rendered over time, with many rewritings or retellings, although certain stories within this larger story certainly have been. To large measure, most of the women with whom I talked have not been exposed to the current explosion of literary nonfiction that has emerged in the academy and among the reading public. Consciously or unconsciously, the women who tell these stories to me are crafting stories for my, and for their, immediate consumption. I am aware that the simple fact of my requesting their stories imbues them with an importance they have probably never encountered before. I believe that during the time they spend telling me their stories, they feel empowered. When they agree to "give" me their stories, I agree to sit alone with them for hours and listen attentively to the lives they have lived—or the version of those lives they choose to share with me. Many of the women in this study are not very well educated, all of them have been abused most of their lives, and most of them are in a position of extreme imbalance at the current moment, in terms of their living conditions and the level of anxiety, fear, and pain they are enduring. And yet every one of them who agreed to participate has taken the time out of her chaotic current condition to calmly tell me her story. She has made arrangements for her children to be cared for by another shelter resident, or a friend, or a relative. She has carved out enough time to sit quietly with me and recount a life of difficulty and confusion. The miracle is that most of the stories I tape recorded for this study are surprisingly coherent by any measure. I agree with Ruth Behar that the genres of life history and life story are merging in some contexts with her concept of *testimonio*, which "speaks to the role of witnessing in our time as a key form of approaching and transforming reality." That might be one way to frame the thesis of this book, in fact. The women in this book are "bearing witness" to motivate listeners, and themselves, "to participate in the struggle against injustice."[2]

In terms of research parameters, I know that my request that they tell me their "life story" and my asking that they include the stories of violence in their lives directed the kinds of narratives I received from them. But those were my goals: to hear their stories of violence and to be able to "hear" these stories of violence within the context of a life lived. At one point in my research I recognized that I was saying more than "tell me your life story"; I would often add: "begin at the beginning with your earliest memories." The one or two times that I consciously did *not* add on the directive, "begin with your earliest memories," I heard a story that was delivered in an achronological manner, beginning with the present moment in the narrating woman's life and looping back, over and over again, pulling in different moments in her life, until she ended with "her earliest memories" as a child. Although this altered the form of the narrative somewhat, the end process and product remained similar.

In principle, most of the life stories adhere to a chronological sequence of life events, beginning with their "earliest memories." I acknowledge my influence on this fact, however. When I tape recorded each woman's story, I told her that I was writing a book about domestic violence and that I wanted to be certain I included the "voices of women who had been abused and battered" in the book itself. I also told them that I wanted not only the stories of abuse in their lives, but to receive from them their "entire life story," with the stories of violence embedded in that life story. My reasoning for this, I explained to each of them, was to try to make some sense of how we encounter violence in our lives, how we deal with it, how we endure and escape from it, how we survive—or don't. This made sense to them. They were willing to tell their life stories and make certain the stories of violence were included. What I did not expect was to discover, as Nelle Morton might have told me all long, that "the journey is home."[3] That is, it became apparent to me as the work progressed that the very act of telling their stories, and our own, is the significance of the project. What is important is not so much what we can learn about a life of violence by listening to the women's stories, although certainly we learn a great deal about that in the process; it is what we can learn about the significance of speaking, through the act of telling our story, that becomes the significant moment, the *now* of the process.

The reader will find that the women's stories differ in many ways, both in content and style, although their similarities are indeed striking. It is also evident that women who are the furthest from violence and abuse in their lives deliver the most recognizably "coherent" stories and their stories are more likely to include thoughtful reflections upon what has happened to them. Stories from women who are newcomers to the shelter, who are perhaps only hours, days, or weeks from living in fear and violence, deliver narratives that may seem more rambling or less sure in their assertions about why things happened, how they escaped, or where they are going next. I find this completely understandable. Readers of this book who are currently living in violent relationships may "hear" in these women's stories many things that parallel their own experiences. They may also hear stories that are unlike anything they have encountered. What I also hope they hear, because it is part of the move toward healing, is that the women who are furthest from the abuse are the ones who offer the greatest hope for recovery, safety, and a life free from violence. The women in the support group *know* they can learn from each other, and they are not asking each other how to dodge the next blow. They are asking for escape routes, for education, for tools with which to work the system, for strategies, for strength, and for hope and survival. The readers of this book can learn similar things. Indeed, it is my hope that the book serves political, as well as many other, purposes.

I intentionally asked the women in the shelter to "begin at the beginning" with their earliest memories because I wanted to test a theory that I had. Going into this work, I believed that women who are living in violent relationships have probably been abused, battered, and violated mentally and physically all their lives. The life stories I have collected confirm this hypothesis. *Without exception,* the women who gave me their stories in this study recounted life narratives that begin with very early accounts of violence, abuse, and neglect, incidents that I firmly believe traumatized and wounded them so deeply that they never recovered, and that the years and years of continued abuse and violence in their lives are a testament to the power those early moments of violence and abuse had on the girls, now women, whose voices fill the pages of this book. I believe hearing the stories in their own words provides insight into the question about just how traumatic early experiences with abuse and violence actually are.

THE DEVASTATING EFFECTS OF ABUSE

Social science research supports the belief that women are traumatized by abuse, and the stories in this book certainly agree with this contention. Mary P. Koss and her coauthors of the book *No Safe Haven* give substantial evidence that abused and assaulted women develop a sense of helplessness, a high incidence of depression, fear, and anxiety, all of which increase as abuse and violence accelerate: "Although just one assault can have permanent negative effects, the severity and repetition of violence clearly affects resulting psychological adjustment." A host of studies are quoted to support the contention that "women victims of severe violence—those who were frequently assaulted, had sustained physical injuries, were sexually assaulted, or had experienced death threats—were much more likely to express extreme levels of distress, including an overwhelming sense of danger, intrusive memories or flashbacks, and thoughts of suicide." The authors conclude that "the more violence a woman experiences, the more she suffers from various forms of psychological distress."[4]

These studies seem to be pointing out the obvious. How much time, money, and energy have been expended to give us these conclusions? Are we surprised or enlightened by quantitative data that indicates that the more a woman is beaten, violated, raped, and in other ways abused, the more helpless, fearful, and depressed she is likely to become?

Diana Russell, in her book *The Secret Trauma,* informs us that in current research concerning incest of young girls, the most prevalent questions still revolve around the lasting effects of early abusive incidents. I am convinced, however, that "hearing" the stories in this book will take us further in our understanding of the effects of violence than more quantifiable approaches. Compare what you learn from the women's stories as told in their own voices with what might be provided to us when women are asked to fill out a survey that asks the following questions:

> 1. Overall, how upset were you by this experience—extremely upset, somewhat upset, not very upset, not at all upset?
> 2. Looking back on it now, how much effect would you say this experience(s) has had on your life—a *great* effect, *some* effect, *a little* effect, or *no* effect?[5]

While much of Russell's research, as well as others working in this area, reflect and reinforce the conclusions drawn in my study, I am arguing that we learn much more if we take the time to listen to the stories told in the voices of the women who are speaking in these pages. In fact, I contend that the act of asking for their stories provides a way for them to "speak" their way out of the deadlocked patterns in which they may find themselves. The stories reflect the process of extricating themselves from the traps that have enclosed upon their lives. In fact, rather than dwell on the ill effects of violence and abuse on the women, I prefer that we focus a bit on another finding that Koss and her colleagues noted:

> Contrary to expectations, abused women reported a high internal locus of control, perhaps because they were so actively engaged in managing their own responses to violence and threat while still balancing the needs of family and other responsibilities.[6]

In the stories in this book, you will most certainly hear some of the fear, depression, confusion, and despair that the battered women in other studies display. But you will also hear a voice that seems to come from their innermost depths, from some center that cannot ever be completely destroyed, one that conveys, loud and clear, another message—a message of survival, determination, strength, and courage.

This book is not only directed to the domestic violence movement as it legislates itself in the United States today, through helping victims to safety and through the intricacies and the confusions of police departments, service organizations, and the court system, it is also directed to all in our society who have the privilege and the obligation to change the way we raise our children. I want this book to stand as a challenge to Judith Harris and others who contend that what we do as parents really does not matter.[7] Harris would have us believe that our children's peers have much more to do with their development into "successful" and productive adults than what happens in the home for the first five years or so of their young lives. I firmly and without equivocation disagree, and I believe the stories of the women in this book will contest that very misguided belief. Such attitudes serve only to let parents off the hook— but we cannot get away so easily. If we insist upon bringing children into this world, then we owe them more than food and clothing and a place safe from the weather. Especially for our daughters, we owe them love and attention. We do not need to be perfect, but we do need to let them know from the moment they breathe air that we will protect them and we will listen to their voices. They need to know without one fleeting doubt that we will believe them when they talk to us and that we want, more than anything in this life, for them to feel safe enough to talk to us and for them to believe that we will love them *unconditionally.* More than anything, they need to believe this simple fact. For I have come to believe in this work that *many men will be violent if we let them,* but we can save ourselves from passively accepting violence in our lives.

The federal and state governments and the National Institute of Justice, as well as other local, state, and federal organizations, continue to pour more and more and more dollars into the growing and thriving *business* of domestic violence. We all share this as a global belief: *many men will be violent to women.* But rather than a global response that legislates, without equivocation, that *violence against women will not be tolerated,* millions and millions of dollars are spent tracking court records of domestic violence, of prosecutions, of recidivism, of arrests, of reported incidents, and even more dollars are spent trying to protect the victims in various ways, by building more and better shelters, spending untold court costs, lawyers' fees, hours of court time, prison expenditures, and money on research about domestic violence—the list could go on and on. Somehow there is something gravely askew about this picture. The *given* of male violence against women is producing a megaindustry based on domestic violence, an industry being played out *on the backs of battered women.* And then, when women retaliate, they are put into prison for fighting back. The prisons are full of women who finally, after years of abuse and violence, cut or killed their intimate partners. Not only is this a double and triple injustice, it is immoral and inexcusable.[8]

I began this work thinking that the well-known "cycles of violence" rhetoric—which is now a standard in all domestic violence work, an easily identifiable formula that scholars, workers in the movement, and even women living in shelters learn and adopt as their own language for understanding the violence in their lives—is, while extremely effective and "true," perhaps does not offer us a full picture of how violence operates in the lives of most women.[9] My efforts to gather women's life stories was also in response to my belief that the full stories of women's lives would reveal patterns that the "cycle of violence" does not adequately incorporate. This hypotheses has also been supported by this research.

Let me acknowledge that women's stories often contain the "red flag" characteristics that we have come to associate with the abuser. No doubt about it. The cycles of abuse are in the women's stories: He is a knight in shining armor come to rescue and love her (she may even use this language); he loves her too much to share her with anybody; he doesn't want her to work; he wants to take care of her; he wants her to dress only for him; he begins to be very possessive and jealous; he tells her to not even worry about her looks because he loves her just the way she is; he takes away the car keys; he follows and monitors her every move; he begins to accuse her of having affairs with anyone she meets or talks to or even mentions in conversation; he goes into fits and rages, hitting the doors, the car, kicking and breaking things; then he hits her hard; and he is very, very sorry; he buys her things, begs for forgiveness, cries, tells her he loves only her—but in a few weeks or months he hits her again, harder; he beats her badly, she may even end up in the hospital; and the cycle begins again, with another "honeymoon" period of sweetness, gifts, remorse, and him treating her like a queen—then it happens again, this time even harder; he may break her nose, her arm, kill the fetus in her womb—and the cycle continues over and over and over again.

It is possible that this prototypical cycle has become, in fact, a kind of master narrative, suggesting a narrative that everyone has come to know well and one that is referenced perhaps too freely as the "typical" narrative for domestic violence. Of course, once the narrative is known and utilized by the more powerful, dominant forces to standardize women's experiences, the use of the "master narrative" no longer describes accurately individual women's experiences.[10] It is, after all, a narrative that privileges male *behavior* over female *experience,* and it is a narrative that has both consciously and unconsciously directed our attitudes and our behavior regarding battering and violence. The cycle of abuse verifies just how much our efforts are reactive rather than revolutionary. We watch *his* behavior; we monitor it, noting it so that we can avoid the next blow; we are crouched down, waiting, praying we know what to expect; we think there is power in understanding how he thinks, how he acts. In describing the cycle of abuse and violence, look at us marking the "red flags"—from behind the sofa or in the back of a closet, possibly there with our children, marking time, marking the indicators of the cycle. We are captive to the patterns of his reality, his behavior. We feel more in control if we think we can predict the next punch, the next beating, the degree of intensity and escalation. What power here, I ask? What have we missed? How can we rise from our crouching position, our furtive stance of watchfulness, and stride toward the door?

Perhaps we can replace this pattern of watchfulness and the anticipation of his behavior with a new story—a kind of "herstory." What can her stories tell us? How can her stories guide us to ask new questions? How can her stories lead us to help ourselves and others? Finding the answers to some of these critical questions is part of the task I set for myself. If we resist the impulse to use the cycle of violence as a template, the question then becomes, what would we hear in the women's stories if we listened carefully, being attentive to these patterns *as well as to others* that emerge from their narratives? Marsha Houston and Cheris Kramarae recognize the importance of telling her story *her way:* "Breaking out of silence means more than being empowered to speak or to write, it also means controlling the form as well as the content of one's own communication, the power to develop and to share one's own unique voice."[11] Women who have been in shelters or who have been in counseling for domestic violence know this identified cycle of violence and abuse. They know the rhetoric for talking about the cycle and they are relieved when they can see their own lives reflected in the delineated and studied cycle of violence prototype. Each woman may even, as she recounts her story, be plugging her own experience into that template. It is a cultural script she has come to learn and trust. She often follows this account with comments about her children and what they have seen and heard—stating that they, too, will most likely follow the "cycle of abuse." But, again, if we can resist the lure of seeing and hearing *only* this identifiable prototype for battered women's lives and listen, carefully, to their stories what else will we hear?

At the core of these stories is the construction of the self of the woman who is speaking. In fact, I would posit that until the moment when she is asked to "tell her life story," she has not ever consciously done this work of self-construction before. Perhaps for the first time in her life, she focuses her mental attention on *her self.* This is *her* story, and she uses this time to shape a life—often with self-reflection built in as a kind of interpretation of that life—as she moves through her story. And in the one hour, or two, or three, or four hours that she speaks uninterrupted to me and to my tape recorder (which I think recede into the background and somewhat disappear as she talks), she tries to make some sense of a life that perhaps has not made a great deal of sense to her as she has lived it.

This is her story. In each of the stories we hear her speak from the interior, from inside the body of a flesh-and-blood little girl. We must listen very, very carefully because this story is not really a "life story"; it is a life honed down to what is speakable. Every word counts, you see, because so much has been left out. Only the most significant markers are here to guide us. The memories that flash across her screen are poignant moments that present themselves as she begins to reconstruct her life.

Not only do the women's stories reveal early abuse, violence, and molestation, the stories reveal that when these women were girls, their own mothers and grandmothers were so wounded and damaged by the violence, abuse, and battering in their own lives, they often were unable to emotionally support and physically protect their own daughters. My research suggests that there are actually spirals of cycles of abuse that occur across generational lines, violence against women that renders mothers broken and wounded. The stories of the women I have met point to the fact that we live in a society that accepts male violence *as a given* and denies girls a safe space for growing toward maturity and women safe places to live their lives and nourish their dreams.

NARRATIVE STUDIES

When I was in graduate school in the late 1970s and early 1980s, there were two disciplines that consciously focused on and understood the importance of "story" and "narrative." These were primarily the fields of literature and folklore. As a Ph.D. student at that time at Indiana University, I gained perspectives from both of these camps and developed a well-rounded appreciation for the significance of story in literary genres, fiction and nonfiction, biography and autobiography, as well as in oral genres, including folktales, märchen, life histories, life stories, ballads, personal experience narratives, and even in sermons. Both literature and folklore, as disciplines, were cognizant of the importance of plot, character development, setting, storytelling style, and reception of audience(s). At that time, the study of folklore was making a radical move from understanding stories primarily as "texts" to be collected, transcribed, and preserved (in archives or books), to talking about how "living" narratives exist not only in the examples of story texts tape recorded or otherwise documented but also in the living, breathing, dynamic act of storytelling. Scholars came to recognize how each told narrative is different from the other times it has been performed, and that storyteller and audience work together to enact the telling of a narrative that is vitally important to the community. Studies of communities that share oral narratives and personal experiences were expanded from the more rural and traditional communities, long recognized by folklorists, to African Americans and immigrant groups in urban centers, as well as to even smaller communities such as occupational groups and families. That stories are told again and again in infinite varieties and nuances, depending upon the storyteller and her or his appreciative audience, was a concept that entered the academic study of oral narrative. This concept influenced the world of fiction, as well, as critics came to understand the intersections between oral story and written narrative, perhaps summarized best by the notion that, indeed, "there is no new story under the sun." What is new and interesting, of course, is the way the story is crafted and shared with an appreciative but critical audience that determines if the story and its telling are appropriate and performed with style.

Certainly, in the nearly twenty years since my graduate school experience, much has happened to those concepts. The literary "canon" has been under attack by a wide variety of groups who claim that, in fact, there *are* some new stories that have not yet been told—black people's stories have not been told, or perhaps not been heard; women's stories have not been told, or perhaps not been heard; and many other groups make the same claims . . . with noticeable results. The canon is expanding, and new perceptions of what "story" is and what it can be are moving in "next door." The whole "neighborhood" has taken on new character, color, and new life. Several texts, such as Gayle Greene's *Changing the Story,* are examining just exactly how these transformations are occurring and why they are significant. Greene sees "tradition" as not a fixed entity, but one that challenges and demands new scrutiny as it endlessly transforms itself and is transformed from beyond itself:

> We should view "tradition" . . . not as a timeless, universal entity, but as "tradition making" and unmaking, as a process wherein fiction performs complex negotiations with the works of the past, negotiations which are both appropriations and subversions.

These moves have been recognized, of course, as political and loaded. Greene's work fits nicely with the claim of Ursula K. Le Guin that "when women speak truly, they speak subversively."[12] It is in this spirit of exposing new stories that have not yet been heard that I embark upon this study.

At the same time, it seems, every other discipline in the humanistic realm has "discovered" the concept and significance of "story." Psychology, sociology, anthropology, communications, film studies, linguistics, rhetoric, and history, to name only the ones that come immediately to mind, have adopted new approaches that hinge upon a new belief in the academy: that "story" and "telling our stories" is a window into whatever task has been undertaken. The book titles themselves tell the story of this new journey toward understanding through narrative: *Auto/Ethnography: Rewriting the Self and the Social; Inventing the Truth: The Art and Craft of Memoir; Lives of Their Own: Rhetorical Dimensions in Autobiographies of Women Activists; The Narrative Study of Lives; Self-Representation: Life Narrative Studies in Identity and Ideology; Autobiographics: A Feminist Theory of Women's Self-Representation; Interpreting Experience; Retelling a Life: Narration and Dialogue in Psychoanalysis; Changing the Story: Feminist Fiction and the Tradition.* The titles of some of these new works indicate the perspective of the writers and the discipline. Certainly, feminists and women's studies scholars and critics have welcomed the notion of "story" as a way to hear and honor the neglected, ignored, and dishonored stories of women historically as well as in the contemporary context, oral and written. Historians and psychologists alike have employed the term *herstory* to draw attention to a shift in what might be called the male-dominated "master narrative." In the burgeoning area of Holocaust studies, memory and story are at the heart of how scholars are attempting to write about the "disaster" in general, and are arguing about whether or not personal narratives embody the "essence" of any holocaust or if, in fact, memory ultimately fails to "speak the unspeakable" and can only point us in the direction of that which we cannot fathom.

Regardless of how it is being employed, the concept of "story," and the recognition of a living, breathing "storyteller," who either speaks or writes her or his story, memoir, personal-experience narrative, and recollections, has garnered a market among both academic and lay audiences. Narrative, many scholars claim, is a crafted entity, even a "fiction," that has been both consciously and unconsciously honed to deploy a certain individual and community-shared identity held by the storyteller. Many even suggest that we tell our stories to "save our lives," recognizing that telling our stories is a positive, therapeutic act that aids the storyteller in trying to make sense of a life that otherwise might appear too fragmented, purposeless, or chaotic. Of course, scholars differ in their opinions about whether or not these constructions are clear examples of how our story "fits" well with other stories in our universe or whether they, in fact, point to our infinite differences across the borders of race, class, gender, regional diversity, cultural differences, and sexual orientation. And both literary and folklore disciplines seem ultimately to be saying that to examine all our life stories, in either of these ways, will in the end help us to become more tolerant, more understanding, more sympathetic and compassionate, less judgmental, and, thus, better world citizens—or as Martha Nussbaum puts it: "Narrative art has the power to make us see the lives of the different with more than a casual tourist's interest—with involvement and sympathetic understanding, with anger at our society's refusals of visibility. [The] narrative imagination is an essential preparation for moral interaction."[13]

It seems that some psychologists, on the other hand, tip the scales a bit to the other side and argue that narrative structures not only guide the way we recount our life's experiences but also dictate our lives. Ruthellen Josselson and Amia Lieblich are the editors of the eight volumes of *The Narrative Study of Lives* published between 1993 and 1999; perhaps their endeavor might be summed up by one of the authors in the first volume. In his article "The Story of Life: Hermeneutic Perspectives on the Relationship between Narrative and Life History," Guy Widdershoven claims that "life and story are internally related. . . . The meaning of life cannot be determined outside of the stories told about it. Life informs and is formed by stories." Of course, his "hermeneutic" perspective on *story* is this: "the implicit meaning of life is made explicit in [life] stories," or, put another way: "human life is interpreted in stories." And again: "Our actions are organized in such a way that we can give an account of them, justify them by telling an intelligible story about them." At times this makes perfectly good sense, as when he claims that "narrative identity" is the "unity of a person's life as it is experienced and articulated in stories that express experience(s)." Other, more radical, points of view might be harder to grasp, such as his claim that "the unity of a person's life is dependent on being a character in an enacted narrative." He expands on this second premise: "We live our lives according to a script, which secures that our actions are part of a meaningful totality."[14]

Whichever viewpoint appeals, we can read these expositions upon the significance of story and determine that this study illustrates how the telling of women's stories helps the narrators to develop a sense of "self." Most of the scholars using story and narrative to talk about how story helps to make sense of a life do not make the second move toward understanding how the construction of story equals the construction of a self. Perhaps Amos Funkenstein comes the closest in his article, "The Incomprehensible Catastrophe: Memory and Narration," in Josselson and Lieblich's first volume. Although Funkenstein is writing about the role of memory and narrative for Holocaust studies, his article is helpful to the discussion of the disasters in battered women's lives as well. Here, his work is especially appropriate because he proposes that "the identity of an individual . . . consists of the construction of a narrative. . . . The narrative construed by and the narrative construed *about* the subject. Such is the making of a 'self.' The making of the self is what I [have] called its *narrative*."[15] Equally important is Funkenstein's notion that during the disaster of the Holocaust, the Nazis robbed the Jews of their "capacity to construct a narrative" for themselves. Without the ability to construct a narrative, he claims, individuals, and even whole groups, are stripped of the ability to create and develop a narrative *construction* of a life, even one that might include escape and the possibilities for a new and different future. This approach, one that seems to equate the paralyzed position of the oppressed subject with the inability to create a life narrative, parallels this study of girls and women who live in such fearful, chaotic conditions that they are sometimes unable to articulate their own stories. The inability to accomplish that enabling act dooms the subject to a terrified site where "self" can never be realized. This is, of course, the goal of the oppressor—to stifle the emergence or development of more positive "selves" who might challenge or subvert the status quo.

I would like to return to the work of feminists for a moment, if only to emphasize how significant women writers and scholars believe the act of breaking silence can be empowering for women who have been silenced and unheard for generations and generations. Unlike many of the other scholars who have turned to "story" for the basis of their work, feminists have recognized the *political power* of narrative for women and other oppressed groups. Sue Monk Kidd, in her revolutionary work, *Dance of the Dissident Daughter,* remembers hearing Maya Angelou remark in a television interview that in order to become a writer, one must have "something to say, the ability to express it, and, finally, the courage to express it at all." For Kidd this led to an epiphany. She tells us that she suddenly knew something she had never grasped before: "And it came to me all of a sudden that becoming empowered as a woman required three very similar things: a soul of one's own, the ability or means to voice it, and the courage to voice it at all." For Kidd, this meant that she (and others who have been silenced) must embark on a new path, one that would enable her to "begin to truly own my experience, to feel the strength of it, to gather it up and put it 'out there.' "[16]

That this is a difficult task, full of pitfalls and negative critiques from the dominant discourse of the times, is recognized by Kidd and others who are calling for women and other oppressed groups to speak up and speak out. The fits and starts, the discomfort of pulling ourselves out of the closets, corners, and recesses of our minds, that accompany our foray into the public discourse have their perils, of course. We shall make this journey neither easily, nor without pain and suffering; the backlash has already been immense. And, of course, it is easy for the established scholars to write and speak about their own life journeys in such glowing, holistic, connected ways that their accounts can only illuminate the difficulties inherent in our own. I am reminded of all the books I have read by Jerome Bruner, for example. An author of more than forty books on the subject, Bruner is recognized as a leader in the field of autobiography. Yet, when I read *In Search of Mind: Essays in Autobiography,* I could almost taste the self-absorbed complacency that comes with the position of white male power and privilege. After recounting for nearly three hundred pages his own highly successful life, Bruner concludes: "I suppose my life has been a good one—as seen from a commanding rock by some mythologically induced member of my reference tribe who is watching the parade. Most of the time it has felt that way to me, too, full of movement, of direction, of surprise, of affection and loyalty."[17]

I could only sit in awe at the language of this confession and wonder if I could believe for one minute that any woman walking the face of the earth at this time could have said those words, used that language, and felt that secure at any point in her life. I can only hope that might be the case, but I sincerely doubt it. It is time to hear the stories of the other half of the population.

In response, perhaps, to Bruner's mythically appropriate life story, Sally Robinson, in *Engendering the Subject: Gender and Self-Representation in Contemporary Women's Fiction,* makes the essential point that if women do not begin to represent themselves, then the representations of women historically presented and enforced will prevail.

> "Representation" is an act of violence, perpetrated by the self-present and knowing subject against, one can only assume, the Others that that subject desires to know and control. Thus, representation is a form of colonization, an imperial move on the part of the subject. Yet representation . . . has another, and contradictory, meaning: representation must also be made to signify the process by which ("invisible") subjects "legitimize" themselves by inscribing their experience, their desires, and their "reality" into discourse. The difference between these two meanings of representation, both political, is in the conceptualization of the subject of representation. . . . That subject is akin to the humanist "self."[18]

Robinson's argument, which draws on the work of gender theorist Judith Butler, is that this "humanist self" has been limited by the normatized, inscribed Western discourse as the story of the privileged, white male subject. Women's stories have been delegitimized and, thus, the woman as subject has been left out of the history of (hu)mankind. The possibility of women as subjects in world discourses and in history can only be realized through women's *self-representation.*[19] In self-representations, argues Robinson, women become (engendered) subjects. It is Robinson's hope and desire that these actions, this reinscribing of the female subject, will *disturb* the dominant discourses. That is my hope for this work as well.

A NOTE ON THE TRANSCRIPTIONS

Only a small fraction of the many stories I tape recorded from women living in shelters (or beyond) appear in this book.[20] I have selected four complete life stories to include in this book. Most are verbatim, given in their entirety as they were narrated to me on tape. Others have been condensed somewhat, with some interpretive material added by me so that the amended stories make sense in the retelling. These particular stories are often drawn upon in the various discussions throughout the book, but many narratives that do not appear in the book in their full version have also been utilized for my thinking and my analysis. All of the names of the narrators and their children, husbands, friends, hometowns, and relations have been changed to protect them all, and to protect me.

Additionally, to respect the confidentiality of sensitive personal information, when writing about any given group meeting, I create a "fictive" construction—no actual names are used and although some dialogue might actually have been said by someone, I've mostly "imagined" a group meeting based on the many such meetings I've attended over a long period of time.

I have given the women in this book first names that seem to "fit" their stories and their personalities to some degree. These names may help the reader differentiate between the stories and the narrators. However, it may prove difficult at times to keep track of all the "characters" as you read. For those stories that are included in the book, you can always refer back to the full transcriptions to regain a sense of a holistic life story. But it is not imperative for you to "track" the narrators by name throughout, or to always recall the entirety of a woman's story as I weave portions of it into a chapter dealing with childhood abuse or teenage years or early marriages of violence.

In some ways, the stories are both unique and surprisingly similar. I use the women's actual words because I believe their words are valuable. I invite you to hear them both in segments throughout the chapters and in their totality in the transcriptions. Either way, they prove to be invaluable to our understanding of the power of narrative for women escaping violence.

Safe and Unsafe Living

THIS MORNING I WAS at the shelter by 8:10. I had an interview set up to tape record a resident's story. This is maybe the fourth or fifth appointment I have had with this particular woman. It has been difficult to get her to commit to a time and date. She keeps saying she will; she tells me she wants to tell me her story. She understands her story has a kind of power, and she is the power broker, suddenly. Last week she gave a portion of her story to a couple of newspaper reporters and her words were included on the six-o'clock news. But she keeps missing appointments, asking if we can postpone, telling me she's not feeling well or is too "messed up today" to do it. I learn patience here; I tell her that's fine. I'm not going anywhere. I'll be around; how about Friday? Sure, she tells me, and by now I know that Friday may come and go and I still won't have her story. But I would love to hear her story; I want it for this study—and so I wait patiently, hoping someday we will sit down together and she will tell me what has happened to her.

So I am here early and the place is short-staffed. I am here to tape record a story, but soon after I walk in, I'm releasing one woman's mail to her from the shelter's safe box even as I'm reaching to answer the phone. Only Karen is in the office, trying to answer three phone lines at once. I answer a line as I try to take off my sweater. I know the script: "Shelter—can I help you?" This time it is a call for Sally, the director. I check to see if she's in; she's not; I take a message. I run to the bathroom before that line or the two others begin to ring again. I make it, barely. "Shelter—can I help you?" This time I don't get off so easy. This woman wants to talk to Karen: She's in jail—her husband beat her Saturday night and so she "cut him." Of course, by the time the police arrived, he was bleeding profusely and claiming she tried to kill him; she told them, no, he'd been beating her all night and raped her twice, and that she was just fed up and escaped to the kitchen and grabbed the closest knife and cut him when he lunged for her. But she's in jail and worried about her kids, could she talk to Karen or maybe Barbara, the DOVE (Domestic Violence Enforcement) coordinator, who facilitates interaction between victims and the police?

The other line is ringing, so I put her on hold and indicate to Karen, who is still on line 1, that she's needed on line 2, while I answer line 3. The phone looks like a Christmas tree, all lit up with blinking red flashing lights, in contrast to the police car lights that are inactivated at this moment as Officer Caldwell pulls into the driveway. He's here to take photographs of a resident's face. She came in last night and is pretty badly beaten. Officer Caldwell has returned today because the imprint of a booted foot is emerging in technicolor on her face and the prosecutor needs a photo of it. Caldwell will take pictures of her back and legs as well while he is here. The bruises often do not really emerge for a day or two; then they are really mean and ugly—the best time for the polaroids. Walt is a good cop. There are good cops and bad cops in this town, and we generally know which is which. Walt is one of the best we've ever worked with. He's the policeman involved in the DOVE unit, a federally and state funded program for arresting and prosecuting domestic violence offenders—wife beaters. Walt wants to put them all away—for a very long time. A good cop. I push the release button to "buzz" him into the building even as I answer the phone again. Then I have to warn everyone that a man is entering the building, a policeman—but he's not here for any of them; they don't need to be concerned. But they do need to hold their children, who always seem terrified when men enter their new safe space. For them, at this moment, all men are terrifying. And policemen are closely associated with the terror they have been living with.

Line 3: "Shelter—can I help you?" The woman on the other end tells me her name and says she is with Community Caring—a group I've never heard of. She is at a local school and has a woman in her office who has a six-year-old daughter in the school. This Caring staff person has just discovered that the woman and her child have been living in a car and in an abandoned house. The woman left another town in the state, about two hundred miles away, to escape an abusive man. He had been beating her daily and had molested the girl; she had called the police there, but they had not helped her at all. So, she put some clothes in a black plastic bag and left town. She thought she would be able to stay with some relatives in Columbia, but that hadn't worked out, so she was living in a nephew's car or in this old house and working for Job Service from 4 A.M. to noon to buy some groceries for her child. The Caring worker wants to know if I think this woman might qualify for coming to the shelter. I certainly think so, but I ask to speak directly to the woman. Within half an hour, we have invited her to come into the shelter; the Caring worker volunteers to bring her over and to bring her child later, after school. Karen takes down her story for the intake interview, and we gather together some clothes and food for her and determine which room to put her in. We ask her to make a grocery list and tell her we will provide food for her, and we give her a cabinet in the kitchen with her name on it. She sits down heavily in the chair in the office and begins to cry. I watch her shoulders heave as she crumples in the old recliner, unable to speak. I can only guess that these are tears of relief. She has found shelter; we are offering her a bed, food, warmth, assistance, safety. No one says a word. We let her cry and hand her the Kleenex box. And then the phone begins to ring again—all three lines at once.

Someone wants to bring in four bags of children's clothes. She had four children of her own, she explains, and she's washed and put into bags all of the clothes they had outgrown. She asks if we need children's clothes. I looked at the woman in the chair and tell her, yes, thank you, we can use those clothes. Another line, another donation of women's and children's clothes. I suggest they bring them right over but warn her I will only give her the address when she is actually ready to come and remind her this is a confidential location and she is not to reveal where we are located. She agrees, slightly put off by this information.

Line 1 is the police department looking for Walt; line 3, a woman trying to reach Sally. The woman is terrified about her husband coming this morning to take away her child. Can't we do a Child Order of Protection for her? I explain, no, we can't do those at the shelter, she will need to go to the children's division at the courthouse and get that. But they are closed. Damn—of course, it's Columbus Day. What to do? I'll find Sally. I hear Sally tell her she could come into shelter with the boy if that is what she wants and needs today, until she can get to the courthouse and get the order of protection. I'm thinking, where are we going to put another woman and child? Even as she's talking to this woman, I'm looking at the resident list. Some residents don't stay long. On the other hand, for most of them there's really no other place to go.

The rules here are pretty strict and rigidly enforced. It's not a hotel. For their own safety, and so the staff knows where they are at all times, the residents have to report "out" and report back "in." If they have children, they must care for them or contract with another resident to watch them; the staff has enough to do. Sometimes, though, they get a break when the children's coordinator plans outings, or play afternoons in the backyard, or games for a dreary winter day. The women have curfews that they must honor; they know it is about safety, but as grown women all these restrictions make them angry. They had to leave their homes, their possessions, their lives to come here into safety, and now there are rules and regulations and fear and curfews. The irony of how safety is achieved at their expense is not lost on them.

Someone left last night, I knew, so there was a room that might be available. But I'm guessing the bed needs to be stripped and the room aired out. That is one of my least favorite jobs, cleaning the rooms. I feel like such an intruder in their space, handling their clothing, their personal items, the children's toys.

I remind the new resident to make out a grocery list, but her vacant look tells me to remind her tomorrow when she's rested. Sally suggests she quit the Job Service job with the long nighttime hours and take a few days here in the shelter to regroup, rest, and decide if she couldn't find a better kind of job. We will provide for her for a while; she might just want to go upstairs and lie down for a bit. She looks at Sally with blank, unbelieving eyes and whispers "thank you" softly as she walks past us and toward the kitchen with Karen, heading for the pantry and food.

Between phone calls, answering the many questions and concerns of the current residents, and helping the latest arrival, Karen, who often also works as a court advocate, begins to tell me about two women she has been assisting who have agreed to give me their stories for my book. This happens a lot. The counselors, or the DOVE staff, or the resident staff, talk to women about my research project and ask if they would be interested in giving me their stories. I have more interviews than I can actually do in a week's time, given that I'm also teaching a full load now at the university and busy with about a thousand other things, as well as driving my two children to all their activities. I feel scattered, to say the least. But each woman's story seems so valuable and courageous. I just keep making appointments and squeezing my daytime hours closer and closer together; then I find myself over here at night taping one more story from a woman who has a day job. This work puts everything into perspective. A very good thing to learn.

Two women come in for counseling and the woman with the boot mark on her face comes to get help with her bruises. Another woman comes in to report that she's still trying to get a job thorough the human services program. I wish her luck. She's been here a long time; gone, come back. She needs to find a foothold in the world, but the footing is quite slippery for her.

A message comes across the TDD from the deaf advocate. I'm not accustomed to this format, but it turns out to be quite simple, really. The operator serves as a translator, and I am able to voice my replies. I have been embarrassed in my interactions with the deaf. We've had deaf residents, and it's never easy. I often must resort to paper and pen, or mouth my responses in an exaggerated manner that must be an insult to the client. The use of interpreters from the deaf advocates and the new TDD have opened a new world of access for deaf clients.

One Thursday evening in January, I get to the shelter a little before 6:30. I would much rather be driving home. It is dark out, and it's cold, a mixture of rain and sleet crackling against my windshield. I try to pull into the shelter parking lot but I cannot: there are too many cars already parked there, jammed in the small spaces, beside the dumpster, lined up along the curb. A big group tonight, I think. As usual. I pull back into the street and park my car, locking the doors. This does not feel like a safe place to park. People are still coming out of the doors of the adjacent social service buildings, entering the streets, heading home or to the corner grocery. They brace themselves against the knifelike wind and the pelting ice that hurts their faces. I am parked half a block down the street and I'm uncomfortable with that, but I have no choice. I get out quickly, stashing my bag under the seat. I never know where it is safer, in the car or in the shelter. In either place a wallet is fair game. I risk the car.

I walk across the parking lot and toward the building, which looks a bit like a real estate agency. Wide front door, windows with closed venetians across the entire front. Smaller windows all lit in the upstairs rooms. There is a number above the door but no signs, nothing to identify this brick structure here on a street of run-down clapboard houses. I push the buzzer to announce my arrival and to gain access. The venetian blinds near the door part with a furtive finger. I see an eye behind the slit. I cannot tell who it is, but I know that my face is clearly visible in the glare of the porch lights. The noise of the buzzer lets me know the door is being unlocked for me. I have only a few moments to turn the knob and enter before the lock is secure again.

The foyer is cool, but I feel the heat from the hallway as I move towards the middle of the shelter. I reach a hand to the inside of the split office door, opening the door from the inside, aware that this marks me as a staff person, an insider. I am pleased to be reminded that I am accepted here. The office staff murmurs greetings; even those on the phone give a nod, a small wave, making me feel welcome. I get some hugs, lots of smiles, and the feeling is warm, comfortable. I like coming into this space now that I'm here. I like being a part of the staff—yet the work, the place, can drag me down almost immediately. I feel a little apprehensive about the next hour. I listen as the volunteers talk in low voices about things they can do with the children during the group meetings. Volunteers make it possible for the moms to sit quietly, without interruption (usually), for an hour of important connecting with other women and with the counselors. The volunteers herd the children, large and small, back into the kitchen area and around the big table already prepared with magic markers, large sheets of paper, games. Later, they will serve popcorn and maybe take the children out to the back porch if the weather permits.

Group meetings are always difficult. It is a time for residents as well as women from "outside" the shelter to come together to share, to comfort, to advise each other. Raw emotions, sadness, anger, tears, and frustrations abound in the living room these nights. An outpouring of souls in danger, who have come together to find a few minutes of safety, solace, and camaraderie in a harsh and uncaring world where pain is the order of the day.

I hang my coat and stash my keys before I move toward the doors that will lead me to the living room. Women are there hugging each other, sitting alone, smoking, crying quietly in a corner, trying to pry their children loose from their necks so volunteers can play with them for an hour while they share adult concerns with adults. It is a noisy space, smoky, crowded; smells from the kitchen are strong; the children are wild and loud, smashing into my legs, reaching up for hugs, smiles and tears all awash on smeared and smudgy faces. I see the Christmas tree is still standing, long after December has come and gone. It looks a bit bedraggled, but the red and blue lights are cheery and welcome. I don't blame them for keeping it here. I would hang on to it, too.

I can see there are not enough chairs, so I begin to bring in more from the dining room, from the smoking porch, trying to guess how many more women will come to the group tonight. At 6:30, Marty, one of the staff people, calls the group to order, welcoming everyone. I'm still enlarging the circle of chairs. Marty tells the group this is "their time," that the group is for them. They are encouraged to share what is on their minds, but there is no requirement to share. And there are only a few rules, she tells them, but they are very, very important to remember. "What are they?" she asks them. They know and parrot them back to her: Do not reveal who is here, for safety is of prime importance, and we must not tell who we see in the shelter, ever. And what is said here stays here—this space is "safe space" and what is said here cannot be repeated. And what is said here must not be referenced later—that is, these discussions stay in the circle and are not to be brought up later in the kitchen or the laundry room, the hallways, or anywhere else. And, finally, all the staff will keep confidentiality, as well, unless they fear someone is suicidal or likely to hurt someone else, or if it is revealed that a child is being harmed in any way. These are the rules. We all know them well.

Marty relaxes visibly and invites everyone to give her first name and describe something good that has happened to her this week—just to get us started, she says; just to encourage us to focus on one good thing that happened to us this week. Their offerings are slim, quiet, tentative.

"My name is Susie and I got work two days this week and that's good. It helped."

"My name is Carrie and I got to talk to my kids on the phone on Wednesday."

"My name is Denise and I've been clean all week. Hurrah!" She holds up a hand in a sign of victory and the others cheer and clap; "that's great, Denise," "good going, girl," "right on!"

"My name is Ann, and I can't think of nothing good that happened this week." She looks on the verge of tears. Her voice is low and muted.

Marty moves on, knowing she will come back to Ann and ask if she needs to "share." Two more women come into the room and find chairs. Marty asks them to give their names and to tell of something good as well. Then she waits a few minutes. The quiet is a bit uncomfortable but not exactly. There is an air of anticipation; most eyes are on the floor. One woman toys with the design on the sofa pillow she holds in her lap, pulled tight against her stomach as if to protect a vulnerable spot there. One woman's arms are crossed against her chest, anger close to the surface. Another sits sideways, her legs curled tightly up under her body, her hair in the crook of her own arm. The room is quiet and still, the only sound being the muted children's voices from the other side of the doors, in the kitchen, making Play-Doh characters and acting out imaginary scenes that have nothing at all to do with their own lives of terror.

Marty asks in a low, soothing voice if someone wants to "go first." There is no response. Gently, she asks Ann if she would like to share. Ann shakes her head in a nearly imperceptible "no" that Marty knows to respect. Jackie says, "Well, I'll start. I'm feeling really pretty down tonight. I've been trying to get out of my lease and they won't let me. He doesn't want me to get out, of course, and the landlord is nowhere to be found. But I need out, bad. It's getting worse all the time and I need to get out. But my name's on the lease and I can't get out of it. And I can't afford to go nowhere else and I sure can't sign two leases. And he won't let me out of it. He wants me there so he can manipulate me and make me do stuff and cook and stuff. He don't want me to go. But I'm sick of it and I'm sick of him and I don't want no more of this. I had twelve years of this crap already and I got out of that but here I am again and I want out. I'm at my wit's end. I don't know what to do."

Marty acknowledges how bad her situation is and asks the others if they've dealt with a similar situation, asks if the law can help get a woman off a lease if her partner is abusing her. The response is loud and clear: "No, the cops can't help." Cathy, for instance, adds, "Oh, no, I'm never calling the police. I've called them before and that was a *big* mistake. No, they won't help me. I been busted too many times for them to come in there, now, and help me. But they know all about this guy; they've dealt with him, too, and they know what a rotten piece of shit he is. But they won't do nothing. They don't want to deal with him, either. No, I ain't going to call the police." The others agreed. They all acknowledged that Jackie was in a really bad situation. And they all agreed there was probably nothing she could do. But they all encouraged her to leave, anyway. "Just get out. Worry about the rent later. Just get out. You gotta think of yourself first. Can't you go to a friend's place or something? At least until the lease is up?"

Next to me, I feel the seething energy of the woman sitting to my right. She is aflame, it seems. I can actually feel the heat from her body, the force of her anger and frustration crossing the air between us. But she does not speak. The woman next to Cathy has been invited by Marty to speak. She is in tears before she can speak a word. She does not know where her daughter is. She is weeping profusely, her shoulders crunched over, her hands on her face. She is apologizing. Marty tells her not to apologize, just speak when she can. A woman brings her the Kleenex, offering her one and setting the box down near her arm. After a few moments, she stops crying and begins to speak in a low, halting voice, still full of the hiccups and wetness of tears in her voice. "She's been skipping school, and now she's gone with her boyfriend, in all likelihood. She left me a note saying she would never be back. She hates me so much. I've tried, but she's still mad about the divorce. Mad at me, I know. She's sick of not having nothing, of getting the free lunches, of not having a car. She hates school. She hates the teachers. She skips all the time. They call me sometimes; often they don't even bother anymore. But now she's gone. I can't breathe. I'm so worried about her. I don't have a clue how to reach her at all anymore. Sometimes I think it's getting better but then that's just the calm before the storm. Now, she's gone . . ." and Joan leaves her words and escapes into tears again. Others are sympathetic. They all know that the children rage at their mothers because it is "safe" to do that. They cannot rage at their fathers, or the men who live with their mothers. It is not safe to challenge his authority. And a part of them blames their mother for all the confusion and abuse. If she would only do what he says, what he tells her to do—maybe she's even responsible for it all. Or, if she would only leave . . .

Another woman offers her own story about a son who ran away and was placed with the juvenile officers for a while, but how that helped and it all turned out okay in the end. "And he's nineteen now, and he's alive and doing pretty well, as well as can be expected, I guess, under the circumstances." Like several in the room, I know this woman's story in intimate detail. She shared it with me on tape several weeks ago, so I feel like I have some insight into the story she has just told about her own son. Most have children who are suffering in unimaginable ways from their lives of pain and abuse. The others may not know her whole story, but they connect at key points.

The woman next to me cannot contain herself any longer. Stella cries out now, slapping her knees, shaking her fist. Her body shifts in the chair as she finds her voice. "He cleaned out the bank accounts. All of them. Not that we had all that much, but the son of a bitch went early yesterday morning and cleaned out all the accounts. I only left two nights ago and I didn't even think. I didn't think once about the accounts. I was just assuming half of that would be mine. I didn't even think. I was just trying to escape before the bastard absolutely killed me. I was concerned, trying to find a place for my kids, and the son of a bitch cleaned out all the money. Got it all. I got nothing. I got not one penny. And he's got the truck, of course, and, now, he's got the house and he's got all my stuff. Everything. I took one garbage bag full of clothes and stuff for me and the kids. Just left. My girlfriend came by at 10:15, just waited at the corner, and we walked out. Just like that. He was watching T.V., drunk on his butt, of course. And we just walked out. I'm glad we did that. But now I can't think. I don't know what to do. I don't know who to talk to. I'm here because my girlfriend came here once and she said you guys could maybe help me."

I feel the energy around her body shift. The anger and frustration are melting, dissipating, moving somehow away from her body. She is still angry, but as she looks though her tears at the women in that room, her eyes soften and her face begs for their compassion, for their help. And, of course, it comes. One after the other they offer her suggestions, names of people who can help her without fees to pay, places to take her children, who to contact in the prosecutor's office, how to get into a shelter if she needs it, how to get an ex parte against him to keep him away from her. Stories are offered as guidance; stories are told to share her pain; stories of encouragement—as if to say, "my situation was at least as bad as yours and look, I'm here, I made it; you can, too."

I know there were other stories, even represented in this room at this very moment, that would not encourage her, stories that might send her right over the edge. But I also knew no one would share those stories tonight. Not here. This room is for finding strength, for clinging to hope, for encouragement and help. Those who have no hope to offer kept silent, biting their lip, tearing the Kleenex held tightly in their clenched hands into tiny bits of white fuzz. One woman gets up from the sofa and crosses the empty space in the middle of the room and puts her broad black arms around Stella's thin and bony shoulders, enveloping her and holding her for a long, steady moment. The rest of us sit in our seats, silent. What else could we do?

Marty notices a young girl in our midst and asks her if this is her first time at the group. She acknowledges that it is, and her eyes meet those of a woman sitting to my left. I can't make out the connection. We wait. The girl tells us her name is Tammy, and she tells us she is five months pregnant. She also tells us she is fifteen years old. "And he beats her up every single day," the woman sitting next to me blurts out. "I'm her mother, and I was the one who got her to come here tonight. I had heard about this group, and I was hoping someone could help her. Can you help her? She can't hear me anymore. He's going to kill her and the baby both. I—" her voice cracks. She looks around the room, begging for assistance, pleading for help for this child of hers who is in such deep trouble.

The girl speaks up. "He doesn't mean to. He's on a lot of drugs and he only does it when he's drugged up or drunk. He really, really loves me and he says he wants this baby. He says he'll take care of both of us. I know he doesn't mean it. He was abused himself—all his life—his dad used to beat him. Broke his nose; he can't hear well in one ear. He's just so messed up and I'm all he's got. I know he doesn't mean it." She is not crying, but her mother is. The girl seems calm, steadfast, but oh, so small, like she might disappear at any moment, just vanish into thin air. I realize she is the same age as my own daughter, safe at home, doing homework, waiting up for Mom to come home from the shelter.

"God will take care of you. Do you know that? God is what's helped me. I pray to God every single day. God has a plan. I don't know what it is. By God, I wonder some days. But God got me out of there. God brought me to this place. And God brought you here tonight, Mom. He got you here and got your baby here. You got to trust in God." All this from the black woman in the farthest chair, who up until this moment has been sitting in silence. She is speaking loudly and with strength in her voice. She reminds me of women I hear in the pulpit. Indeed, she is preaching. "God brought me here. I was nearly dead. I'd had seventy-two stitches in my head. God brought me here. He put me through trial after trial to make sure I would not crumble. But then, he saved me. It was by his grace alone that I found my way here. Into safety. I am safe now and I praise him every single day."

I am always uncomfortable with these outbursts. I wonder if the others will recoil, think Edith's "God-talk" a little out of place, not appropriate for our group. But no, to my surprise, Grace agrees with her. "That is so true. I'm not a religious woman. I haven't darkened the door of a church in twenty-five years. But I know God is here by my side. I know Jesus walks beside me every single morning when I leave here at four o'clock to go stand in line for whatever work they might find for me that day. I walk through the projects and the men, they talk to me, and they harass me, and I just keep on walking. It's pitch-black dark, you know, and I'm thinking, What am I doing out here in the dark, walking through the projects? But that's all the work I can get. So, I get up and I go and I know God is protecting me. He brought me here, too, and I know that he is my strength. I know that's where my strength comes from. I know that for a fact." Some of the others chime in and agree with her. "Amen, Sister." "You got that right." And some say nothing. I don't know if their silence is disagreement or discomfort, but they'll never say it. This God-talk is hope-talk, too; it is a rope thrown out to help the newcomers. This is where many women find their strength. Who am I to question? It sounds *so* good. Maybe they're right; maybe God is protecting them. That would be nice.

Violet quietly brings up the fact that she must go to court and face her abuser tomorrow. She has to prove to the judge that the bruises on her face and body were put there by him. "He will be looking so good," she tells us. She thinks he is friends with the prosecutor. "He is smart, and speaks so well, and he will smile that million-dollar smile and tell the judge I'm hysterical and crazy. He will make them believe that I was out 'whoring' and came home looking like this—again. He will convince them that 'my story' is a total fabrication, that I have completely made it up to get him into trouble with the law." He will tell them he has married "beneath" his status in the community and has lived to regret it. "She is a drug addict and a whore. She does not take care of the children. She leaves in the middle of the night and doesn't come home for days."

I know this last part is true because she comes occasionally to stay at the shelter until the bruises and the swelling go down enough that she can go back to work. We know her story and we have no trouble at all believing it. He is well known, a professor at a small college in a nearby town. A quiet-spoken, credible, friendly man, an educated man. We know what he was done to her, too. We have called the ambulance and helped her get to the emergency room. We know they rarely ask about the bruises. They write on the report: "She fell down the stairs." Again. And again. And again. She will lose her children tomorrow, she fears. We fear it, too. She probably will. No one was there to witness how he dragged her through the mud in the driveway by her hair, pulling out great sections of it, leaving gaps in her scalp three inches across. No one was there when he kicked her repeatedly in the stomach as she crouched on the ground. No one was there when he got into the car in a blind rage and backed it over her legs, put it into gear, and drove off into the night. The children were in bed. The mailman found her the next morning and helped her into the house.

Her husband told the police he had been away, giving a lecture in another town, and came back to find her in this shape, the children cold and hungry, the mailman in their house. He supposed he would have to commit her. She's out of control, he tells them, looking stoic but respectable, his shoes spotless, his jacket and tie immaculate. "Just look at her," he had said to the police, as he walked away, heading toward the kitchen to feed and console his confused children. The women in the group shake their heads, believing her every word.

It is not until the group has been dismissed and the children released back into the arms of their mothers that I hear the women begin to talk about the news reports. A woman we knew from the shelter and from the group had been killed the afternoon before by her former boyfriend and stalker. She had come in only a few days before to get an ex parte filed against him. He would watch her, hidden in the grass in an abandoned lot next to her house. She had called the police. The neighbors had called the police. They would circle in their patrol cars sometimes, but they never got out and kicked around in the grass. They just cruised from the comfort of their cars. But he was there. She knew he was there. Her kids knew he was there, too. Kirsten was five and she would watch from the kitchen window that sat just above the tabletop, the curtains pulled just ever so slightly so that she could see out but he could not see in. Crystal was too young to know exactly what was going on, but at two she sensed the danger in the air. She knew her mother was frightened. She saw the patrol cars for days on end. They were out of food but her mommy didn't want to leave the house to go get anything right now. They could eat these pork and beans, this stale bread maybe just one more day. Maybe he will go away. Maybe the police will get out of their cars and tell him to leave—for good.

She jumped when she heard the pounding on the door. "Who is it?" she pleaded. "It's Sam; open up." It was her stepfather. He knew she was afraid. He knew that her abuser was bothering her again. He'd called the police, too, telling them where this guy was hanging out, telling them to keep an eye on that piece of shit because he was for sure going to hurt her. He knew that it was only a matter of time.

We had all heard this last week. We knew this girl's story. She was terrified. Crystal was his child. He thought he owned her and the child both. But he was strange, scary even. She had asked him to move out. She had told him to go away and, no, he couldn't see Crystal, not right now, not until he got his act together. Go get cleaned up; stop drinking; get a job. Then come back and talk to her, that's what she told him. But he didn't. He just set up camp among the broken-down machinery in the vacant lot, watching her every move, lying down in the tall winter grass, parting the stalks so he could see straight into her trailer space. He had his eye on her. All the time. He never ate, just steadily drank, and drank, and drank. He didn't even feel the wet, winter soil beneath the thick army jacket he got on free-clothing day at the Salvation Army. She never saw him leave the grass. And she never saw him cross the packed dirt in front of her trailer where a car would be if she had one. She never heard his hand on the metal door latch, either. She did not hear his muddy boots on the kitchen floor or down the hallway or into the back bedroom. And she did not hear her children scream and scream and scream as he left the trailer and walked back across the packed dirt to pick up his gear and move into the trees beyond.

"That is just so sad," Marty agrees with the others as she stands by the Christmas tree, holding one of the children on her hip as though it were her own, shaking her head in resignation. "She was just here. Last week. She got the ex parte filled out. Fat lot of good that did. Just a piece of paper. Just a piece of paper." But there is no need to dwell on what might be the inevitable. The women do not need to remind themselves of this girl's story, of her terror, her pain. No one needs to acknowledge her story as their story. Any of their stories could end up like hers. The end; he killed her. She tried to tell the police. She tried to make everyone understand. She knew; her stepfather knew. She had been in the shelter before, but she hated to come in again. Besides, he would watch her. He would have followed her if she came here again, and then we'd all be in danger. He was dangerous, that one. Nothing in this world was going to stop him, and in the end, nothing did. The newspaper announced: "Alleged Killer Apprehended."

"Alleged." Remarkable.

I move among the women murmuring good-byes—a pat on the back here, a hug there, a smile, a little wave. See you next week. Good luck. Be strong. Try to keep your chin up. Be safe. Please, please, be safe. They are in no hurry, really, to leave this room, this safe place created for sharing, for communion, for hope. Leaving the room means going back home, or going upstairs to one of the rooms up there, or getting into a car and trying to decide where to go—what's next, what can I do?

I gather up my keys and coat, say good-bye to the volunteers and to the staff who will be there all night, guarding the doors and the precious human beings upstairs putting their children to bed, taking showers, reading, but probably not falling asleep. They cannot sleep yet. It is too soon.

I take a deep breath, tie my scarf, and push open the bulletproof door. I leave the light of the porch and walk through the parking lot toward my car, halfway down the block. There are no streetlights here but I realize the sleet has stopped. I fumble with my key a little bit trying to get into my car quickly.

I lock the doors, start the engine. I pull away and drive several miles out into the starlit countryside, driving to my home, where my family waits for me, safe from the demons that crawl into the minds of the women pulling out of the shelter's lot and the women settling in for the night in a lighted room upstairs. Although it is bitter cold, I roll down all the windows in my car and breathe in the clean, sharp air and listen to sweet, light-hearted flute music loud all the way home.

2

Powerful Words

Atlanta (AP)—An abusive husband killed his common-law wife by setting her on fire, then died in an explosion when he apparently yanked out a natural gas line in hopes of making the blaze look accidental.

Police said William Reese, 45, doused Rosemary Flournoy, 41, with gasoline and set her on fire early Thursday. . . .

A badly burned Flournoy died in a hospital.

[A neighbor] said she had been "afraid something bad was going to happen." The couple had had a 15-year relationship. "She took a lot off him. . . . People say when you take a lot of abuse, you love them. I don't see how." . . .

Battery and false-imprisonment charges were pending against [Reese] for allegedly tying Flournoy to their bed with an extension cord in 1997.

The police report said he told her "he was not going to let her out, feed her or allow her to go to work."

[The neighbor] said Reese [when incarcerated previously] would spend his time in jail writing poems and drawing pictures of the couple in wedding attire.

Columbia Daily Tribune,
April 10, 1999

ONLY A DAY OR TWO after I began answering the hot line at the shelter, I took a particularly disorienting call. At 9:30 one morning, I answered the phone and could barely hear the small, young voice on the other end. The line was crackling, thin, far away. The woman's voice was breathless; she was nearly in tears; I could hear the sounds of babies in the background. "How can I keep my children away from him, if I leave?" These were her first words. No time for hello; no social niceties. Here we were. I asked her the proper questions in the correct order: Are you safe? Are you in a place where you can talk with me for a minute? Should I call the police? Have you called the police?

She answered my series of questions with more gasps than words, then said: "I'm in the car. He stole his ex-wife's child and they didn't find her for three months. How can I keep that from happening? Can you help me keep him away from my kids? Can you guarantee that he won't take my children? That's the main thing; I don't want him to steal my babies."

"Where is he now?" I asked her, trying to remain calm. "What do you want to do?"

"He's in the house and if I go back in there he'll scream and yell and beat up on us. And if I try to leave, he'll go nuts. I don't even know if I can leave."

"Is that what you want?" I asked her. "To leave? You have the children, can you drive to Centerville, which has a shelter—the closest one to you. Do you want to go there?" I could hear her and I could hear her children, in the car. There was a long pause.

"I don't have the keys. I'm out here in the car on the car phone, but I don't have the keys and I don't know what will happen if I go back in there and try to get the keys. I don't know if I can get the keys and leave."

I talked with this young woman for several more minutes, as the already bad reception of her cellular phone drifted in and out. I don't know what happened to her; I probably never will, unless I hear of a homicide somewhere in that part of the state and I put two and two together and guess it was her. I never really heard her full story.

Another day, not too long after I began working at the shelter, I cleaned out a room vacated overnight in the whirlwind departure of a young woman and her small baby. I don't know what happened to her, either. My job that morning was to clean out her room and prepare it for a woman and her three children who were arriving with help from the Salvation Army that afternoon at two. I thought of James Agee's *Let Us Now Praise Famous Men* as I collected this woman's most personal belongings, wondering what she looked like (I couldn't even remember if I had met her or not). I boxed up her shoes and the baby's toys. I picked up a red barrette from the floor, a baby's bonnet, the baby's car seat, and a lone, tiny white cloth shoe. I dragged black plastic bags of this woman's belongings into a hall closet for storage. All she had to her name had been thrown into those plastic bags, and now she had left those behind as well. But before I made any presuppositions about this woman, I marveled to find on the desk a copy of the *North Colorado Review: A Literary Journal for the Mental Traveler,* and under the bed a novel entitled, *All My Friends Are Going to Be Strangers.* What did she take with her? Where did she go? What is her story?

Working in the shelter on a regular basis, we often do hear women tell their stories to each other as they move through their days as residents in this "safe house." In the kitchen while cooking, in the family room, the smoking room, the back steps, the office, we hear their stories. They are relating them to each other and to us, the staff. And, in the weekly support-group sessions, we hear their stories anew as they try to connect with the other women in the group, both residents and women living outside the shelter who are currently enduring abusive and violent behavior in their homes, or women who now live alone or with a roommate after leaving the shelter.

The effect of the storytelling in this venue is to shore up support for their newfound friends. They often refer to each other as "sister." They can cry here because, in the shelter, they have come to know other women as friends, completely separate from their families and their abuser. They smile when they look around the room and realize why their abusers isolated them and did not "allow" them to have girlfriends. Now, they claim, they have a room full of "girlfriends," women they can talk to and have come to love in a very short, intense time. They come to realize, perhaps for the first time in their entire lives, that having women friends is an act of empowerment and solidarity. Often they move out of the shelter together, find new housing, and try to create a life free from their marriages and abusers.

Perhaps the support group sharing time is the most poignant example of the transformative power of narrative in the shelter context. Here, women are able to speak openly, to encourage others who have not come as far, perhaps, as they have, and to explore new possibilities, ask questions, get support. Simply being there in that room with other women they see as *like them* provides the discursive potential for transformation. They are invited to share their story, and "story" here carries the weight of power and potential. However, that potential can be illusory, since the very institutions that have been established to "help victims" of domestic violence can actually victimize the victims again and again as the women seek to escape their physical abusers.

I hear the word *story* all the time in the shelter office. For example, when a policeman stopped by to pick up an ex parte order this week, he glanced at a woman sitting in the far corner of the room and asked me, "So, what's *her* story?" On the other hand, the house manager speaks of a woman's story in different ways: "Well, her *story* is . . . ," or "Her *story* is that . . ." She tells the new residents: "Keep your *story* simple, don't make it all complex with lots of different details about all the stuff that's going on. Stick to *one story,* that'll make the process go more smoothly."

I hear the difference between the policeman's comment and the house managers as critical. The policeman's "What's *her* story?" seems to equate the woman with "her story"; his language also implies he is suspicious of her story. But, to him, she *is* her story; he sees her sitting there as a "battered woman." The house manager and those of us who try always to work in the best interest of the women we serve recognize that a woman at the shelter is much more than just "her story," and furthermore we understand that her story has nuances and it changes. It is often a confused story, especially at first, days run into weeks and disappear behind the beatings and the pain. And gradually, as we cajole and urge and support her through "the system," we facilitate the work of those who seek to create a coherent story, a story that will "fly" in court, that will gain her services, that will satisfy the prosecutor, that will be in the language others have devised—language that is far, far from the flesh-and-blood violence she still carries in and on her body, in her mouth, in her most private parts, on her head, in her ears. Ironically, as we and all the others work with her through the "system," she is learning, with our assistance, how to use *language,* the proper language, the rules of the game; in fact, we teach her to learn, as John Austin put it, how to "do things with words."[1] She learns what to say, what not to say, how to phrase things, how to imply. This is about *using* words—to gain her safety, to make others hear her (perhaps for the very first time in her life), and to get the criminal justice system to work for her (a seemingly preposterous notion for many of the women I meet in this context).

The woman telling her story may believe that she got into the shelter and received help because of what "he did," when, in fact, she receives aid and shelter based on what *she says.* By picking up the phone and calling the shelter or the police, this act and the words she chooses are *doing something.* Furthermore, we must recognize just how affirming and transformative the telling of a woman's story actually can be. Last week she tried to use the words: "Please, No, Not again, Stop, Don't hit me, I'll leave, You leave, Don't touch the children, Go away, No, no, no," and her words carried no weight whatsoever.[2] If anything, her words only brought more grief, more pain, more anger directed her way, a punch in the mouth. But this week, she learned a remarkable thing. Her words are valuable. Her words just might save her. She is learning how to do things with words—powerful and saving things. And maybe, if she's lucky, someone will hear her and listen. But I want to point out that our power to disempower her is only a breath away. In fact, we have perhaps already participated in her disempowerment through our first phone interrogation.

Let us suppose that the young woman on the telephone in the story above does sneak back into her home and somehow, miraculously, gets the keys and drives into the nearest town. If she *does* make it to a town with a safe shelter for women being battered, in all likelihood she will call that shelter from a phone within the city limits. She does not know where the shelter is, nor does anyone else. Shelters are always at an undisclosed address. In fact, even if she knows where the shelter is, she must place a call asking permission to come into the shelter. This call will be a more structured phone conversation than that first crisis call from the locked car, when the best I could do was just listen and reassure her that there was a way to get out of there, even though I did not really see how she could. She will be calmer than she was before, and the staff person will fill out an "action card," listing her name, which she must give if she is seeking shelter; what her situation at home is; when the latest beating or abuse occurred; how the violence started and how it was concluded; where she is now; how many children are with her; whether or not she currently is taking drugs or drinking; and what she wants to do at this point.

There are many reasons for this litany of questions and answers. The staff members are concerned that they admit only women who are in immediate, dangerous crisis situations of abuse and violence. There are other agencies specifically designed to aid addicts and the homeless. The shelter is only for the woman who will be beaten again in the next few hours or tonight when her abuser returns home. Those in the gravest danger get first claim to the limited beds. The staff members are also concerned that they speak directly with the woman in crisis, not the police or a service worker. It is important to hear her say, in her own words, that she wants to get out of her violent situation and that she is seeking shelter in order to escape abuse. This is critical in terms of the woman's ability to voice her desires and to commit herself to this avenue of self-protection and escape from abuse. The staff has learned from experience that when someone else seeks shelter and escape *for her,* it rarely succeeds in helping her change her life situation. This must be her decision; for if it is, there is a better chance that she will actually begin to develop some patterns that could lead toward permanent and healthy changes. The phone call to the shelter and the request to "come in" are the first critical steps.

In thinking about women's stories and the efficacy of women's words, I might point out the two stories given early in this chapter are "my" stories, not theirs. These are the stories I tell about my work at the shelter, working with women trying to escape from the violence of their partners. But imbedded in my story are fragments of what we might recognize as *her* story, but at this point in time, she has not yet developed this particular moment into a recognizable "story." Story follows experience. Think about the woman in the car. She has not yet taken that necessary step away from experience and circumstance, away from immediacy and moment, to recollect for me an incident, a narrative, a recounting of what has happened to her. At the present time, she is *in the moment,* sitting out there with her children in that car. When she telephones again, she is more removed from the crisis situation and begins to develop a story that has more breadth and depth. She locates that moment of terror into a week and a month and, perhaps, years of terror. She realizes it was not, in fact, an isolated incident, and eventually, she will begin to tell her larger, more developed story, one that is empowering because it becomes self-reflective; the act of telling her story helps her heal her concept of her self.

Once a woman arrives and is settled into the shelter, she begins to tell her story in more and different contexts: first in the office during the "intake interview," then perhaps in the living area or in the kitchen as she is greeted by the other residents. She may tell only fragments or the most recent incidents, something to warrant her inclusion into this select group of women escaping. She will come to the support group and share again; she may meet with a counselor and share her story there. This is the natural context for her telling of her story. At the shelter, her story is valuable. She is honored for her words and for her ability to tell her story in ways that incorporate her presence into the group. Her story gains for her admittance, inclusion, support, respect, and empowerment. She, like the other women in the shelter, has escaped the horror, the pain, and the shame. Here she is included, accepted, even embraced, without judgment.

But in the world of seeking shelter and protection from the man who beats her, she will learn very quickly that she must also develop and relate a story that will help her get assistance. And she will learn in short order that the story for public, institutional consumption may be a far cry from the story she came into shelter telling. Which makes us all ask: What *is* her story?

When I first met Cathy, she was staying in the shelter, recovering from deadly bruises and a concussion that were the results of an online romance she had struck up with a man twenty years her junior. She "met" this young man on the Internet, told him the entire story of her abusive and violent marriage, and then went to live with him when she was escaping the out-of-control anger of her husband, Ron. In a short amount of time, this young man began to hit and beat Cathy as well. When she first arrived at the shelter, and even when she gave me her life story on tape, the stories about her husband and those of the subsequent boyfriend would seem to merge. We all remembered, however, how she lost her hearing in one ear and how her ribs still ached even years after the following incident. Her account of the response of the police and the prosecutor to her stories is typical of many of the stories women share in the support group. Clearly, in order to get any assistance from the "system," Cathy would need to modify her stories in such a way to get the official to not only believe her but help her gain the kind of assistance she needed.

> Anyway, the upshot of it was the judge never really ruled for him to have to pay my attorney's fees or anything. We ended up having to sell the house. I got fifty dollars a month maintenance and he got everything. And that was four years ago. And the county sheriff's department was not cooperative with me at all as far as keeping him away from me, honoring the ex parte

orders. He came back about two months after he had left, came in his mom's car, because he knew they were watching for his truck. He came in his mom's car because I wouldn't let him in the house, knocked me down in the driveway, gave me a concussion, fractured my collarbone, broke two of my ribs, and then proceeded to try to run over me with his mother's car. And I rolled out of the way, which I was hardly capable of doing; I couldn't breathe very well at the time. And I went to the doctor the next day. He told me everything that was wrong with me was because of domestic violence, and I went to the prosecuting attorney of the county—well, I went to the police station, to file charges and then went to talk to the prosecuting attorney.

He said, "I'm not gonna file these charges."

And I said, "Why not?"

And he said: "Because it's just your word against his—you don't have any witnesses or anything."

I said, "Excuse me! I'm the one with the injuries. Okay? That kind of supports my story a little more than it would support his saying he didn't know anything about it. How's he gonna explain his whereabouts during the time?"

And he was like, "Uh, I'm not going to file that!"

In response to Cathy's tale, another woman told about how she had to learn to "tell her story" about how she was raped by a man with whom she had had a romantic relationship at one time.

Yeah, I tried to be very honest about it. And that's not always in a woman's best interest in the courts. It makes me angry that to be taken seriously I would have to lie about it. But women *are* raped even when they are attracted to men. It doesn't mean you've done anything wrong. And I wasn't going to lie about it. I was attracted to him and he still raped me. *He still raped me.* [By telling,] I jeopardized everything I had worked for. So, finally, it came to the pretrial hearings and it was suggested we settle out of court.

I believe we should honor and listen to the actual stories of women who live in and seek to escape from abusive and violent men. I believe their words are important. I believe they tell the truth when they talk to me. I believe they are honest when they first call for help on a hot line. I also know from experience that we teach them to disbelieve and to dishonor their own words and stories by the ways in which the institutions that are supposedly in place for their assistance seek to reshape their words and rewrite their stories to fit the discourse of the service organizations and the courts of law. We tell them this is "for their own good" so that they will be heard and helped. But, in truth, the irony is that domestic violence has become "big business." This is a particularly insidious situation because a tremendous bureaucracy within law enforcement and the court system has been established on the backs of women who are being battered, but who are not listened to when they speak!

SOME OF THE HARD-TO-HEAR FACTS

According to international reports from the National Institute of Justice, millions of women in the world are beaten badly, are belittled and emotionally traumatized, and are violated physically and sexually on a regular basis in the privacy and supposed safety of their own home.[3] They are beaten, abused, and violated by the men they cohabit with—fathers, uncles, sometimes brothers, and, most often, by their spouses and partners. In the United States alone, the statistics now claim that a woman is beaten by her husband or partner every four seconds.[4] So, by the time you have read this paragraph, another woman has been hit, beaten, kicked, slapped repeatedly, dragged by her hair, or raped in her own home, often in front of her children, by the man who is her closest human companion—a man she claims she loves and who will, most often, also claim to love her. That this is so is a grave and sad personal, social, cultural, and political reality. To be fair, not all women are beaten and violated by their spouses and partners; to be sure, these statistics may, in fact, reflect the fact that many of the same women are beaten again and again by the same man. On the other hand, those who are working with data on the number of reports of violence, abuse, and murder, the number of court cases that appear on court dockets, the numbers of prosecutions, ex partes issued, the data on recidivism (recurrence of the same crime by the same offender), and the number of phone calls to shelters and hot lines, all suggest that the figures are probably not reflective of even *one-tenth* of the number of women who are actually beaten, abused, and violated, but who never report it.[5]

Research and scholarship on the issue of women being beaten by their spouses and partners in their private homes has been dominated by social scientists, and the predominance of research funding for domestic violence comes from the mental health divisions of various constituencies, most of them connected to the National Institute of Justice, which makes me wonder whose "mental health" they are focusing on. The topic is treated in the scholarship as a "social problem." Additionally, sociologists, social workers, psychologists, psychiatrists, theologians, and a host of lay writers who offer popular self-help books to the general public have entered into the conversation about this "national problem."[6] Criminologists and lawyers, of course, have also entered the dialogue; they are interested in issues of how domestic crimes are treated by the police and by the court system, and in the shaping of new laws to curb the violence against women by their spouses. The National Institute of Justice offers reams and reams of data and official reports based on grants written and conducted to collect data from reports, arrests, prosecution, sentencing, recidivism, therapy for batterers, safety networks for victims, and active community response teams that will, hopefully, increase awareness of the problem and serve to aid those seeking assistance.[7] Most of the grant possibilities under the 1984 Violence Against Women Act involve tracking databases and providing more and more figures on these aspects of violence against women.

Even a quick glance at the website for the National Institute of Justice would lead one to believe that we have, in this country, created a monster to keep the monster that lives among us breathing like an overstuffed slug that must be kept alive at all costs. These bitter thoughts arise when I consider how all the millions of federal dollars being spent on statistics gathering and computerized data collection, as well as building more and better shelters, seem, somehow, to have missed the mark. Perhaps the best illustration of the current interest in domestic violence and violence against women would be to note that in the year 2000, a World Wide Web search for information on "domestic violence" yielded 859,502 entries, a search for "violence against women" yielded 4,383,822 entries, and "wife beating" yielded 1,129,768 entries. Serious web searching on other search engines and linked sites could easily yield four times this many entries. *Think about it:* all this discussion about men who think they have the right to hit, kick, and violate the women who live with them.

The sheer volume of scholarship and published materials on this problem attests to its predominance in American, as well as international, family life. The overwhelming amount of data, reports, analysis, articles, and books is daunting and perhaps even diffuses the immediacy of the problem for women who actually live in fear and pain every day of their lives. What must be acknowledged in the midst of all this statistical evidence is: Women are seldom successful in winning their cases against their abusive husbands. Few men are actually put in prison because they beat their wives; they are much more likely to be imprisoned after they have *killed* her.

THE "FACTS," FROM HER VIEWPOINT

I am hoping that this book, filled as it is with women's stories, will add a dimension to this topic that has been lacking. I hope to put real flesh and blood, literally, onto the page called "domestic violence," and let the women's voices call us back into connection with them. To that end, I want to draw attention to the use of language to talk about male violence against women in domestic situations, both by those who are involved in violent situations and those who write about those situations. Feminist scholars writing about male violence against women have drawn attention to the global reality of this problem. They have shown how male violence against women is really about gender, power, and domination; and how inadequate, unfair, and unjust the police and court systems are in their reaction, response, and prosecution in situations involving domestic violence. Additionally, they have pointed out how language is used against women who have been abused and violated. They have also demonstrated how the sociocultural norms of most cultures throughout the world continue to support worldviews and belief systems that implicitly and explicitly condone male violence in general and maintain a deep-seated, but often unexamined, belief in the male right to "rule" his "own household" and "control" (beat, batter, and violate) his wife and children, who are viewed as his property. Feminist scholarship has also shown that women have internalized most of these beliefs, as well, and expect to be abused, belittled, and violated because they are, as they have been told over and over again, *only women.*[8] Unfortunately, most of the world's religions also support and reinforce these notions of male dominance and female submission and in doing so perpetuate the myths of a male's right to dominate and violate and a woman's submissive and "weaker" nature.[9] Too often in my work, I hear that a woman's pleas to the church, to a minister, or to her own pastor are not well received, and she is often enjoined to return to her home and "try harder" and to search her soul to determine what she might be doing to "provoke" his anger and hostility. What has been done to her is, in other words, *her fault.*[10]

The picture painted by the paragraph above, unfortunately, supports an image of woman as victim. And, in fact, that is the language that is used to refer to women who are beaten and violated by their spouses and partners. They are referred to as "victims" and as "battered women." Men are referred to as "batterers." Of course, the active participant in this portrayal is the male; the passive one, the female. "Victims" are generally thought of as unfortunate persons who are harmed by outside forces beyond their control. These are not personal crimes. We think of "victims" as being in the wrong place at the wrong time—it was fate, circumstance, an inexplicable, unfortunate coincidence. But, for women who are beaten by their spouses and partners, this crime is indeed personal. The situation is her own home. The abuser is the man she loves, has married (or is committed to), shares children with; the man who says he loves her, who will apologize profusely for the beatings, only to repeat them tomorrow or the day after and the day after that. To refer to her as a "victim" is to use language to veil the harsh reality of her life of terror *in her own home from someone who lives there with her.* And, of course, as we have learned from feminists, *the personal is political.*[11]

While the term most often used to describe situations where men are beating their wives is *domestic violence,* feminists advocate not using the term because mere "violence" could imply random incidents in a domestic—which could be read as "comfortable"—situation. They insist on more honesty in the use of terms, an honesty that acknowledges that in almost every instance, the truth is that *a man is beating, hitting, kicking, violating, and raping a woman in the privacy of their shared home.* This violence is *not* "domesticated," and the violence is not randomly distributed among the members of the household: Men are beating women.

But we are a bit embarrassed about this unleashable male violence toward women, so we couch this behavior in euphemisms like *domestic violence.*[12] This is one way we use language to "soften the blow," if you will, of the reality that men are hitting women. In fact, with words like *domestic violence* we in effect domesticate the crime. We can erase the perpetrators, the pain, the abuse, even the "victims" with such terms. The success of *domestic violence* as a completely opaque euphemism was most evident when the term was first used in Congress to garner support for the 1994 Violence Against Women Act (see the National Institute of Justice website). When the discussions about the bill began, many congressmen and -women thought "domestic violence" referred to terrorist attacks on American soil. Indeed—had it been, a great deal more money probably would have been allocated. It is to the credit of the shapers of that bill that it is named the Violence against Women Act and does not use *domestic violence* in its title.

Domestic violence was at one time called "wife beating."[13] On the surface, that term seems to be a better alternative. But, if we think more about it, this term, too, erases the perpetrator, dramatizes the act of violence, and draws attention to the recipient of the beating (i.e., a wife), making it seem as ordinary a phrase as "dog catching" or "rabbit hunting." Wife beating. Although our work in the movement is certainly meant to assist the woman who has been beaten, one of the most frustrating things about our work is the fact that culturally and socially, even globally, these euphemisms and phrases arise because there is an *assumption* that men *will* beat, rape, and abuse women and that we need to find ways to *assist and protect* women from acts that we presume *are going to happen*—as if "wife beating" is here to stay.

While it will be a challenge, I have determined not to refer to the situations of violence and abuse in private homes where men are beating women as "domestic violence"; and I will try not to refer to the women who live in constant fear of being hit and beaten, raped and violated as "battered women" or merely as "victims." The women who are now living in shelters or who have moved beyond shelters into other forms of independent living separated from their abusers are not currently "battered." And even when women are being beaten and hit on a daily basis, they are more than simply "battered women"; they are women who have been beaten up by their husbands and partners. And they may be victims of a sociocultural matrix of beliefs and practices that oppresses and harms women. But I find it demeaning and inaccurate to refer to them individually as "victims." And, certainly, in the shelter space in which I first interact with the women in this study, they are no longer being beaten and do not view themselves as victims of their husbands' abuse. They are survivors; they are warriors; they are fighters. Unfortunately, they may face the court system with this new-found determination to survive and move forward in their lives, only to find themselves victimized by the impersonal, inadequate, institutionalized, and biased system once again.

AN EXAMPLE OF AN EVOLVING STORY

The following is typical of a story as it emerges from the lips of a woman who has just arrived at the shelter, perhaps in a police vehicle. We are not clear what has happened, although we know from her first call that she has an ex parte against her abuser and he has threatened her life. Neither she nor the police know where he is right now, but there is concern that he is trying to find her to kill her. We gather there has already been a fight; apparently, she knifed her boyfriend and will be facing charges herself, most likely. That's all we know at first. She is alternately angry and raging, then crying and incoherent. We don't even catch her name at the beginning.

> I can't believe the son of a bitch came at me like that! He comes and he goes when he wants to. But he is the father of one of my kids, you know. But he really doesn't live with me. He's just a freeloader. Coming when he wants to. I'm not even sure he's got a key; but he must have a key because he's always in my place. I told him if he hit me one more time I'd kill him. He never believed it, though. He'd just push and push, you know. That's why I put that knife behind the toaster. I put it there, knowing he'd come after me. I knew he would. I was ready this time. We'd both been using all weekend and drinking—at least he'd been drinking. And when he's drinking he gets really ugly and mean. But when he's using, you know, he can be real sweet. That's why I use. Really, it is. If we're both using, everything goes pretty well, considering. When we shoot, things

slow down, shift, everything mellows out, so to speak. He doesn't hurt me then. When we can afford it, it can be real good. But that rotgut crap he and his brother buy and drink in my house, I can't stand that stuff. And it makes him real mean.

I've heard many stories like this one, told in a style that is fast and furious. Often the narrator begins to weep uncontrollably, tears falling down her bruised face. This woman is still wearing bloody clothes, her hand wrapped, with a dirty bandage around the side of her head. She seems to be missing patches of her hair. I try to guess her age, but I know from other similar situations, I will probably guess wrong. Women I think are forty-five turn out to be twenty-seven. Battering takes it toll.

We let her talk, cry, and rage over the course of several hours and even days, as she moves in and out of the office at the shelter, the rooms, the kitchen. We listen quietly and sympathetically. But as we listen, the staff is making mental notes. This is a raw and honest story, but when this woman tries to get an ex parte against her partner, or if she is prosecuted for cutting or even killing him in the course of a fight that ensued the night she is describing, the staff knows that this story will destroy all her chances for any kind of sympathetic response from the police, a judge, a prosecutor, or a jury.

We can hear her story and sympathize. And when this woman goes to the smoking porch and tells her story to the other shelter residents, they can identify with this woman's story. They've probably done the very same thing. But they will begin to warn her, as the staff will, that she must begin to reframe her story. She must leave out some of these raw truths; she must be careful how much she reveals; she must develop a story, a simple story, that does not reveal what living like this is really like.

What must she drop of her story? First of all, she must never repeat again for anyone to hear that she actually threatened his life. No matter that he had held knives to her throat and guns to her head while he raped her in the anus with a Coke bottle and repeatedly threatened that he *will kill* her. He can deny all that in court and yet she will be the only person in the room admitting that she did, indeed, threaten to kill him. That's enough to incriminate her right there. The other residents say, "Shhhh, don't say that. Don't ever say that again. You mustn't tell that you threatened to kill him. Don't tell anything you said to him. Not anything."

And the alert reader, who knows and recognizes that this woman has been beaten every single night for a bloody month, will already deduce some of the other things this woman must not tell. One morning, as she limped through the house while her 240-pound husband was still passed out on the sofa, she vowed she would never, ever again allow him to beat her to within an inch of her life, or rape her until she bled and her body screamed in pain. She knows what the scenario will be when he awakens, and in an empowering moment of desperation, because she knows her hundred-pound frame cannot withstand much more from his fists and his attacks, she puts a small, sharp knife behind the toaster. It's out of sight, but it makes her feel good just to know it's there. She sees just how to reach in and retrieve it if he comes after her. She maybe even practiced pulling it out quickly with her right hand, noting that her left hand cannot reach it at this angle. She does not know if she'll actually have the nerve to grasp it and pull it out to threaten him. She certainly does not know if she has the courage or even the physical strength to plunge it into his flesh, but she feels better all morning just knowing it is there. But if she tells this part of her story, her actions in the kitchen become premeditated, not instinctive acts of self-defense. No, she planned to kill him, or to hurt him very, very badly at the very least. This would not go well with the police, the judge, the prosecutor, or a jury. No, indeed, it would not go well at all. She'd better lose that part of the story, now.

And she has revealed that they were both using drugs; she was using drugs with him. That makes her a dope addict, a no-good user, herself. She's as bad as he is, they will think and say. No matter that shooting drugs with him was a devil's bargain to get him to mellow out and not hit her, a way to avoid the cheap liquor that always made him a mean and ugly drunk, surly, moody, and unpredictably violent. She should leave that part out, the other women warn her.

So, what has become of her story? The warnings of the staff, the advice of the other residents, the interjections of the counselor who leads the support group that night, and the court advocates who work closely within the "system," all point to one imperative. She must not tell her story, or at least she must not tell the story the way she's been telling it here, in the shelter, for the past few hours and days. "But what *should* I say?" she questions the women around her. "What *can* I say?" She seeks assistance in knowing how to tell a story that will not indict her, provide just the fuel the prosecutor wants to hear. He will ask, sarcastically, "And where were your four children, Ms. Rogers, while the two of you were shooting up?" "And he doesn't even live there, does he? So, why is he there all of the time, if he doesn't actually live there? You say you don't want him there? Then why is he there? Actually, you gave him a key, didn't you, Ms. Rogers? You gave him a key, because you actually want him to be there with you, don't you, Ms. Rogers? Truth is, you like him being there; he supplies you with your coke. You could get away from his abuse, couldn't you; you just don't want to." They warn her how his questions will corner her and make her look bad, really bad. "But it isn't like that," she protests. But she already knows they are right. She must change her story quickly.

THE ACKNOWLEDGED POWER OF WORDS

The women's shelter provides a unique context for storytelling, a venue (with several different yet interconnecting arenas) that recognizes how words and language can indeed operate to change circumstances, a context that by no means "hears" or understands this storytelling as traditional, as expert finesse, as celebratory, validating, or transformative (even though, I would argue, the stories potentially could be all of these things). Audre Lorde's comment about the frustrations of trying to use the master's tools to dismantle the master's house has haunted me ever since I first encountered it; yet, the pragmatist in me acknowledges that it is precisely through our reappropriation of language (the "master's tools") that we are able to transform our lives.[14] What other recourse do we have? It is the acknowledged power of women's words that enables me to at least critically examine Lorde's assertion.

Therefore, at this point, I will focus on women's stories about violence and abuse in their homes, violence against them largely from their spouses or partners, and sometimes their fathers—men who say they love them. These are stories told by women in the process of gaining shelter from, court protection from, and (hopefully) prosecution against their abusers. They also relate their stories to other women in the context of the women's shelter where they are currently living and in the support group sessions when the telling of their stories is transformative, as the women come to know their collective unity. In the group setting, they come to realize they are not alone in their grief and fear and that their experiences are shared with other women just like them. This context for telling a woman's story of violence and abuse is obviously multilayered. By looking at how a woman's story is honed, performed, and adapted over the course of her journey toward safety, we can see how women learn to "do things with words."

Given the process of building a story for the benefit of services, I am interested in how a story of crisis evolves through the various stages of "using words" to gain safety, and I wonder two things: Why is the story she is taught to tell better than the one she came in telling? And have we noticed that at the same time she is learning how to formulate words that will gain her services, which is a form of empowerment, we are, by telling her what to say, and when and how, serving only to disempower her once again by replacing her words with those created by the very institutions established to help her?

It occurred to me very early in my work in this context that some of the "stories" I was hearing were not well-formed, easily discernable "narratives," but rather they were fractured stories, delivered very much *in medias res* (into the middle of the plot). They contained no obvious story beginning—to be sure, beginnings were implied and could be fleshed out over the various tellings to come, but in that initial story, her story began *in the middle.* And often the stories have no endings. There is no neat tying up of these stories, no easy, confirmed ending. Even if they find shelter, they are left hanging; indeed, that's where the women are today, in this moment: "We are alive now; we have nowhere to go; we don't have a clue about tomorrow. But we are here in safety tonight. That's all. The end"—for now. So my question is: When a battered woman tells her crisis story in crisis, is that her story? When she tells it later and fleshes it out, is it a "better story"? If she might relay this story within the context of other abuse narratives and weave them together into some kind of coherent life journey of a woman who has been violated would that be even better? To our discredit, the women in these situations learn quickly that their more developed stories, complete with all the requisite information, will help them more within the various government resource services and institutions. Carefully crafted stories will serve them far better than honesty or the plain "truth" will ever get them.

Generally, after the first crisis call we get from a woman in danger, we get a second telephone call. She has managed to remove herself somewhat from the immediate situation and she calls us to find out more about coming into the shelter. Her situation at home is terrifying; she needs to escape. Often she ends this conversation by saying she would like to come into "shelter," to become a resident of the "safe house." In order to do this, she must tell her story in somewhat more detail than in her first, panicked phone call. She must tell us what is going on and over what amount of time; she must relay in detail when he hit her, how many times, how he has hurt her recently and if he is hurting her children. Did he hit her? Where? With an object? Did he threaten her life? With an object? With a gun? This story, too, is assessed, and the determination about whether or not she will be provided with safety at the shelter depends upon how she tells her story—what components are there, which ones are missing, how dangerous her situation is, if violence has occurred before, and if she has been drinking. If her story "holds up," she may—via the power of her own words—be provided with shelter. While I am aware that the contemporary scene of drug abuse and the crisis of the homeless renders the shelter staff helpless to provide housing for everyone who calls in, it is, nevertheless, imperative that we notice what the system at large is doing when "clients" are admitted or denied justice and assistance based on the story they are able to tell at any given moment—and in crisis, at that!

A woman's story about the abuse she suffers at the hand of her abuser is developed during the time she is participating with the "system," as she moves from seeking assistance from the police and working toward getting her abuser arrested, to finding safe shelter, attempting to have an order of protection against her abuser secured, and, finally, moving toward prosecution of her abuser and his sentencing to jail or prison. Again, with the way the system works, the "truth" of her account may disappear long before she receives any benefits, and, of critical importance, to a woman in this situation, this is yet another example of how her own sense of herself can be *both empowered and damaged.* No one has heard or bothered to listen to her "real story," or else she has been too terrified to tell it. Why should this be any different, she wonders? This has been the case all her life. And while this new "safe" situation *should* be different, in reality, it is not. Her words and experiences are *not* honored and respected in connection with all else that is transpiring.

When she calls the state hot line number or the shelter or the police the very first time, she must tell a story that reflects a certain degree of danger and harm to herself and to her children. In order to get the police to her home and help her, she must say certain things. Based on what she tells the police, her call will be ranked in terms of its priority in relation to other calls coming in at the same time. Whether or not she has called the police before, if they came to her assistance on other occasions, and how consistent her story is will determine how they continue to respond to her calls and assist in her safety. Women who live in a violent household and are always trying to sidestep an abuser's verbal, emotional, and physical assaults often acquire a calm, steady demeanor. While this may or may not act as an actual deterrent to her husband's flashes of violence and uncontrollable rage, she believes it will. "Walking on eggshells" is a daily routine. She believes her steady calmness just might avert a crushing blow to her face, her belly, her back. She hangs on to every shred of control she can. If she just doesn't provoke him . . . maybe she won't be beaten tonight. And she teaches her children these same soft-shoed moves. "Don't aggravate your dad; don't get him upset; it's better just to go on out than stay and risk a blow or being yelled at."

Ironically, this survival mode will work against her when she calls the police. If she is not hysterical, weeping, and incoherent, the police are less likely to take her call seriously or to respond immediately. Her calm voice and demeanor are not indicative of the danger level in that house. She certainly does not know about this strategy of the "first story" when she initially calls the police, but she quickly learns the language and the necessary framing of her story for best results in assistance to her—and how not to get arrested herself! But all of this knowledge may still fail her, for in the state of Missouri, for example, there is now a police "rule of last blood," which provides a rationale for which party the police should arrest when they arrive at a chaotic domestic scene. If they arrive and the male is bleeding from a knife injury, for example, and the female exhibits bruises (indicating earlier violence but not immediate assault), then the *female* will be arrested for inflicting the injury that resulted in the "last blood." No matter that her body testifies to months, perhaps even years of abuse at the hand of her house partner, if he shows signs of the most recent assault, she will be arrested. In many states, there is a current police rule that in cases of domestic violence, *someone* on the scene must be arrested.

If the woman is lucky and her abuser is arrested, she may then try to get an ex parte, a legal order of protection, for herself and her children, at the county clerk's office. Here the court advocates will assist her in telling her story once again. This time she dictates a narrative to the advocate or clerk, who helps her write it into the appropriate boxes on the form that will find its way to a judge. Again, her story in this instance must carry the most effective language, must include pertinent and specific details, must be couched in certain ways to insure that the judge will actually sign it and provide for her the legal protection against her abuser (of course, this paper may not at all keep him away from her; she knows this). The clerks and the advocates know how the story should "sound" and what should be included and what deleted in order to best insure that the order will be made and that the police will try to enforce it. Wendy Hesford would call these prescribed sentences part of the "cultural script" of domestic violence, scripts that guide us both in our actions and in our narrative retellings of events.[15] If it is the middle of the night and she is seeking an emergency ex parte, then the language is doubly important, because the story will determine whether or not a sleepy judge will get out of bed and actually sign it. And finally, of course, her story must ultimately be told to her defending attorney, and, if the case goes to court, to the court, the judge, and the jury. Unfortunately, too often her plea for justice will go unanswered. She comes to believe that here, as in all other spaces in her life, the decisions will not be fair. She is not equal under the law, and her story, honed or not, prepared and well-articulated or poor and disjointed, will probably make no difference. Too often it is his word against hers and he knows the rhetoric, the discourse of the public arena. He knows some of the men in the justice system in the town they live in; he is friends with the cops. He is a respected citizen and is known to others. He may even be a policeman himself.

In feminist and women's studies circles, attention to women's lives and women's life stories, women's ways of knowing, women's friendships, the bonds of mothers and daughters, grandmothers and tradition, have taken us all, in Alice Walker's words, "in search of our mother's gardens."[16] Our attempts to fill the silences, to reinstate women back into the historical record, to celebrate women's lives and the telling of their stories, has been both celebratory and romanticized. "Tell your story," we say, and we will listen because that story is real, is true, and it validates you and, in extension, all women. Usually we hear stories of strong and bold women, women struggling against all odds, women who "run with the wolves." But what of the stories that we may *not* want to hear, or are embarrassed by, or do not know how to respond to? What about the painful stories that are told in furtive voices because they may bring only shame and potentially more violence to the women who tell them? And more than that, do we really want to hear her story? How many other painful, heart-wrenching, devastating stories have we not ever "heard" because they are difficult to hear or they don't fit the profile of the stories we have come to expect, or even demand, in exchange for safety and services?

I want to move our attention beyond the "reading" that would foreground these stories as examples only of the victimized woman, suggesting, instead, that we "hear" a story of an empowered woman who is determined to change her circumstance. The narratives in this study are all from women who have left the homes where they have every right to live in peace and safety. They have left all of their belongings, clothes, jewelry, toiletries, books, furniture, everything, to risk coming into the shelter to prevent "him" from hitting them again. These are women on the move. One minute they are angry, strong, and determined. In the next, they will admit to being apprehensive, even scared; in the shelter with other women who are also escaping, they are willing to articulate both their strengths and their weaknesses, their fears and their aspirations, to be vulnerable to the pain as well as open to the lure of new possibilities. In this chapter, I have examined the ways in which some of their stories "do" things, noting, however, how the system teaches them that the raw truth is never their best avenue for success. The next chapters examine the transformative nature of words—or how women use language to speak about the unspeakable. The key for this analysis is, of course, to remain attuned to the words and phrases, the language and the nuance of the women's own stories, their own words. Grounded in their use of language lies the transformative power and possibility for change.

I want to end this chapter by commenting that I do not want to reduce women's stories of violence to some kind of structural analysis or discourse critique. In *Passing the Time,* a wonderful book about a man who listened to an entire community's stories told slowly and heard carefully, Henry Glassie reminds us that "Good work is not the end of our task. Scholars are citizens, in debt to their society. Our study must push beyond things to meanings, and grope through meanings to values. Study must rise to perplex and stand to become part of a critical endeavor."[17] As with Glassie's characters, the women I study do not occupy some misty island from distant days. The women I know have been living in a dark corner of the same world you and I inhabit, but they are reaching for the light. The sacred heart of their existence has been split by intimate terror: We must not only hear and listen and respond to their stories of pain and violation. Could it be that *we* should learn to *listen* better, rather than teaching *her* how to *tell her story* "better"?

3

Describing the Unspeakable

A headstone resting on a cemetery plot in Cedar Rapids, Iowa, bears the name of a woman murdered 13 years ago. The family of Susan Wray Davis holds out a dwindling hope that her body might yet be found. . . .

Susan Davis disappeared in 1986, at 35, after she had become estranged from her husband. A victim of domestic violence, she feared her husband enough to buy a German shepherd for protection after they separated.

When she vanished, Ralph Davis told police he didn't know what had become of her. . . .

. . . Only a few months after Susan vanished, . . . [her brother reported] Davis [had] told him he didn't believe in God . . . "Because I don't want no one judging me when I get through with life. I want to do whatever I want to do in life, and I don't want no one judging me."

Columbia Daily Tribune,
April 25, 1999

LATE ONE AFTERNOON A police car pulled up to the door and a young officer helped a rather well-dressed woman out of the car. He rang the bell indicating that I should let them in. I did. And he proceeded to bring the woman, Charlotte, into the office for the third time in three days. She had arrived first on Thursday evening with numerous bruises all over her body and her hair shaved in three places showing all of the seventy-nine stitches she had received on her head. Charlotte had gone back to her own home late that first afternoon to retrieve her two cats, but she had miscalculated. She did not think her abuser would be at home. He was, and he greeted her at the door with two gunshots—one over each of her shoulders, near her ears, and he proceeded to beat her nearly to death with the butt of his revolver. As she lay in a pool of blood on the floor at his feet, he miraculously emerged from the dark cloud of rage that had propelled him to beat her senseless and called an ambulance. Charlotte had been back to the hospital twice because her ears were ringing, her equilibrium was off, and her head was hemorrhaging.

This was near Christmas of last year. Two weeks ago, Charlotte came back to see a counselor at the shelter, where she had been a resident for more than two months, and told me she would like to share her story with me for this research.

Keep in mind that the story I have just recounted to you is *my* story about something that happened to a woman named Charlotte from *my* point of view, as someone working at the shelter. These are not her words. In fact, when she did tell me her life story, she talked nonstop for my tape recorder for two hours and forty-five minutes, reaching only up to age thirty-five (she is now forty-five); at that point, she announced that she would have to continue another day because she really needed to go. When we met a second time and I let her hear the end of the previous tape indicating where she should pick up her narrative, she talked to me for less than ten minutes, became agitated, told me she felt ill from some medicine she had been taking, and asked if we could reschedule again. She assured me several times that this was not an emotional issue for her but "just" a physical one (she just didn't feel well). Up until this point in her life story, she had recounted no physical violence or abuse, although her parents were alcoholics and abusive in their own ways to her, the only girl in the family. In her account of the first thirty-five years of her life, she did not indicate that she had suffered beatings and violence. But when she arrived at the place in her life where violence began to dominate, her story splinters. She was unable to continue. There is a definite "gap" in her narrative. She apparently did not want to, or could not, continue with her story after that point.

But the account of Charlotte's taping comes later in my story about my research, and I need to go back and fill in the gaps in my own story.

After working in the shelter for several months, I realized that I was hearing well-developed personal stories told by the residents within the building. In the office, or in the living room, a woman might begin to relate her past life— her childhood, other abusers she had escaped from, and so on. Sometimes, if the office was relatively quiet for a few minutes, we might sit, sipping coffee, while a woman traced her story back to her early years, to other abusive partners, to a father who was mean and sadistic. Often one of the other residents would come to the door of the office, trying also to sort out what had happened to her and where she was going next. We are always good listeners; that's part of the job. The spontaneous context for storytelling led me to believe that the telling of her story was, in a way, therapeutic for the woman speaking. This was not a therapy session, to be sure, but the simple act of voicing what had happened to her and trying to sort out the various ways in which she had been abused, and her responses to that violence, seemed important.

What the women told us in these stories led me to believe that it would be important for me to get their entire stories, their life stories. I wondered how we might put the stories of violence into the whole of a woman's life. Had she had a "normal" childhood, or had she been terribly abused as a child? Where had she lived? What was her mother like? Had she felt secure as a child or terrified? I wondered if the women would be willing to share with me their life stories in a controlled but safe environment. I began to ask different women if they would tell me their life stories on tape. I told them I would not mark the tapes with names, dates, or places; I told them I would transcribe the tapes and change all names of persons and places, even dates; I told them I thought their stories were extremely valuable to the kind of study I wanted to do about women's lives in dangerous and violent domestic situations. They agreed. And they began to share their stories with me on tape.

"HEARING" THE GAPS

I began to accumulate stacks of tapes of life stories from women living in shelter. I transcribed them, reading and rereading the transcriptions, trying to "hear" the women's voices, their stories, and understand both what was there, on the tape, and what was missing. One of the first things I noticed was that sometimes, when the narrator would get to an incidence of horror and violence, she would, like Charlotte, narrate *around* the violence in such a way that left what appeared to be big gaps, holes in the story—she might imply hitting, punching, violence, anger, yelling, and blood, but give few graphic details. She seldom really articulated how being hit felt, or how she reacted. She often sketched out the scene in bare outline.

The story I related at the beginning of this chapter, about Charlotte, who could not tell all of her story to me but left in confusion and fear, was not the only story that reflected a kind of roadblock to the recounting of her experience. Another woman filled three tapes, talking for hours. The driving force of her narrative, tape after tape, was urging me toward the disaster: Somewhere in the future, on November 12, a monstrous thing happened, she was near death, and her story was a promise to take me there to that eventful day, that ultimate moment of pain and violation. After hours of recounting several years, she finally reached that horrendous day when her life had to change or she would die. She told me about a party she and her live-in boyfriend had gone to, how he had been drinking and doing some drugs, how she had been drinking, too, and was surprised when he pulled her up off the floor where she had been sitting with other friends, and loudly announced they should leave. She did not want to leave, she said, and told him so, but he insisted and got louder and more aggressive. She paused for a long moment (a narrative device in all these stories when the narrator tries to voice the violence), took a deep breath, and said, " . . . after Andy, I knew I had to keep living; I had to go on."

Stunned, I broke my own vow not to interrupt the narrators in this study. "Wait," I begged. "Go back, if you can. I don't want to push you, but do you realize what you just did there? You reached November 12 and you skipped over the event, the disastrous moment, in a heartbeat, and said 'Well, after Andy—' Can you go back? Can you fill in that gap?"

She did go back, but I could tell it was very difficult. When he grabbed her off the floor, she said, he pulled her elbow, wrenching it, she thought, possibly out of its socket. He shoved her into the door frame, trying to push her out the back door, still with his fierce grip on her arm, yelling and calling her a bitch and a slut. He shoved her up against the car, took her long hair in his hand and began to smash her face into the windows and the side of the car, again and again and again. All she knew then was blood in her mouth, her hair wrenched from her scalp, and she was on the ground. She heard the car as it drove away. Somehow she dragged herself to the door of another apartment of someone she knew, and that friend helped her and took her home. Andy was there when she got home, but he ignored her, so she went upstairs and fell across the bed.

This incident seemed traumatic for both of us. Should I have left her story the way she gave it to me? Was I wrong to ask her to go back and fill in the gap? What have I learned from the details she provided at my request? Was her "voicing" of the violence important for her to do at this time in her life? Was it beneficial or harmful for her to recount the bloody details, to voice the violence and the pain as best she could?

I have concluded, actually, that I should not have asked her to go back and fill in what she had originally left out. She was not ready; she had already made a narrative decision. I am convinced, now, that we must hear and "read" these stories as they come to us, even interrupted and broken by the gaps and ruptures. In fact, to ask trauma survivors to go back and to fill in the gaps may be to ask them something they are not ready or able to do. Respecting the gaps and ruptures and learning how to peer through them where they bleed into the narrative event but away from recognized language is, rather, our task.

But in exploring the places in women's stories where language seemingly breaks down, where they are not able to speak the unspeakable, we must also acknowledge that there are other places and other stories where the "unspeakable" *is* spoken. I hope to shed some light, or at least pose some possibilities, for why and when and how the women telling stories are able to articulate some horrors and not others.

I suggested earlier that we think about words as transformative—or how women, newly empowered, "do things" with words. But I have also cautioned that in the process of teaching women how to use language to "get things done," we also run the risk of disempowering her and deflecting the significance of her experience as told in her own words. The key for this analysis is, of course, to remain attuned to the words and phrases, language, and nuance of the women's stories, as they relate them *in their own voices,* complete with the gaps and ruptures. I think the same cautions are appropriate for this examination of what appears to be "missing" from the women's stories—that we must be careful not to assume failures or discredit what is narrated before we have carefully explored the evidence.

In this examination of the women's life stories and the embedded stories of severe abuse and violence, I want to explore what might (at first glance) be deemed the narrative failures, the places in the narratives where language breaks down, where the women "fail" to locate words and language to depict events that go beyond the ordinary and take us into what some scholars and thinkers might call "the disaster."[1] However, my analysis will not suggest that the women or their narratives have "failed." Rather, my analysis will point our gaze directly toward the disruption, toward the "tear" in the "fabric" of the narrative and invite us to "read" the silence, the void, the muted voice of that moment. What will we hear and see if we peer into the rupture? And could there be several different messages occurring simultaneously?

LOCATING THE UNSPEAKABLE

During the time I was beginning to seriously read and reread the transcriptions of the women's life stories, thinking about the ways in which their narratives often moved *around,* even avoided, explicit and graphic details of pain and violence, a colleague, Mike Bernard-Donals, gave a Friday afternoon talk about his own work with recorded narratives of Holocaust victims. He explained how he was using the work of Maurice Blanchot to think about when, how, and why language fails to actually articulate the *essence* of the Holocaust—how even personal accounts (as witness) are not able to capture the overwhelming, unfathomable horror of that event. In his talk that day, Mike discussed Maurice

Blanchot's notion, examined in his now often-quoted book *The Writing of the Disaster,* that when we *try* to describe events within the disaster, we actually do the disaster a disservice, because what we can say can never really even approximate the horror of the actual event. In fact, the more we say, the further we get from the actual disaster—at least that is Blanchot's idea about our attempts to describe and even evoke the reality that was the Holocaust.

So I began to wonder how this might help me think about the women's stories of pain and violence, the horror of their lives, and I read Blanchot, several times. His book is difficult and I find him pompous; he makes generalizations and offers single-line "truths." He seems to write from a center far from reality, waxing poetic, playing the guru for all of us. And yet there are no citations in his book; he appears to have relied on no one but himself for these ponderous statements—or so he would have us believe. He speaks with patriarchal assurance. He is adamant about the unspeakable nature of the disaster and about the failure of language. He warns: "The disaster ruins everything, all the while leaving everything intact. There is no reaching the disaster. Out of reach is he whom it threatens, whether from afar or close up, it is impossible to say: the infiniteness of the threat has in some way broken every limit."[2]

For those who listen to the disaster stories that belong to someone else, he claims: "The disaster, unexperienced . . . [i]s what escapes the very possibility of experience—it is the limit of writing. . . . [It] is beyond the pale of writing."[3] According to Blanchot's bleak view, even the person who experiences the disaster cannot portray it. The narrator will encounter the failure of language in describing that which cannot be described. In describing the moment of the disaster, he says, when the victim is closest to the pain and violence, she or he can only recount the barest of details, a kind of "witnessing" chronology that cannot do justice to the situation but at least is an honest attempt to do so. As the witness moves further from the scene of pain and horror, and as she or he begins to formulate a narrative about that past event, Blanchot would say that this "testifying" narrative begins to eclipse the event; it will fail in its attempts to recount the reality of what happened and becomes a story separate from the event.

This is not, I would argue, a case of "coding" in women's narrative, as Joan Radner and Susan Lanser have explicated in their important work, "Strategies of Coding in Women's Cultures." While certainly "coding" is occurring in many of the narratives I have tape recorded, the examples in this book illustrating gaps, interruptions, and other fractures in the narrative are not examples of coding as much as they are muted screams of what cannot be spoken.

According to Bernard-Donals, who writes about recorded Holocaust stories, the resolution of the debate about memory and history turns on the ability to identify—not discursively, and not even through an examination of the rhetoric, the logic, or the documents—the presence of an event by means of the *disruption* of the logic or rhetoric of the documents and language. Bernard-Donals draws on the work of historians who search, ultimately, for a language for historical writing that leaves room "for the *presence* of an event to *bleed through* the writing or method of the historian." According to this view, it is the disruption itself that "presents the disaster in its failure to represent it," suggesting the possibility of a kind of "redemptive history," as suggested by the works of both Walter Benjamin and Blanchot—a history that might offer more "truth" than the constructed kinds of history most of us encounter on a regular basis.[4]

READING THE GAPS

At first this seemed to make sense to me as I listened to the words of the women's narratives, and I agreed with Blanchot: That which is inscribed already on her flesh and body cannot be spoken. The unspeakable is, in fact, unspeakable. This seemed reasonable to me; it offered a way to help us read and understand the gaps in a woman's story. Even the women narrating these stories seemed to recognize that they were, at times, skirting the disaster, and they said things like: "I'm leaving out a lot here"; "I haven't told you everything"; and "You don't want to hear the bloody details." Continuing with Blanchot's theory, I wondered: If we are listening carefully to a woman's story and its gaps, could we, in these narrative ruptures, get a glimpse of the disaster, even though she does not speak of what has happened to her? I wondered if, even though the narrator at times is *unable* or *unwilling* to find words to re-present that moment, the disaster might nevertheless be available to us through the silence, the rupture in the narrative.

It seems plausible, in Blanchot's terms, to think of women's stories, the remembering of the pain and violent moments, as a kind of after-the-fact "testifying," rather than the more immediate "witnessing," a recounting that he characterized as raw and unarticulated, but nevertheless closer to the disaster. When speaking from a distance, the woman is largely trying to make some sense of the past events. But these narrators know, as we must, that to re-present the moment of the disaster creates it anew for them. In retelling it, they must relive it: Memory becomes reality; the past emerges and converges with the present. This view of the women's narratives suggests a different reading of Benjamin's notions about what might be available to us through the gaps, a less historical and collective narrative but a more personal one. This reading of the "presence of the event" does not so much restore the events of history as it does "tear the fabric of memory" so that we glimpse, in Benjamin's terms, "the time of the *now*"—a now that requires a conflation of the past and the present.[5]

For those who believe we must not risk the peril of forgetting the Holocaust, glimpsing the "real" of that disastrous *now* is a driving imperative. But for women who cannot or will not honor the horror of the violence inflicted upon their bodies by men who supposedly love them by recounting it in its graphic details, the "now" may be something else altogether. Perhaps several of these imperatives can operate simultaneously. Women narrating disastrous moments in their personal lives try to find a way to articulate that horror and pain; their attempts are often difficult, and speaking the violence is often avoided, narratives are truncated, narrative plots dissolve. Women recognize the power of language and they recognize that to name the men and to name the violence they have wrought upon their bodies is, possibly, to torture their bodies anew. A woman does not want to use language to portray him as powerful and her as victim. Hence, the gap in her narrative calls for us to discern at least two messages: the reality of the disaster, the horror, the pain, the torture; but also the *now* of her release, her escape.

This proposal might offer a way to understand the Holocaust memories as well as those of women who are recalling beatings and near-fatal experiences. Blanchot and others are terribly concerned about preserving our understanding of the monolithic horror known in its totality as "the Holocaust." Everyone knows the history: Six million Jews died at the hands of the Nazi murderers. This is a horrific truth we are afraid to lose sight of because it harbors the reality that such an event could occur in modern times, because there are people who deny that it ever happened, and because we want to believe that if our memory is strong enough (that is, if we can maintain the essence of that disaster), we can somehow prevent it from ever happening again. On one level, the disaster that is violence against women in their own homes, and the epidemic proportions of this assault upon the bodies of women globally, is also a kind of holocaust. And the narratives of the women who have survived this violence attest to the *essence* of this disaster in their narratives. Glimpsing through the "rip in the fabric" of their stories, we are able to "read" the reality of the disaster, both the monolithic reality and the personal one. This is what appears to be missing from Blanchot and Benjamin's perspectives on the narration of the disaster. Their analyses and their concern are attuned more toward the "greater" disaster of the Holocaust, the totalizing effect of the disastrous event. Yet the narratives they are reading—both the cryptic "witnessing" accounts and the later "testifying" narratives that attempt to articulate more from a safe distance—are *personal experience narratives* that beg for the listener to "hear" the pain and violence that has been inflicted upon that one person and on her or his immediate family members and community. The cultural readings of memory and history are absolutely necessary for our totalizing historical efforts, yet the personal narratives that make up that all-encompassing history are living, breathing components of the larger narrative—what Lyotard might suggest is a kind of "master narrative." This is not a "false" master narrative, nor a misleading one, to be sure, but we fail in our readings of narratives if we can only discern, in the end, the overarching historical narrative at the expense of the smaller, more personal stories.

Therefore, I would like to propose that both images are available to us through the gaps and the ruptures of narratives of disaster: the *essence* of the event we recognize as *the disaster,* which may, in fact loom as largely unarticulated in its horror but evoked in the silences, as well as the *now* that Benjamin talks about. But the *now* that is also discernable in these stories, in the gap, might suggest another story, a more personal story the narrator hopes to convey. For the battered women, I propose that the stories they tell of violence and pain invoke at least three distinct but interrelated "truths." One has to do with the essence of the disaster, one has to do with both the essence and the reality of their personal disaster, and one has to do with their invocation of the *now* that is radically different from the *now* of the disaster. Allow me another diversion to demonstrate how I have come to claim the viability of these multiple "readings."

PAIN AND SILENCE

We seem to be at an impasse. Is the disaster unspeakable or not? And if not, why not? How do we read the gaps in the narratives of pain and violence? Do they operate best as only references to a horror that cannot be articulated, only surmised by those gut-level faculties that have nothing to do with logic or knowledge? Perhaps no single work has helped me think about these issues in relation to women's narratives of abuse more than Elaine Scarry in her ponderous and tortuous work, *The Body in Pain.* Yet she seems to contradict herself all over the place. Scarry claims, "Physical pain has no voice, but when it at last finds a voice, it begins to tell a story"; on the very next page, she admits that "whatever pain achieves, it achieves in part through its unsharability, and it ensures this unsharability thorough its resistance to language."[6] I want to explore both of these possibilities, beginning with the second quote first, and examine why the pain might be "unsharable"; perhaps the resistance may not be with the language but with the impulse of the narrator.

Embedded in the life stories of the women in this study are stories of abuse and violence, much of which began very early in the women's lives. Furthermore, the pain and torture they have endured often mirror the lives of pain and torment their mothers endured as well. While it is certainly obvious that pain and violence inform their narratives and are as common to them as breath and food, in many of their stories there is a point where acute violence enters and where the narrative appears to "break down," where language and words, apparently, cannot do justice to the pain and the violations, where the narrative becomes erratic, loses its coherence, and *resists failure* by deferring to silence in order to do the event justice. This would be a kind of Blanchot reading.

On the other hand, I have suggested that the women narrating these life stories are aware that to name the evil, the violence, the abuser, is to continue to give it/him continued power in and over their lives, a power they are attempting to diffuse by their life choices to escape and move into shelter, to hide, to try to use the court system to protect themselves. Scarry agrees that to *name* the agency of the pain is to credit that person with power.

> Nowhere is the sadistic potential of a language built on agency so visible as in torture. While torture contains language, specific human words and sounds, it is itself a language, an objectification, an acting out. Real pain, agonizing pain, is inflicted on a person. . . . The physical pain is so incontestably real that it seems to confer its quality of "incontestable reality" on that power that has brought it into being.[7]

This notion bears further scrutiny. It may well be that, for a woman who has been battered, to describe the abuse upon her body is to inflict the pain anew and to identify her own body as the site of the objectification, the violence. She becomes the abuse; she becomes the pain. Torture, claims Scarry, contains language, but it is also "itself a language, an objectification, an acting out." Narratives of abuse, centered as they are on what "he" did, shift the subjectivity from her to *what he did to her.* Intuitively a woman narrator may know (but perhaps could not articulate) that one of the reasons she is reluctant to tell her most violent stories is that the storytelling or reporting mode focuses on the agent of the violence as well as the object of that violence. In that act of narration, she acknowledges his power at the same moment she is objectified by her own pain. She may resist that telling. Such a reading of her narratives suggests agency on her part in the telling of her story and shifts the subjectivity of both the event and her telling of the event.

VOICING THE STORY OF PAIN

Now, I want to return to Scarry's other contention, that "if violence and pain can find a voice, then it will tell a story." What voice would provide such an opportunity? And if, as I have suggested, the women telling their stories are making conscious, and perhaps unconscious, decisions about what to tell and when, how can the women find a voice and tell such a (new) story?

I teach several women's studies courses at my university, and certainly one of the major ideas that has emerged in feminist thinking over the past several decades is the acknowledged importance of "silenced" women finding their voices and, of course, using those new-found voices to express themselves and to counter the oppression of women. In literature, we explore the various ways women write, positing that they often write differently from men. We see evidence that in their use of language, in their constructions of the world they live in, and in the way they write about their experiences, they are shifting subjects and shattering the notion of a single, monolithic "master narrative" that includes everyone on the face of the planet. How does this call for women to speak, to write their experiences, to find their own voices and tell their own stories help us if, in truth, what women are trying to "speak" is actually "unspeakable"?

Other writers have helped me with these questions. Janice Haaken, in her new book about women remembering childhood incest, *Pillar of Salt: Gender, Memory, and the Perils of Looking Back,* applauds women's efforts to find a new voice for their storytelling, particularly when they are breaking taboos against their voices being heard. And she is dealing, in this book, with one of the major, long-standing "silenced" arenas evidenced around the world. Girls are, and always have been, molested, tormented, and raped by their fathers, brothers, uncles, and other family members on a regular and constant basis. Yet she claims that remembering is a "gendered activity," meaning that girls and women have been taught *not to speak*.[8] She asks what it means to listen to women's stories with a "third ear," and she reminds us how important it is to take into account the "ego-involvement of the storyteller." Women have suffered from too little ego-involvement and are all too ready to yield to the position of the "other." In fact, they know they have been associated with hysterical/emotional storytelling and have been punished for displaying female outrage. Hence, Haaken wants us to acknowledge a "complex subjectivity" in women's narrations that takes into account women's historical relationship with *not speaking*. She has forced our attention upon the difficulties posed for women to, first, remember incidences of incest, and, even more problematic, to *tell* these stories of pain and violence.

What has compounded the problem, Haaken tells us, is that the world really does not want to hear their stories. We are in denial about incest, and the backlash has created an entire discourse about how professionals and lay persons alike are discounting stories of incest as "imagined rememberings," and claiming that they are largely fabricated and untrue. In response to these reactions, Haaken is encouraging women to tell all and is admonishing us, as listeners, to hear their stories and understand how significant the *act of telling* the stories is for the narrators.

The stories in my study reveal how narrative operates for the female storytellers in both acknowledging and contesting what has been acted upon their bodies and upon their minds; the narratives seem to break down where *language* breaks down. But perhaps language does not fail either; perhaps the failure is in the receiving of the stories, in the failure to discern what is being said. How can we listen to her stories without second-guessing the narrator, without pointing to her *inability* to "tell" the pain and abusing her even further, and without generalizing to an entire population what it is she cannot speak?

At this point in my reading of women's stories of abuse and lives of torture, I was obviously confused. I was seeing both the gaps in the stories as well as the attempts to speak pain into story; I was determined to honor both, yet without resorting to seeing one or the other as some kind of "failure." I was also beginning to notice some patterns regarding when and where narrative ruptures were likely to appear within the stories. First, some stories clearly exhibited a gap or rupture in the narrative sequence, at the points of severe and acute pain and violence. Second, I recognized that some stories were told in such a cryptic and minimalist fashion that they were not so much examples of narrative gaps as they were simply underdeveloped as narratives. Yet even in the second pattern, there were certainly examples of places in the narrative, particularly in the childhood accounts, where the "silenced" narrator kept her silence and was not able to voice an event into story, as Scarry proposed might happen. I determined to explore these two different kinds of stories in different ways.

I recalled a book that could help me think about our awkwardness when we try to speak about difficult or painful memories. Jill Ker Conway, in her book *When Memory Speaks,* noticed: "Abrupt transitions and shifting narrative styles are sure signs that their authors are struggling to overcome the cultural taboos that define women as witnesses rather than actors in [their] life's events." And I recalled something else Blanchot had claimed: that the witness to disaster or the survivor in disaster cannot remember the disaster because she "does not believe in the disaster. One cannot believe in it, whether one lives or dies. Commensurate with it there is no faith, and at the same time a sort of disinterest, detached from the disaster. Night; white; sleepless night—such is the disaster; the night lacking darkness, but brightened by no light."[9] Thus, Conway and Blanchot provided a way to think differently about the women's accounts of their earliest abuse and molestation by family members. And the conception of witness versus testimony appeared with renewed possibilities.

SILENCES AND GAPS

After hearing and transcribing perhaps thirty women's stories of pain and violence, I began to realize that the women narrating these lives seemed, at the *beginning* of their stories, to actually stand outside their lives, watching, eerily, as though they were but witnesses to a life that had very little to do with them. And the narration of these early childhood experiences consisted of truncated, compressed accounts. There were no details and little reflection on the part of the narrator. As examples, I recall the first words of two women, Sherry and Margaret, in their life stories told on tape. Sherry began:

> Well, I'll start. My earliest memory is, I was, I'm going to call it three, and—this is a screwed-up first memory—I witnessed my father get murdered by my uncle. This is my earliest memory. My mom was a drinker and so was my dad. And they got into it one night and my uncle came in and shot my dad. From there I moved to an apartment and I got a new dad. . . . And he was abusive. . . .
>
> And then when I was in kindergarten, first grade, she [my mother] got cancer and we moved from the city to a small town and we had long years of cancer. . . . My stepdad was still there and there was all kinds of boyfriends. But my stepdad molested me when I was seven. And then Mom died and I was eleven.

Margaret's story begins:

> You know I really don't remember a whole lot about my childhood. I think that's really odd, because when I talk to other people they can tell me incidents that happened in their childhood, and I'll sit back and I'll think and I just don't remember. I don't remember having a happy childhood.

Like Conway's assessment of Virginia Woolf's stance in "A Sketch of the Past," where she recounts her own abuse at the hands of her two brothers, the women narrators "exhibited more ironic detachment than rage; *repelled* by 'the compulsive style of victimhood,' "[10] But I want to defer this discussion of the girls' "witnessing" accounts to the next chapter. For now, I want to return to the women's stories that involve a gap and that apparently grapple with the issue of how to portray violence.

I began this work believing, with Conway, that memory is important. Memory, along with language, according to Conway, is the force that makes us human: "We need to cultivate the goddess of memory because it matters how we remember things."[11] But, she warns, the new postmodern narrative for all those marginalized persons whose "life falls outside the central narrative of worldly success" will not involve reflections on the unfolding of a long and thoughtful life, but rather will focus on urgent questions of identity.

If we go back to Sherry's accounts of her first memories, we find that the child who witnessed her own father's murder remains completely detached from her own story. And this child who could not speak is still trying to locate her voice when she narrates the violence and abuse she encountered in her marriage. Even when she is telling stories that chill us to the bone, Sherry's narrative style is distanced, detached, and deceptively calm. Yet a close analysis reveals that Sherry has grown in her development of "self"; this story of pain and violence moves the paralyzed child into a new place of subjectivity and eventual reflection about her position.

> I've got a scar here, right underneath my chin here [gestures to show scar]. My first husband, I fixed him dinner one night, and I don't know why our fights were always over dinner—I must be a bad cook, man [laughs]. We had pork chops one night, and his pork chops had to be broiled first so they'd stay tender. . . . And I don't know what happened, but he bit his meat and he said, "This tastes like shit." And the only thing I said was, "I did it just like I've done it every night." And this "other guy" came out of him—that's what he said, it was "the other guy"—and put a knife through my chin, trying to cut my tongue out so I couldn't back talk him anymore.

As serious as this experience is for this woman, her account of the event is not particularly graphic or detailed. She does tell us he "put a knife through my chin, trying to cut my tongue out so I couldn't back talk him anymore," but as Elaine Scarry might point out, this account is not delivered as an "active" memory, with the victim talking as the subject of the violence. She does not use language that helps us feel or understand the pain inflicted upon her face, language such as, "I felt the knife; it cut into my chin; there was a lot of blood; it hurt a great deal; it was really painful; I jumped up to escape the knife; he came after me." Rather, the account is passive on the part of the narrator and foregrounds *his* state of mind more than it does hers: "he bit his meat and he said, 'This tastes like shit.' And the only thing I said was, 'I did it just like I've done it every night.' And this 'other guy' came out of him—that's what he said, it was 'the other guy'—and put a knife through my chin, trying to cut my tongue out so I couldn't back talk him anymore."

The earlier sentences in her account reveal that she is not trying to "back talk" him at all; she has merely remarked that she cooked the food the same way she always cooks it. We are to comprehend the understatement in her final phrase: "so I couldn't back talk him anymore"; actually, this is *his* account— "I'm going to cut your tongue out so you can't back talk me anymore." She has portrayed herself in this narrative as logical, sensible, and soft-spoken. We are to read in the rupture made literally by his knife his own irrationality and rage as he tries to cut out her tongue. Our dismay at his actions is her dismay as well. She has warned us of his quick temper and irrational responses to things like how the meal is cooked. The reference to the "other guy" here involves her own diagnosis that her husband has a split personality and the "other guy" is the part of his personality that beats and cuts her. In a way, this rationalization of her husband's behavior absolves him of any responsibility for "his" actions.

In other portions of her story, she recalls a number of similar events. For example, she goes on to reveal that by the end of this incident she is lying on the floor, presumably in a pool of blood, possibly in shock or unconscious. She even admits in one brief sentence, "yeah, it got scary." But her narrative does not explicate these specifics of the horror. She does not use language to talk about the pain, the fall to the floor, the blood; in fact, in this narrative she diverts the point of view *away* from herself lying there on the floor by talking about several other aspects of her life story that she can relate to this dreadful moment.

Rather than painting a picture of her pain and wretched form on the floor, rather than focusing our attention onto her subjectivity, she instead draws our attention to the face and eyes of her young son as he stands looking down at her. But even this position in the narrative event is too close and difficult to maintain, so the narrator tries to remove her son from the disastrous moment by telling him, "Go to the bedroom—go to the bedroom." He cannot move, however, and the locus of her narrative becomes not *herself,* wounded and in pain on the floor, but rather the frozen body and terrified eyes of her son, who is transfixed by this horror.

> And my oldest son, he got to witness it. And he was old enough to scream and know that I was hurt. And there was one time I remember I kept trying to tell him, "Go to the bedroom—go to the bedroom," and he wouldn't listen to me and he just stood there, and I remember just laying there and looking up at him and I'll never forget the expression in his eyes. I won't ever forget that look. But he couldn't look away, you know, it was like he

couldn't look away. I don't want him to grow up and think that's right.
And I don't want him to ever see it happen again.

Her concern is for *him:* He has seen the disaster in his own kitchen, executed
upon the body of his mother, and she sees the terror and pain in his eyes, and,
like a good mother, she vows never to let this happen again because it is not
good for him to see. We are drawn back to the first lines in the transcription
of her life story where she describes *herself* as a "witness" to the horror and
violence in the kitchen of her own childhood, watching her uncle kill her father.
I would suggest that the silence she adopted as her own in her first three years
of life, and for the next ten or twelve, dodging the undesired attentions of the
uncle left to care for her, had a direct impact on the way she was able to narrate
this disastrous event during the taping of her life story. This event, she claims,
was "the final thing."

> With Dale, that knife was the final thing. And I remember Aunt Susan
> hitting that tree [trying to kill herself to get away from her abusive
> husband], and it was just like, I was ready to commit suicide, but I sure
> as hell didn't want him to kill me *for* me [laughs]. If I'm going to go out,
> I want to do it myself, thank you. But yeah, it got scary.

If we return, at this point, to the discussions earlier in this chapter about
what is unspeakable, what we might discern when we peer through the gap
in women's narratives, and how silenced pain might find a voice, then we
might find a way to understand this narrated story of violence. Sherry does
not, in this gruesome tale, construct her being as merely a victim suffering
at the hands of a powerful oppressor. By deflecting the story away from the
language of pain, she can, through her expert use of language, point to his
shortcomings, his possible split personality, his unwarranted rages, and his
lack of logic. Her account becomes reflective. She tells us "that knife was the
final thing," meaning that this is the point of her departure from the house
of violence, her escape into the world of the shelter. She becomes reflective,
too, upon the life and attempted suicide of her aunt Susan, noting without
elaboration how she does not want to end up like that. And she takes agency
back from her abuser, saying if she is going to die *she* wants to do it rather
than let him. And her understatement is profound: "But yeah, it got scary."

In listening to women's stories—and actually learning to "hear" them—I
find little to support the suggestion that these girls turned women developed
any sense of "self" early in their lives; rather, they first portray themselves as
passive witnesses. Their stories confirm that they grow up feeling invisible.
They claim no agency nor subjectivity in their stories until they appear to

recognize that their self is embodied in a site separate from the abuse endured by their physical body. In Sherry's narrative, it is not until the end of this account that she moves toward embodiment, and it is through the dead and battered bodies of other violated women that she seeks to shape her own:

> Every now and then [at the hospital where I worked] we'd . . . get in a woman who had just, had been—just beat to hell. And they would have to go in and like remove her spleen and shit, where she got beat. And it was one thing, it was weird seeing a dead body that got beat, and then a woman go through all that shit in surgery from being beat, it was weird. When it was me going through all that pain and stuff, that was one thing, but to actually sit there and watch these other women go through it—it would—it was never going to happen to me. But it did.

Haaken reminds us that, "[f]or Lot's wife, the story ends before we know what she has seen. Her fatal rebellion creates a disturbing void, one [which] may be employed as a metaphor for a generative, symbolic space opened up for feminist analysis. Like Lot's wife, women have their experiences entombed in men's accounts of the past. Unraveling entombed memories is, then, both a creative and revelatory project." I have accepted Haaken's challenge to investigate what has not been explored. Haaken claims that "important truths reside at the periphery of what is most readily noticeable." She explains what she calls a "complex subjectivity" in women's narratives, suggesting we talk about the kinds of remembering that women do, rather than talking about memory as a fixed entity. She calls this the process of "transformative re-membering," which refers to the recollection of an event that serves as a psychological marker from an early to a later form of self-knowledge; that way, "the motivational and active dimensions of mind are in the foreground." For the women in this study, the term "transformative re-membering" is appropriate, for the process offers them, as Haaken says, "a new vantage point from which to view the past." She continues: "The activity of remembering stands at the threshold between body and mind like a translator." Or, put another way: "transformative re-membering refers to the creative use of the past in *redefining the self*."[12]

For months, as I have read and reread these stories, I have been squinting through the disruption, the gap, trying to glimpse the disaster that Blanchot assures me is there if I can only discern it. But I have come to realize something new and radical. It is not the disaster I can see through the disruption of the story of a woman's pain and torture, it is the transformed woman who refuses to recount the disaster and privilege the subjectivity of her abuser. Benjamin claims we can glimpse the "now" of the "presence" through the rupture and the "now" of these women is their *escape*. Only if we refocus the lens can we both hear and see her, transforming, remembering, redesigning her person, her self. It is our task to listen carefully and welcome her presence. *She is a survivor.* Her story attests to this fact and by the end of it, this is what she wants us to hear.

This reading of how we might hear stories of the disaster, and recognize what is discernable in the gaps in personal narratives, may point to the difference between what we can come to recognize as the personal disaster and the collective one. The proponents of the master narrative have forgotten that the whole of its reality exists in the essence of its smallest parts. Is there an *essence* that is truly larger than a single person's pain? If one narrative evokes the larger whole, how can we justify discounting her story as mere testimony, as inadequate to tell the story of the disaster?

4

Hearing Silence

Two mothers in tears embraced yesterday. One woman's 17-year-old daughter was shot and killed Monday; the other's son is charged with pulling the trigger. . . .

About 150 people, primarily teenagers and young adults, filled the church for the 1 1/2 hour service to honor the teen who was shot multiple times outside the apartment she shared with 23-year-old John Carl Sanders Jr.

The couple had filed for a marriage license just days before Leanna [Myers]'s death.

Sanders remains in Boone County Jail charged with first-degree murder and armed criminal action in the death of Myers.

At the funeral, there were no signs of the couple's 2-month-old daughter, Lea-Johna.

Columbia Daily Tribune,
June 11, 2000

THIS BOOK HAS BEEN extremely difficult for me to write. By the time I arrived at the more articulated stories of violence against women by their partners, I was exhausted, drained. I thought perhaps I could not type one more story, one more account of pure horror. But as I reflect on the writing of this book, this chapter—on young girls' *silences*—is actually the chapter that breaks my heart.

As I wrote this book, I was reading Mary Pipher's book *Reviving Ophelia: Saving the Selves of Adolescent Girls* with a reading group I belong to whose members are mostly women who have daughters. We are concerned with the way American culture is erasing girls' independence and strong notions of "self" and replacing those with images of too-thin models and concepts of beauty that are technologically produced and never achievable, causing girls to despair and lose themselves in the process. Pipher believes there must be a revision of the culture before young girls can find the nurturing they need to grow into independent, thinking, whole human beings. Adolescent girls, she tells us, are "saplings in a hurricane. They are young and vulnerable trees that the winds blow with gale strength." Adolescence, she says, is "fascinating. It's an extraordinary time when individual, developmental, and cultural factors combine in ways that shape adulthood. It's a time of marked internal development and massive cultural indoctrination." Further, Pipher tells us: "Early adolescence is a time of physical and psychological change, self-absorption, preoccupation with peer approval, and identity formation. It's a time when girls focus inward on their own fascinating changes."[1]

As I read Pipher's book, I felt as though a chasm stretched far out between the girl's adolescent lives as depicted in her book and the lives of the women as I was hearing them in their stories on tape. These descriptions of childhood and adolescence did not apply to the girls whose stories were being told on tape to me. Pipher might be right when she claims that self-absorption and reflection are prerequisites for healthy female development, but I could only surmise what damage is done when spaces are not provided for the growth and well-being of a growing girl. The girls in this study have been crouching in corners, closets, and basements for most of their young lives. They have been dodging blows and worse from their fathers and their mothers, their brothers and their uncles. They tell stories of lives full of danger, dark and threatening pain and suffering, unpredictable rages and blows upon their bodies, and emotional trauma and abuse inflicted upon their minds, on a daily basis. Some of them are able to articulate that such experiences early in life left them confused and often unable to speak or act.

Perhaps more appropriate to this study is the work of Jill Taylor, Carol Gilligan, and Amy Sullivan, whose new book, *Between Voice and Silence,* follows a group of adolescent girls who begin life secure in their right to speak, but who learn as they grow that silence is valued over voice. These researchers are concerned with how life experiences teach young girls to "learn" to be passive and to not question. They explore how dangerous the messages are for girls to conform, to fit the norms of proper "femininity," and the psychological dissociation that comes when they lose their sense of self and their right to voice. Importantly, their work was developed over a long period of time, based on intense *listening* to the voices of young girls. Not only were the researchers interested in who was talking, they were also keen to discover *who was listening* when the girls talked.

That is why this is the chapter that breaks my heart. For the women in this study, there has been a lifelong, grave danger to their emotional and psychological well-being, as well as to their physical health and survival. The danger that greets them at birth and hovers over their daily lives in its darkest and bleakest form is *violence.* It holds their lives in its tenacious grip and strips them of their right to the more normal fears and dangers of adolescent life. In the crouched and silent forms of these young girls we realize just how crippling early years of violence can be.

When we listen to the life stories of women who now live in shelters to escape abusive and violent men, we find many persistent and significant patterns. We also find important clues about how critical it is that we actually listen to and hear their stories *as they tell them*. Some of the most formative experiences, I think, are inseparably linked and need to be presented together: early molestation and not being able to speak that violation, speaking the violence and being further abused for the telling, and feeling betrayed by those the girls trust to help them. While the realities of beatings and babies, pain and despair have made their mark upon the minds and bodies of these grown women, the women say they felt invisible as young girls. They learned it was in their best interest to be invisible, because that was the easiest route. Marcie's story is representative of how these young girls felt growing up:

> My dad's brothers, one of them—my uncle Bob and my aunt Martha— they were heavy-duty alcoholics and they lived near us, and her parents were also alcoholics and we would go visit them a lot, and they would just sit around and everybody would just get wasted, and then my dad would just sort of pass me around between my uncle and [my aunt's] father and everybody—I was just handled a lot. Everybody was drunk and nobody knew what was going on except me. And nobody really paid attention to what was happening, and it was just pretty gross. And if I wouldn't—my uncle Bob was a pretty angry drunk, and if I wouldn't go sit on his lap and kiss him and let him feel me up and all this stuff, I'd get in trouble. And I felt like my parents were there [but weren't any help], and my mom didn't drink. My mom was the only one that wouldn't drink. My mom never had more than one drink. My mom never got drunk— [laughing]—God, I wish she would have. My mom is very tight-knit, but my mom was around and saw this and she would just pretend like it didn't happen. And so it didn't. And so I was sort of in the middle of all this with no ally.

. . . "With no ally." Invariably, the narrators' fear, sense of invisibility, and lack of feelings of self-worth seem to reflect back to their early years of abuse and silencing and certainly led them into the arms of men who would only abuse them further and use their vulnerability against them. Early in their stories, the women often recall that their mothers were largely absent, abusive themselves, or unwilling to hear the young girls' stories and come to their assistance. And while their stories note how the girls felt about their mothers, the women are reluctant to locate the mother as the source of their confusion and fear. Several found mother substitutes in older sisters, friends, or aunts. Susan told me:

> My sister, although she was quite a bit younger than my brother was, she and I were really close. She's been probably the most consistently close person to me in my life. She was wonderful to me when I was little, like taking me on dates with her. And her steady boyfriend in high school was really good to me. My mom, she was a great mom for my sister, she was always there, very reliable, but when it came to a need for nurturing, she wasn't, well, she wasn't as emotionally nurturing and really couldn't meet the emotional needs for the kind of child I was.

Dorothy's story makes it clear how significant the mother was for these girls, and how difficult it was for them to deal with the "absent mother":

> I don't remember the birth itself, but I know what happened to me. . . . [M]y understanding from other family members [is] that my mom had me in prison. She had gotten in a lot of trouble and she had to do some prison time. When she went into prison she was pregnant with me. And she had me and they put me in foster care for probably, I think, about three years until she got out of prison. And she came back for me when she got out of prison.

Accounts such as the following from Cathy seem to sound the same refrain; though slightly different, they still point to how these little girls did not feel loved, or even wanted:

> And—as a little child I always felt—unwanted—I was the youngest of five children; only four of us lived with my parents; my half-sister lived with her mother in a different place. My mom told me, when I was about eight years old, that when she found out that she was pregnant with me, that she wanted to have an abortion, because they already had so many children, and they couldn't afford children. But abortion wasn't legal in 1957, so she went to find out how much it would cost her to have an illegal abortion, and it was going to be seventy-five dollars, and she said it might as well have been a thousand, and so she went to my grandmother and asked my grandmother for the money, and my grandmother wouldn't give it to her, and, otherwise, I suppose I would have been aborted at that time. So I've always had really strong feelings

about abortion for that reason, because I'm kind of glad I'm here in spite
of everything.

Sherry's mother died when she was nine. Her story reveals the gap left by
the departing mother, yet even in life her mother could not be there for Sherry.
Sherry herself connects her early abuse with her mother's lack of attention to
her. After her mother's death, she definitely links her early drug habits to the
fact that no one was really watching her.

> And then when I was in kindergarten, first grade, she got cancer and
> we moved from the city to a small town and we had long years of cancer,
> and through that time she still had lots of boyfriends, lots of parties.
> My stepdad was still there and there was all kinds of boyfriends. But my
> stepdad molested me when I was seven. And then Mom died and I was
> eleven. But from seven to eleven we went back and forth with my grandma
> and my uncle and all our relatives. She was up here in a hospital. After
> Mom died we went and lived with my uncle back in the city. And that's
> where most of my memories are. He was abusive to his wife. There was
> me and my brother and my sister. We moved in with him and he had at
> the time two kids.
>
> And he was drunk and abusive and my aunt Susan was a real—what
> I call a real lady. You know she'd do anything for us, you know, she was
> just wonderful. And he just always beat the hell out of her. Then we left
> the city and moved back into the country and he was still mean to her.
> And that's when I started getting onto drugs—but years before that—see
> here's where it gets confusing—
>
> When Mom was sick, I started getting into—I made friends in town,
> we lived out in the country and I started—I think my drug use has to do
> with my abuse. The first time I ever did any drugs I was like seven. . . .

Listening closely to the tapes of the women who shared their stories suggests
that the lives of violence are mirrors of the lives led by their mothers and
grandmothers, aunts, cousins, and sisters. Often, the broken lives of their
mothers move in slow motion in the background and weave silently into the
lives of the daughters. We sense that their mothers were so terribly wounded
themselves, they simply could not respond to the desperate needs of their own
daughters. And the daughters, in turn, find themselves as young mothers with
no resources, no reserves, and no energy to provide the love and support their
children in turn require. In the stories, the women identify their childhood
needs for love, nurturing, close attention and affection; they are also quite

clear when they articulate how they felt when these needs were not met. For example, Cathy continues:

> But I always had a feeling growing up that I really wasn't wanted. My mom was the kind of person who always took good care of me in the sense that I always had all of my physical needs met as far as, you know, clothes and food and, you know, being watched. She watched after me, she didn't abandon me. I was lucky in that sense. She took good care of my clothes. It was more like: She would dress me up, show me off, and then send me to my room. You know, I just always really felt that I wasn't wanted and wasn't loved. My mom was a very critical person. She criticized and criticized. And it made me very withdrawn. I was a very withdrawn child. . . .
>
> When I was nine years old, my mom called me a "whore" one day, and I had no clue what the word meant. And so I got a dictionary and a flashlight and hid in my bedroom closet and I was looking up the word. And I just was looking under *h,* trying to find the word *whore,* and I couldn't find it anywhere, and, being a halfway intelligent child, I thought, "Maybe it starts with *w,*" you know. So I looked it up and I read the definition. I don't remember what the definition said, but what I remember was this horrible sense of shock that came over me that this was the reason that my uncle had done these things to me all my life, that basically men treated me the way that they did, because somehow I was born that way, that it was a condition you were born with and that's what was wrong with me. And I internalized that very much, I guess because my mother said it to me.

Cathy is still not sure why her mother called her a whore, but describes the situation where she first heard it.

> When she would get angry she would say all kinds of things, but that was the first time I had ever heard that word or at least heard it from out of my mom's mouth, the first time I remember hearing it. And, at the time, she was very angry with me and had knocked me down in the kitchen. I was between the kitchen cabinets and the stove. There was a space there where the trash can usually was and for some reason the trash can wasn't there that day. She had knocked me down on the floor and she took off her shoe and raised it up to hit me with it and that was when she said—when she called me a "little whore."

At age fourteen, Cathy tells us, she ran away from home. When she was found, her family placed her in an institution for incorrigible girls, and then she was moved into a home for mental patients. Eventually, she claims, testing documented that she was not mentally ill and they allowed her to leave. It was clear to her, though, that she could never return home. So, at fifteen, she asked a friend of hers, a young man who was a soldier stationed on the West Coast, to marry her just to get her legally away from her home and parents. He agreed and they shared one year amicably enough before she fell in love with the man who would eventually become her abuser. Cathy says of her mother: "I guess my mom just has a lot of unfinished business."

ON SILENCES

Writers such as Tillie Olsen and Virginia Woolf, as well as feminist critics, have taken seriously the role of "silence" in women's oral and written constructions. Silence was never construed as "nothing to say"; rather, they suggested that silences can speak a muted message of oppression and hint at furtive attempts to speak an opinion, to lash out, or to defy. In a far different manner, we recognize how silence, the stony stare, and a mastery of the tongue can all be part of a power play (as long as your opponent knows you are "playing" in his game—or he in yours). Different writers have probed the silences to see what we might glean in that seemingly barren field. At once invoking and imagining, Virginia Woolf created a fictional sister of Shakespeare who clearly had no voice, or none anyone in her time might have heard. Mary Belenky and her coauthors in *Women's Ways of Knowing* recognize that silence is the first stage in the development of young girls and women who have never located their voice or have been silenced by their families, communities, or both. Their analysis of this stage is prefaced by the words of Adrienne Rich: "Where language and naming are power, silence is oppression, is violence."[2] It has become clear, through analyses of girls' development, that many never leave this first silent phase, even as they become adult and older women.

In the introduction to her excellent collection of articles, *Violence, Silence, and Anger: Women's Writing as Transgression,* Deirdre Lashgari comments: "Little has been written on the specific conjunction of these issues with women's culturally shaped responses to violence." She is, of course, talking about written or scholarly responses, those "culturally shaped responses" to violence. But I would like to pose a different kind of "culturally shaped response to violence"—the silences employed by women for self-preservation, silences that simultaneously save at least some women from more battering and abuse but, at the same time, provide little opportunity for the creation of positive and healthy self-constructions in young girls. The women's life narratives outline a process learned early in their lives. To tell is to suffer. To not tell is to suffer. The choice is devastating. As with the writer who is "writing from the margins" and dares to challenge the status quo, the woman who dares to speak knows at once the cultural injunction against "making noise" or "causing trouble" as well as the risk and the utter necessity that the self-silencing cease as a mode of interacting (or not) with the world. Her preservation of self is closely connected to how she solves this dilemma. When she does dare to "break through" with her voice and her story, her action implicates us. As listeners, how do we receive her story? Are there ways in which we can hear her voice and her story? Lashgari says we have a responsibility to "in-corporate the pain of violation, to take it into our own bodies where it can force us to respond."[3] These are not stories to be ignored or defiled.

To a large degree, the feminist scholarly community has taken the view that women's silences should be explored, mined for meaning, and broken. But the imperative to hear voices from the margins, from women and minorities, from voices forgotten or ignored, must be tempered by an understanding that the most critical factor is whether or not the stories can be told and heard within the context in which the previously silenced speakers live. For the women in this study, such as Cathy, the view that stories must be told is not nearly so determined; to "not tell" meant years of knowing their bodies and minds had been violated by men whom they had every right to trust for safety, not for violation. Cathy recalls what her childhood was like.

> My earliest memories are of an uncle that I had who, I guess, spent a lot of time with our family, although I don't know why. He was actually abusive. To the best of my knowledge, that started about the time I was three or before, but that is the first memory that I have of it.
>
> And I can remember when it used to happen, thinking, even as little as I was, that he can hurt my body but he can't hurt me, and I always had this sense of kind of being outside of myself watching what was going on. And I don't know if he threatened me. I don't know why that I had to cover this up or hide it, but I do know that when I was sort of outside of myself watching what was going on, I would think things like, "Oh, that is going to leave a bruise. I'll have to cover that up. I can't let Mom see that"—those kinds of things.

"To tell" meant to suffer the anguish of either not being heard or suffering the consequences. Marcie tells about what it was like after her mom got out of prison and married a man she could not stand to be near.

> The second year he started messing with me. Sneaking into the bedroom. My mom worked second shift and he worked first—so they wouldn't have

to have a babysitter. We was living in Arkansas then. My mom worked at a little doughnut shop down the street and he worked in the coal mine down in Arkansas. And every night at the same time every day, when he started messing with me, it was right around *Jeopardy.* When *Jeopardy* would come on, and still to this day, when *Jeopardy* comes on I start shivering and have to leave or turn it off or something. He would come in there in the bedroom and he would mess around with me quite a bit. Make me do this to him and he was doing that to me and just off and on did this stuff. That went on for probably a good two years. And he was threatening me. You know—"If you say anything, I'm gonna hurt you and hurt your mom", blah, blah, blah—and I remember dreading—being scared to go to bed.

I think it was on a Saturday—I was sitting on the porch and I remember this real clearly. She was sitting on the swing and I had formed a sore around my mouth. It looked like a huge ringworm is what it looked like. And my mom asked me, "What's wrong with your mouth?" And I wouldn't answer her. I wouldn't even look at her. And she picked me up and she turned me around and she said, "What is wrong with your mouth?" And I told her. I said, "Michael is doing bad things." I would never call him Dad. Never.

And she said, "What do you mean, Michael is doing bad things?" And I told her—I was crying—I remember crying and telling her I couldn't tell her because he was going to hurt me and her and she started shaking me and she was like, "What do you mean, what do you mean?" And finally I told her. She had shook me and slapped me so many times that I just told her that he was making me have oral sex with him and that was causing it—and she beat me. She beat me bad. She didn't believe me. She said I was a lying, instigating little bitch—just beat me bad, real bad.

Toni Morrison has said that "Cultures . . . seek meaning in the language and images available to them."[4] This would also pertain to women, who seek meaning in the language and images available to them. In terms of their early experiences with sexual abuse, incest, and molestation, the language and images available are nearly nonexistent. Had they told their stories and found receptive ears and humans ready to help them out, perhaps these stories would not have withered, leaving only a dark, angry spot to fester in their most inside parts, perhaps they could have constructed childhood stories that spoke of empowerment instead of fear, stories that could have been the foundation for positive self-construction. In the narrative tellings included in this book, the women who have shared their stories have tried to articulate these childhood experiences of molestation, fear, and loathing. Here, then, is the record of the silence broken. These are not necessarily well-articulated, carefully honed and fleshed-out stories, but they are stories finally told—to listeners who, they trust, will hear and not respond with abuse and disregard for this breaking of the silence.

INCEST AND EARLY CHILDHOOD MOLESTATION

Research on the lasting traumatic effects of early molestation in girls reveals that naming this violence and dealing with it often takes many women a lifetime of therapy to heal, and perhaps an equal number of women never get the chance to heal at all. Researchers Ellen Bass and Laura Davis, in their acclaimed work, *The Courage to Heal;* Matthew McKay and Patrick Fanning, in their book, *Self-Esteem;* and Diana Russell, in *The Secret Trauma,* all point to the devastating effects of sexual abuse and molestation by fathers, brothers, friends, and neighbors—all men who represented trust and safety to young girls and who violated that trust. The act of the molesting is traumatic enough, but the added fact that the girl is cautioned not to "tell" adds increased stress to her life. Judith Herman, writing about father-daughter incest, notes that, "From the psychological point of view, especially from the child's point of view, the sexual motivation of the contact, and the fact that it must be kept secret, are far more important than the exact nature of the act itself."[5]

Elizabeth Fiorenza points out, as well, that in our mainstream, largely Christian culture, values such as love and forgiveness help to sustain relations of dominance in domestic sexual violence. Religious texts make victims feel guilty if they do not patiently and lovingly submit to abuse and forgive their abusers. She notes that children, especially, are taught to love, honor, and obey their parents—which produces a double bind for them: "It becomes virtually impossible for them, particularly little girls, either to remember and to speak about sexual abuse by a father, priest, relative, or neighbor, or to recover their damaged self-image and self-worth."[6]

Perhaps even more devastating is the fact that when some girls do choose to risk telling what is happening to them their mothers do not believe them, or worse yet, accuse them of telling vile lies and punish them for telling. Diana Russell, in her book *The Secret Trauma,* reports that girls who were disbelieved or blamed when they *did* reveal sexual abuse often suffer the most extreme aftereffects. She emphasizes that, as adults, these women had the most difficulty disclosing the early abuse against them and continued to feel the most guilt.[7] I could see the evidence of this over and over again in the stories I collected for this study. Nearly every woman includes some indication that she was molested by her father or stepfather, a close neighbor, uncle, or friend. Some

of the survivors never tell about these experiences until they are adults; as
girls, some did try to tell their mothers, but they met with resistance, denial,
or worse—more abuse, from their mothers. In her story, Marcie is clearly just
as wounded by her mother's disbelief and punishment, for telling the story
about why she has the sores on her mouth, as she is by her stepfather's sexual
molestation, and perhaps more:

> And I think it was a few years later they finally got divorced, but the whole
> time she never did apologize to me for beating me or anything. She just
> said, "lesson learned." So then we moved back to this state, to a little town
> right outside here.

In *Between Voice and Silence,* the researchers tell us: "In this book, we enter
a landscape that is strangely silent—where girls for the most part are not
heard in public, or if heard are generally spoken about in the third person.
These girls have voices; they are perfectly capable of first-person speech, but
as they will say repeatedly, nobody listens, nobody cares, nobody asks what
they are feeling and thinking." Their work grew out of the Harvard Project on
Women's Psychology and Girls' Development, a research project that has led
the researchers to conclude that girls "could speak, but for the most part felt
that few cared or listened to what they had to say. Having a 'big mouth' often
got them into trouble, but silence, the slow slipping into a kind of invisible
isolation, was also devastating." Not only did these words ring true in terms of
the stories I was hearing, but also, I could see evidence of Elizabeth Fiorenza's
contention that many women feel their suffering has been willed by God
because they were bad, unworthy, or too alluring.[8]

If Taylor, Gilligan, and Sullivan are correct in noting the importance of
female role models, then the opposite must also follow.

> [Other strong] women were perhaps the best protection against the risk
> of disconnection and psychological dissociation. A resonant relationship
> with a woman, meaning a relationship in which a girl can speak freely
> and hear her voice clearly resounded as a voice worth listening to and
> taking seriously—a voice that engages the heart and mind of another
> and calls forth response—was associated with psychological health and
> development and what are commonly regarded as good outcomes for the
> girls in this project.[9]

But girls who *cannot* locate this woman listener in a mother or another
significant female figure, then, are at greater risk of losing psychological health
and development. Taylor and her coauthors hypothesize that what helps girls

in their growth and development is hearing of the experiences of older women. Yet, if their mothers and aunts and grandmothers cannot speak of their own experiences because they were too painful, then this process is aborted.

I am reminded here of Sherry's kind and loving aunt, who was so beaten and battered by her husband that she tried to leave the violence by attempting suicide; the resulting head injury caused her to have essentially "left them anyway." Sherry recognized a lesson in her aunt's story, but it wasn't a lesson of encouragement and support; it was a story of defeat that provided no new road maps for Sherry to follow. Cathy, too, hints of the possibility of help from other female family members, but the fears of exposure and subsequent abuse are greater than her desire to break the impasse of silence:

> I don't remember there being anyone in my immediate family that I could ever go with to talk to or to feel that I was safe with.
>
> My dad's mother, my grandmother, was a very gentle, kind human being. And her sister, who was my aunt Ginny, she was my great aunt, she was a very kind, gentle person, and she had had a very difficult life. She grew up in Denmark and she became pregnant before she was married, which, in that day, was absolutely scandalous, and the family pretty much banished her from the family, would have nothing to do with her except for her sister, my grandmother, and they were very close and I loved these two women a lot. They were a great influence in my life and I used to spend a lot of time talking to them, but I always felt like there was so much about myself and about my experiences in life that I just couldn't talk about. And I think they probably would have accepted it, but, at the time, my feeling was just that "I can't talk about this."

EARLY ABUSE

In the language used by women to describe early sexual abuse, we find that their voices are largely muted. Words are at a minimum. These are not narratives that have been reflected upon or developed. "I was molested when I was three"; "My father molested me when I was three"; "My stepfather molested me when I was four." In many of these accounts we get no details at all. In some, we get a bit more. Judith Herman, Diane Russell, and Elaine Scarry all warn that there will be gaps, negations, and displacements in narratives of traumas endured in childhood and recounted as an adult. And Anne Dalton, writing about Harriet Jacobs's slave narrative of abuse and sexual violations, notes the "tensions between what she states and [what she] metaphorically suggests" in her story.[10] We might use these same tools to "read" the stories of these girls' early experiences, when they say, for example, "He would mess around with me quite a bit. Make me do this to him, and he was doing that to me, and just off and on did this stuff"; or when they say, "And I can remember when it used to happen, thinking even as little as I was, that he can hurt my body but he can't hurt me, and I always had this sense of kind of being outside of myself watching what was going on."

In the women's stories, words such as *"stuff"* or *"it* used to happen," or *"it* got really bad then" are encoded inscriptions for details they cannot or will not inscribe for the listener. Since "telling" has more often than not resulted in even more devastating reactions and punishment, Taylor's research group found that: "In the face of increasing relational crises, a preadolescent resilience can give way to an increasing uncertainty, a hesitancy in speaking, a tendency toward self-doubt that questions the validity of their feelings and dismisses the value of their experiences." The researchers caution us to "listen for the first-person voice, the *I*. Listening to the *I* is crucial: researchers hear how a girl speaks about herself—how *she* thinks, what *she* feels and does." They also stress that we must "notice what she does *not say*—where she sounds sure of her words, where she sounds tentative or confused."[11] We listen to how she builds her narrative and to what end.

Similarly, the work of Joseph de Rivera and Theodore R. Sarbin, in their book *Believed-In Imaginings: The Narrative Construction of Reality,* which explores the remembering of childhood incest, suggests that building this narrative of past abuse is a critical step in recovery. The construction of the narrative itself provides a framework for the women to begin to deal with the incidences and begin to heal. Obviously, in most of these narratives, the women have not reached that place of narrative and positive self-construction. George Handley, writing about personal testimony in *Violence, Silence, and Anger,* warns that "language is [only] a signification of, a pointing to, the suffering that we can never directly know; what we read"—or hear—"cannot be a direct presentation of the events." And it is telling that Belenky and her coauthors' stages of knowledge include a section on "conceiving the self" as a portion of the "Silences" chapter. Belenky and her coauthors comment: "Describing the self was a difficult task for all of the women we interviewed, but it was almost impossible for the silent ones."[12]

Early childhood molestation is described by one woman as "When I was three, my stepfather molested me." While it is true that the speaking woman has used words here to tell a "fact," that is all she has managed to do with the language and the words available to her to describe this experience. Whether it is because she was too young to recall the incidence(s) clearly, or whether she has repressed the details, or whether the trauma of that event in her life has not yet been dealt with to the extent that she can "speak" it any further than this simple statement, it is, at any rate, still below the surface and "unshareable."

I want to return to a closer reading of Sherry's early recollection. She identifies this beginning as a "screwed-up first memory," saying, "I witnessed my father get murdered by my uncle. This is my first memory." Interestingly, this is a twofold passive construction. The girl identifies herself as a *witness*—an important word in this study. She is not a participant; she is an onlooker, and that is the way she describes herself and, obviously, the way she felt at the time—on the outside looking in. Her father is the focus of the uncle's murderous intent—he "gets murdered" by the uncle. The effect of these beginning lines is akin to a kind of black-and-white, silent, slow-motion film. There is no action deployed, no blood, no details. But she *implies* chaos: Her mother and father "got into it one night and my uncle came in and shot my dad." Her parents are drinkers, she says, and her mother loves to party and has a long series of "boyfriends." Her parents fight while the girl watches; she is a bystander to their activities but not really integrated into the scene or their lives of parties, sex, and alcohol. She relates all of this in a matter-of-fact voice with a paucity of words. A great deal happened that night; it is her first noteworthy memory—yet none of the sounds, the pain, the fear, are conveyed by her words. It is important to remember that she says she is probably only three when this event occurred, so this memory may in fact be grainy or fuzzy in her mind's eye. Can the girl (in the scene, at the time) hear any sounds? Does the remembering woman recall sounds, screams, thuds, crying? Does she hide, cry, scream? There is no way to know what she knows or thinks about this event. She only marks it as her "earliest memory" and she does not elaborate. This is nearly a silent account. The unspeakable here is left to the imagination; the event is not communicable from the remembering three-year-old girl through the lips of the adult woman.

This first introductory portion of Sherry's story is actually a narrative of *implied violence*. None of the violence is portrayed *in language* to the reader/listener, nor does Sherry include any of her own feelings about the incident—either how she felt at the time or how she might reflect back on that incident as an adult speaker. As with much of her story, and similar to stories of childhood incest, she is for the most part separated and distanced from her self in this account. We "see" her as though she is outside her own body looking in on the events in her life. Her narrative voice suggests that she is disembodied, disengaged from her own story and the violence that abides there because, she has retreated to the farthest corners of her inside self—a safer place than the one on the front lines.

Sherry's description of the early sexual abuse she suffered is delivered in the same distanced manner. She does not give us details about the molestation by her stepfather nor do we know how she felt about it, at least not until later in her story. There is no shame, guilt, fear, pain, or anger revealed in the account as she gives it at the beginning of her life narrative. It is straightforward and chilling in its detached presentation. There is no representation of *herself* in this account. The act is presented as a dead fact: "But my stepdad molested me when I was seven. And then Mom died and I was eleven." Astonishingly, in these two brief, bare-bones sentences, four years of traumatic experiences remain nearly unaccounted for. Does her stepfather continue to molest her? Is her life one of fear and pain? Does she tell her mother? Does she tell anyone? We are led to believe, at this point, that the most important "facts" here are that she was molested by someone very close to her and whom she expected to protect her, or at the very least not harm her, and that her mother dies when she is eleven. The reality of the abuse compressed into these brief sentences cradles a buried excess of loneliness, isolation, and abandonment.

SPEAKING THE ABUSE AND SUFFERING THE CONSEQUENCES

What happens when a girl is silenced for telling about sexual abuse? She is abused again by those who will not listen and, sometimes, even worse, she is punished or blamed for the violations against her body. Even though the term *self-esteem* may be under scrutiny as an overused or popularized concept, Matthew McKay and Patrick Fanning, in their book *Self-Esteem,* find it extremely useful in their examination of what builds a strong self-construction and psychological well-being. They claim that "self-esteem is essential for psychological survival. It is an emotional *sine qua non*—without some measure of self-worth, life can be enormously painful, with many basic needs going unmet." One of the main factors differentiating humans from other animals, they claim, is the "awareness of self: the ability to form an identity and then attach a value to it."[13] Clearly, in the stories of the girls in this study, their self-awareness and self-worth are connected with their earliest memories.

> And I can remember when it used to happen, thinking, even as little as I was, that he can hurt my body but he can't hurt me, and I always had this sense of kind of being outside of myself watching what was going on. And I don't know if he threatened me. I don't know why that I had to cover this up or hide it, but I do know that when I was sort of outside of myself watching what was going on. I would think things like, Oh, that

is going to leave a bruise. I'll have to cover that up. I can't let Mom see that—those kinds of things.

So I felt like I had done something wrong. . . . So I got to the point where I would wrap myself up in sheets and blankets thinking that was going to protect me, and it never did, but I was a child, you know—you think of anything you can to try to protect yourself.

In these reflections, we get the image of the girl trying to make herself invisible, recoiling deep inside herself, hiding, making herself numb. Sometimes, in a reflective moment in the narrative, these women can articulate some of what they think happened to them. But the ability to reflect back and understand what hindered them in the construction of a healthy self comes at a point when they have enjoyed some time in safety and perhaps some therapy to help them sort things out. Margaret and Sherry articulate this position perhaps the best, but certainly from the standpoint of being further from the abuse. As Margaret puts it,

And what I saw in him, I don't know. You know, when I sit back and reflect on the two men—I've been married three times—and two of those men I don't understand what attracted me to them. I'm actually embarrassed to talk about it. So, I think that's where it all started. It started with a lack of self-esteem. I really think if I had believed in myself more, was in touch with myself more, liked myself more—I think I used sex as a tool to get guys to like me, especially him. Actually, I even tried to get pregnant. It didn't just happen. I really was out to get my parents.

Sherry is similarly reflective about the ways her childhood created the self-esteem problems that hindered her as an adult:

A lot of the reason why I got into abusive relationships is like my family—I think family is a big support system and if your family doesn't support you, then nobody is ever going to. And I know when my mom didn't ever ask me about what had happened, you know, that really—I remember that bothered me, you know. So, I knew my mom really didn't give a shit, you know. And if your mother doesn't care, then who in the world is really going to care? You're not going to have that. And then when I finally [did tell]—it takes a lot to tell somebody that you've been molested, you know, when you haven't dealt with it yet and then, when my family didn't believe me, that bothered me.

RELATIONSHIPS WITH MOTHERS

Typical in this study are stories told by women whose mothers were absent—either in reality or in other, perhaps even more damaging, ways. Sherry's story begins with her mother, really, but the thread is so thin we know why Sherry felt alone, invisible, deserted as a very, very young child. It is quite easy to see how her mother's own abuse at the hands of her father, her father's death at the hands of her uncle, and her mother's illness, drinking, and subsequent death must have revolved around this young girl, causing her to feel as though there were no supports for her. As is often the case, she was molested as a young girl, and it is also typical that no one believed her or came to her assistance. Her mother was practically a ghost. Sherry never describes her mother in concrete terms, just notes that she was a "good-time party girl"; the girl is only responding to the behavior of the adults in her life. Her mother is not her confidante and is not able to support or protect her. But close reading of this and other stories makes it evident that her mother, too, is an abused woman, who may be protecting herself through drinking and pulling away from the household scene that causes her pain. The result is that, as a young girl, Sherry feels completely abandoned, alone, unloved. Her mother's death, combined with the fact that her stepfather is molesting her, can only suggest the depth of the possible feelings of alienation and fear for a girl of eleven. We note with interest that she mentions three times in the first portion of her life account that her mom dies when she was eleven, stressing through repetition alone the import of this profound truth. She is alone without her mother, who, although she was never particularly attentive anyway, is now forever absent and unavailable to protect her from her stepfather or the other relatives who lurk in the background.

Young Sherry's behavior is typical and predictable as well, if we think collectively about the women in this study. Her early adolescence includes promiscuity at an alarmingly young age, drug use, and attachments to older men who always eventually hurt her. Although her story appears at first to be chronological, it actually loops back several times to pick up threads that Sherry wants to emphasize as her narrative unfolds and she begins to make sense of it.

The ultimate betrayal for this young girl is not the physical abuse she endures from her uncle, it is the fact that her mother and others in the family do not believe she has already been molested by her stepfather. When she talks about how her uncle reveals his sexual desires for her, we see the first window into her feelings and her thinking about this intrusion upon her personal self. However, when she tries to articulate just how disgusted she is by her uncle's sexual advances, language *fails her*. Rather than describe what makes his actions seem "perverse" to her (a word she does employ at one point), she resorts to body language, contorting her face and mouth into an expression that clearly tells us "his advances were repulsive to me." Rather than *speak* this infringement upon the sanctity of her self, she *grimaces* instead, clearly communicating her sense of repugnance at his perversity. But his advances apparently do cause her to recall her experiences with her abusive stepfather, and this somehow prompts her to share that earlier childhood story with this uncle and her other family members.

Clearly, her family's response is the critical aspect of this narrative. She finally tells about the stepfather's abuse and sexual molestation but reveals, in her typical matter-of-fact fashion, that they did not believe her:

> And Uncle George got drunk one night and told me that he wanted to be "with" me, sexually, and I thought that was real perverse, because this is the man that raised me; my mother had entrusted him to take care of us and stuff. And he told me he was attracted to my other cousins, my other female cousins, and we were all blonde haired and blue eyed. And I thought that was kinda—[pauses, grimaces]—so I started sorta watching how he was and *I told them about my stepdad, who lived there with us in the city. I told them how he had molested me, and they never believed me.* [emphasis mine]

Many of the authors in Deirdre Lashgari's collection, *Violence, Silence, and Anger,* as well as many others, have identified several aspects of early sexual molestation. Most scholars agree that the negative effects on girls are more severe: (1) if the abuse is from a close or intimate family member, one thought to be in charge and there to protect the girl; and (2) if the girl believes she cannot tell anyone about the molestation, and, especially, if she risks telling about the sexual abuse, and no one believes her. In Sherry's narrative, as well as many of the other women's stories, this seems to be the case. Sherry seems disgusted by the advances of her uncle, but she is equally disturbed (even after several years) with the reality that when she does tell her family about her stepfather's behavior, her family does not believe her. This is the ultimate betrayal. The girl's recognition that it is not in her best interest to tell anyone about abuse is second in impact and importance to her learning that the reality of her story will be denied. This denial carries a tremendous price for her welfare and well-being and her development of a healthy sense of self.

In another convoluted, but sophisticated, narrative twist, Sherry moves within her story of this uncle's attempted molestation back in time to her stepfather's actual molestation. We learn several significant things in this remembering of her life narrative as she reattaches portions of the narrative she did not reveal at the beginning. For the first time, she reveals that she previously *had tried* to tell her mother about her stepfather's sexual abuse, but that her mother never acknowledged her story, did not seem concerned about Sherry's situation, and did not try at all to protect her:

> And when my mom found out about it, when I was younger, she never once, never once—I told a friend of mine, and she told her mother, who told my mother—my mother never once took me to the doctor, never once asked me about it, and I thought that was really [weird]; and my stepdad still stayed around. She kicked him out, but he'd still come back and stuff and she wasn't even around home. That was really sick.

Here the only comment we have from Sherry about her mother's lack of attention to her crisis is an apparent sense of loss. She is not willing or able to articulate how she feels about her mother's inaction; she resorts to a gesture that I must decipher—a shrug and a grimace, which I have interpreted as "weird," or "strange," or "inappropriate." Later, she says, "that was really sick." She does suggest that her mother's inattention to her story of being molested is confusing to her—her mother "never once" took her to see a doctor, "never once asked [her] about it." Her story suggests that she has never come to grips with these facts. Had her mother responded in some way, it would have been an acknowledgment of the fact that something had truly happened. Her story reveals that at the time she was reaching out, that she is trying to "tell" the story about her sexual abuse at the hands of her stepfather in the only way she can imagine telling it: "I told a friend of mine, and she told her mother, who told my mother." She must have expected some action. In fact, she names two that would have been appropriate and would have signified her mother's concern: she had hoped her mother would talk with her about it, and she felt it would have been appropriate for her mother to take her to see a doctor. Implied in the next words of her narrative is another implicit desire: She could only hope that her mother would care enough about her well-being that she would not leave Sherry home alone with the stepfather. But that did not happen, either. Sherry says her mother was ineffective in any attempts to protect her daughter, who by now must have been feeling extraordinarily vulnerable: "My stepdad still stayed around. She kicked him out, but he'd still come back and stuff and she wasn't even around home. That was really sick."

What is said here and what is missing? When her mother was not at home, her stepfather continued to "come back and stuff." What is he doing to her? She does not admit to fear here, yet if we read these lines carefully we can begin to feel the terror and the pain of the seven-year-old girl who has "told" to no avail. Her pain is even greater because her mother knows, now, of the abuse and yet does not really try to save her. Can we smell the fear in these lines? Can we know the way this girl felt when her mother left the house? She does not recount for us the number of times he returned to molest her, but the words she employs here are indicative of perhaps years of sexual abuse by her stepfather—abuse she identifies as "really sick," if ignored and therefore tacitly endorsed by her mother. Sherry is right; it is sick. By her seventh young year, she has learned a great deal about her world. She will be ignored; she will be molested; she will be lonely; she will feel forsaken. And the way she can detach herself from the reality of her life is to distance herself from the world around her. She does not tell us what he did to her. Like the other women in this study, she found ways to numb herself and endure without involving her mind or her body in the actions imposed upon them.

Somehow Sherry knows, even as a young child, that everything that is happening to her is wrong, but she also knows no one is able to help her. Even her beloved aunt is, like her own mother, suffering at the hands of a violent husband and "leaves" her own children in a desperate attempt at suicide that fails, rendering her mentally disabled. Sherry feels the loss deeply. It is obvious that the women in her life will not be able to help her. She recounts that she and her siblings are shuffled back and forth among the relatives, staying mostly with an abusive and violent uncle who "beat the hell" out of his wife, the beloved aunt whom Sherry believes to be a "real lady" and not deserving of his abuse. And, we must note, there are no words here, no language employed to convey what these years were like, at least not at this point in her narrative. The only words she uses that convey any emotional feelings at all are about this aunt: "You know she'd do anything for us, you know, she was just wonderful."

Mothers who are absent; mothers who are abused; mothers who are drunks; girls who are molested; girls who are silenced and feel lost; girls who feel invisible, unloved. How does this get translated into the stories of their childhoods? The beginning of Margaret's story is a good example of a narrative that appears eager to conform to a kind of "normal" standard of childhood memories but that later dissolves as she begins to remember more of her own story.

> You know I really don't remember a whole lot about my childhood. I think that's really odd, because when I talk to other people they can tell me incidents that happened in their childhood and I'll sit back and I'll think and I just don't remember, I don't remember having a happy childhood.
>
> I think that we had a really good home. I loved my parents to death, and they were the best parents ever. But growing up, I don't think I ever found "happiness," and I think I struggle with that today because I tend to become more depressed or get in a "funk" mood. I think that has a lot

to do with when I was growing up and I don't remember a whole lot of it. So, about my childhood, I don't remember a lot, and that bothers me a lot when I can't remember it. I know that we went on family vacations and that was a lot of fun. I was the youngest of three children; I had two older sisters. And I can't understand why I can't remember more. My parents always let my friends come over.

Margaret is perplexed by her lack of memory. In fact, as she speaks, she seems curious, as though this stroll through her past allows her the opportunity to sort through her feelings and perhaps even question her own glossing of what life was actually like for her in her home.

I don't think I got a whole lot of self-esteem growing up at all. I remember when I got a job in a convenience store as a manager, my mother was very skeptical that I could actually run that store and handle the money. She's never really given me the "open door." You know how today, I'll tell my kids, "The sky's the limit; go for it—I'll support you." I didn't ever get that. That might be one of the reasons I got pregnant at the age of fifteen. I wanted to get out of there.

Like Margaret, many of the women in the study begin their stories quite differently from Sherry's devastating earliest memories of her uncle killing her father. Some, in fact, seem compelled to begin with a nostalgic tone, but move away from these healthy and positive, perhaps fantasized, images that are quickly shattered by the remainder of the story. For example, Delores begins her story this way:

The very first memory I can remember in my life is a big red apple hung on the wall. And my mom. And I've seen pictures of it and it's where she used to change my diaper. I've been taught that you cannot remember things before your preverbal time, but I remember the image of the big red apple and wanting it, that's the thing I remember first, and I think it's kind of interesting, not even knowing what it was and Mom's [saying], "No, you can't remember that, but I can."

I guess the second thing I remember is waiting for Santa Claus. I was probably two, maybe two, waiting for Santa Claus, sleeping on the couch and waking up and seeing someone there by the tree and closing my eyes really quickly, because I was told that if you saw Santa Claus he wouldn't come, but those are not bad memories or good, they are just kind of neutral memories.

Delores's romantic images of apples, her mother, and Santa Claus are contradicted almost immediately in her narrative. While they may represent the peace and tranquility Delores longs to recall and the evidence of a happy home, Delores is already ambivalent by the time she says, "those are not bad memories or good, they are just kind of neutral memories." Lest they sound too idyllic, she catches herself in the lie. Hers was not, in fact, a loving household. It is telling that even in her narrative her mother is there to contradict her nostalgic beginnings, telling her that she could not possibly recall those times and that red apple. Her mother is probably right, but it is significant that the girl remembers her mother's denial of her own childhood memories, as well as the treasured memories she cannot relinquish.

Like so many of the other women, Delores tells the story of a girl who tried to survive in a household where violence was commonplace. It is apparent from her story that the abuse inflicted upon the mother in her marriage came, then, to be inflicted upon her daughter.

> Mom was the one who was difficult to deal with. She angered quickly, got her feelings hurt very easily, was a perfectionist. I remember most of my preadolescent life was trying to stay out of trouble, stay out of her way, because you never knew what would set her off, and I can't say I was extremely, physically, abused, but I do remember being spanked frequently, not to the point of leaving bruises or anything like that. But the strangest thing is, I can't remember what I did wrong, you know, I cannot. . . . What I do remember is always trying not to make her mad.

Delores recalls that she believed her father "sapped" the very energy out of her mother. Her subsequent fear about her mother's anger being turned on her becomes painfully clear when, in her story, she relates that she was sexually molested by her babysitter's sons. At the time, however, she is not willing nor able to share this with her mother because her fear of her mother is greater than her fear of the molesters.

> It's just that I was worried about who would take care of us. So I was scared, and I never did tell anybody that until after I was an adult. But it was really scary, really humiliating for me. And I had to keep going back there. I can't remember for how long.
>
> So I felt like I had done something wrong and she said if I told my mom that she [the babysitter] would never take care of us again, and I remember feeling so alone and thinking, "Who would take care of me," you know, if I told?

Not surprisingly, we learn that Delores left home at a young age and shortly decided to marry a devout Pentecostal boy. She left to get away, seeking solace in a marriage of her own choice rather than that of her parents, and in a new religion that was as strict as her mother but held promises that were attached to this striking young man. She says she made a poor choice and knew it fairly quickly. Her dilemma, at the point in her story where she realizes she needs to leave her soon-to-be husband, reveals her despair and highlights her relationship with her mother, who she believes fails to help her in her darkest hour:

> So, I felt isolated. I remember calling my mom and asking if I could come home, and she said she would have to talk to Dad about it. But Mom never did get back to me, never did get back to me. She never told me I could come back home. There was a time before that, when I had asked her if I could come home, and she didn't think it was a good idea. She used to tell me when I was a teenager that she would be glad when I was gone. As a teenager she would—I really do not see myself as being a "smart aleck" or anything like that—but if I said one little thing that she took that way, she would just haul off and slap me. So, I couldn't go back home. At least that's how I felt.

As in the narrative Delores tells, many times in this research a woman would begin her story with kind and loving things to say about her mother or about her parents, but as her story evolved, a radically different picture would begin to emerge, different from the one painted at the beginning. Janie tells this about her mother:

> My mother has always been—if anyone—that has been my support system. I have always known that no matter where I was at in the world, if I was in trouble and I needed help, all I had to do was get a dime, call my mom, and she would either help me out of it or she would be there or whatever.

We have to wonder, then, why this young girl leaves her home at seventeen and gets married. It is not clear from her story if her early molestation by a neighbor man was ever revealed to her mother. She tells about this part of her childhood in a straight, matter-of-fact manner:

> When I was probably four years old I was molested by a neighbor who was older; my brother's ten years older than me, and this gentleman was kinda retarded and he was probably in his thirties then. He never actually

did anything, as far as penetrate me; he would just touch me in private places.

Did she tell her mother? Her story suggests that she never told anyone, that she knew what the consequences might be. Later in her story, for example, she revealed this about her mother:

> But in some ways I guess my mom [got frustrated with me]—? I can remember, math has always been a hard thing for me to comprehend— and I'm into computers now!—but I can remember so many times [her] sitting and helping me with math, and she was excellent, you know, she didn't even need a calculator. But if I didn't get it the first time, she would be yelling at me, I mean, if I didn't—if she tried to tell me more than twice, she would slap me, you know. So, finally it got to the point where I wouldn't even ask for help.

Although Janie began her story with: "My childhood . . . Going back as far as I can remember, I had a happy childhood overall," she commences, in the *very next sentence*, to counter that statement in every way imaginable. This is *not* the story of a "happy childhood":

> I had a father who was an alcoholic. I had a mother who was manic-depressive, who basically raised my sister and me on her own. We moved around from place to place a lot until it became later on in my life, I guess between ten, eleven, twelve. . . . I saw what she was going through, going to bed crying every night and having nervous breakdowns, medication, things of that nature. And I helped raise my sister quite a lot when I was that age. . . . Mom was still very depressive. There was a time period in her life, as I became older in my teenage years, that she became very manic-depressive and had to go and be hospitalized. At that point, I took care of my sister. I began raising her [takes a deep breath].

Like the other mothers in these stories, Janie's mother cannot provide a safe haven for her daughter. And in her depression, she herself became abusive to the young girl. At the end of her story, I asked her a question about her relationship with her mother. But again, she framed their relationship as strong and supportive by saying: "My mother and I were very, very close. She was a good woman. She just did everything in the world to please anybody. But she was very suicidal."

The following story reveals just how difficult it was to live with this pained, abused woman, whose husband kept moving her further and further from civilization, ignoring her signs of deterioration.

There was a time when I heard the gun go off in the basement of my home. That was a time that my dad was gone from seven o'clock, six o'clock in the morning until nine or ten o'clock at night. She didn't have a vehicle. She never had any money. He wouldn't let her have any money, and if she didn't have money, of course she didn't have a way to go spend it, because she didn't have a vehicle, you know, she just didn't have any friends. [Crying] One time she just lost it. She went into a nervous breakdown. She didn't know who she was.

One day, and this just brings tears to my eyes to say, one day I remember I was a young teenager, about thirteen. My dad was working all the time, doing drugs, was an alcoholic, and my mom went through the same abuse I went through [with my husband], with my dad. She had a loaded .357 Magnum laying on the table and I walked in and she says, "See this gun?" I was scared to death of what she was going to do. She says, "I'm going to pick it up as soon as you walk out the door, and I'm going to shoot myself, unless you can give me ten reasons not to." And me being only thirteen, I had to give her ten reasons why. And that was a hard thing for me to do.

As with many of the women in this study, Janie was forced to be an adult long before her years. She tells how she took care of her sister, herself, and her mother. Janie goes on to recall that she impulsively "got pregnant" at fifteen and moved into an apartment with her boyfriend. Eerily, as though her life is already patterned, destined to shape itself into her mother's life, she talks about how quickly her young husband became abusive, how he moved their mobile home ever farther out into the country, isolating her more and more. She tells how she signed custody papers to raise her younger sister because her father left the state, and how she became pregnant with one baby after another.

Mothers are absent, abusive, or distant, and they are unresponsive to the needs of their daughters. This is the story told over and over again in the narratives of women who are escaping violence in their domestic lives. Recall Marcie's story about the sexual abuse of her father, her uncle, and their friends, and her mother's lack of a reaction to the situation. Although her mother eventually got a divorce, her lack of a direct response to Marcie's abuse is devastating. She clearly remembers the day she tried to tell her mother. She learns several lessons—about trust and support, and how not to get beat. Silence is enforced for her. She will not turn to her mother again.

Her mother must have partially believed Marcie's story, because a few nights later she actually spied on her husband and caught him in the act of molesting the little girls. Mustering all her strength, she does an amazing thing, but what

Marcie wanted was her mother's acknowledgment of what was happening to her. Marcie remembers:

> There was one night she didn't go to work, but everybody in the house thought she did. She didn't go to work, but she went downtown to the bar and was waiting for dark—for it to get dark—and she snuck back to the house, and she looked in the bedroom window—us girls' bedroom window—and she saw for herself what was going on, because he would always leave, not the big light itself, but the night-light on, and she saw for herself what he was doing and she come in with—I'm not sure if it was a sledgehammer or something—it was a hammer but one of those big hammers—but she come in and she started raising all kinds of hell, and she ended up leaving, making him leave.

This is a remarkable narrative sentence, long, extended; she adds on the events one after the other, building to a crushing blow—with the sledgehammer. All in one breath, Marcie recalls what her mother did that night. But Marcie's memories are not quite clear here; she cannot actually recall whether her mom left, or if she forced her husband to leave, so she tells us both things happened. What is clear, however, is that this act of strength on the part of her mother does not absolve her of not "hearing" and sympathizing with her daughter's dilemma. What Marcie does recall is that she never talked with her mother about what happened, and she has never forgiven her mother for not believing her and for beating her for telling.

The reader can hear the patterns in these stories, the early years of pain and fear, silence and suffering. Some of them begin to be reflective about where they have been. Some, like Sherry, are able to reflect on the significance of these early years of feeling abandoned and relate their invisibility and despair to their adult lives that are filled with violence and abuse:

> I don't think a child is born with self-esteem. I think it's up to the parents and the people who love that child to build that self-esteem and make them strong and make them—you know. A child is not born with self-value, self-worth; you know, that's something that is taught to them. And if you don't have that, you just—you're just not going to go anywhere.

5

Looking Back

Russellville, Tenn. (AP)— Joyce Hanson Newberry had finally met and married the man of her dreams. But her ex-husband was the nightmare that wouldn't go away. . . .

[E. C.] Cobb, 52, cut the phone line to [his ex-wife's] mobile home and threw a road flare through a bedroom window. As Joyce Newberry ran out the front door with her new husband and her best friend, . . . Cobb fired with a 12-gauge shotgun. . . .

Cobb, a former deputy with the Hamblen County Sheriff's Department, was a quiet man with a volatile temper who had been depressed for weeks about his ex-wife's [new] relationship. . . .

"He was a very jealous-type person. He couldn't take rejection," [Sheriff] Long said.

Columbia Daily Tribune,
May 12, 1998

IN THE PREVIOUS CHAPTERS, I have sought to discern how women talk, or do not talk, about the violence in their lives, how they tell their stories to receive services, how their life stories reveal the debilitating effects of early molestation and sexual abuse, and how the stories show the ways the development of a healthy "self" has been thwarted at every turn. All of these young girls grew into adulthood, still trying to be invisible and trying not to call attention to themselves, still seeking assurances that they matter as human beings, grateful for the attentions of men who unfortunately became their abusers as well. In group meetings, many of the women repeat Teresa's sad cry, "Is it stamped here [on my forehead], you know, 'abuse me'?" Their stories reveal a pattern of violence and abuse that has a tenacious hold on their lives. Breaking free from a life of abuse at the hands of men in their lives—men who may ultimately kill them—becomes one of their primary goals. Of course, the mental obstacle here for them, and for us, is the truth that *they* don't have to do anything different, or change. This is not about them at all.

I discovered, as I tried to sort out the different aspects of this project, that the material never easily divided into "neat" categories for each new chapter, especially as I moved from the chapters on self-esteem, the issues of silence, and the "unspeakable" into new chapters that would examine more deeply when and how violence *is spoken* in the women's narratives. And I had to ask myself tough questions—like where does childhood molestation and abuse stop and "violence" in the home begin? Is a mother's lack of support and silence a kind of abuse, or does that aspect belong with silence and pain and the trauma of growing up without role models and a way to develop self-esteem? I am aware that sometimes the material in these chapters overlap; I am aware there are repetitions; but this story is *not* neat and clean and easy to dissect and present in an unmessy fashion. Violence permeates every single page of these stories, in one way or another. A word, a glance, an assault, a violating touch, neglect, a blow, a punch, a death, a suicide all in their own ways are part of the mix that made the survivor who she is today. I heard many narratives about growing up that echoed these words from Tina:

> I hung with the dudes. I went to Tyrone's. Tyrone was this great big black guy, and he and his mother dealt drugs out of his house in a really bad section of town, and that's where we went to get drugs, and it was all about drugs and guns and money. I moved in a man's world—in an underground man's world in a really tough world. And I was this little tiny thing and I was hitchhiking all over the city doing drugs, and I looked so young for my age. I'm twelve and thirteen and I'm sure I looked eight and nine, and I'm smoking and doing drugs and hitchhiking all over the place, and some pretty scary stuff happened hitchhiking around. I'm real surprised I survived that time. I really feel like I was being taken care of. And not too many horrid things happened. Some pretty bad things happened but nothing—I could have disappeared in that world really easily. I was the only girl that was getting loaded besides one other girl that I knew of, and so she and I hung out with my brother. My brother and I were best friends and we dealt drugs and got loaded on a lot of stuff a lot of the time and my mom just pretended it wasn't going on. Friday and Saturday night it was just a constant trail of people in and out of our house. And my mom just watched T.V. and read her book and pretended it wasn't happening. By the time I was fifteen I was pretty dependent on any kind of a substance. I didn't drink that much; I mostly smoked pot every day and hash and did psychedelics and speed.

Compare Tina's story with Charlotte's fear of her mother's husband:

> Pretty much most of my abuse and stuff started when I was four years old, when my mother was married to my first stepfather, but I thought he was my real father. He sexually molested me and he also physically and verbally abused me as well. I was left-handed and the only left-handed person in our whole family. And he threatened me, if I ever used my left hand again, he was going to break my arm. And so I quickly learned how to use my right hand.

In this chapter, I want to examine in more detail some of the more graphic portions of the women's stories. After noticing that there are definite gaps in many of the women's narratives of pain and violence, and that in their accounts of their early childhood abuse there are compressions that suggest an unarticulated narrative that has not yet emerged for them, I now face the task of discussing some of the more violent aspects of the stories that they *were able* to tell me. There are gaps and compressions here as well, to be sure, but there are also examples in these complex stories of incidences of violence, some complete with many details. It seems to me the details are still told from a "safe" distance; you will notice this as well. But what I want to do in this chapter is examine how the women are able to "speak the violence," and in so doing, I hope to develop an argument about how this speaking of the violence serves to create a site for the development of a new "self." As I write this chapter, I am thinking again about Audre Lourde's contention that "the master's tools can never dismantle the master's house." If the "tools" Lourde refers to are words and language, I must then side with the American feminists who claim that, in fact, it is through the manipulation of language that we *must* find ways to dismantle the master's house, for what other language do we have? I know the French feminists would have us move toward image, symbol, and *écruiture féminine,* or ways of writing on the body with what they might call "white ink," referencing female secretions as an alternative avenue that would move us beyond language.[1] But here I will not move us in those directions; rather, I will examine how women are able to use language to speak the violence and voice themselves into being.

"FICTIONS OF POWER" IN THE HOME

I have mentioned how Elaine Scarry's book *The Body in Pain* has helped me think about how difficult it is for women to use language to talk about pain and violence against their bodies and their minds. In her book, Scarry notes that an abuser or torturer is able, through the use of physical pain, to create the illusion of total power. Excruciating pain or complete and total fear, she argues, blinds us into accepting this "fiction of absolute power" and strips the mind of the ability to transform a painful incident into speech and language that would deny the abuser this position, or offer any subjectivity to the victim. She says it this way: "The political advantage of [delivering] physical pain is that it can deconstruct speech and transform the reality of pain into a 'fiction of absolute power.' "[2] As Scarry sees it, the political "master" is able to "unmake the world" of the victim while forging his own political discourse and identity—and hers.

In the case of violence in our homes, this argument would translate into how public and private, popular and religious, discourses conspire with the oppressor to support the following "master narrative": The man is the head of the household; the man is boss; the man is dominant and the woman is submissive; what goes on behind closed doors is "our" business. The women in this study have heard more than once: You are my "woman" and I own you and I can do anything I want to you; you are useless and worthless and I have every right to beat, strike, push, shove, and rape you; I do this because I love you; I am so jealous because I love you so much; I keep you at home because I love you so much; if I check on you constantly it is because I love you so much; know this—if I can't have you, no one can; do not ever forget, you are *mine*. This language, the rhetoric of the politically powerful man who is endorsed by our society as justified in his oppressive actions (covertly, if not overtly) "unmakes" the world of the women and children who must live with him. Fear and pain reign supreme in households where the man's rages and demands fill every living moment, day and night. There is no world outside the boundary of fear he creates for those who dwell with him. Tina describes this kind of life perfectly:

> If you cried in front of my dad, he beat you until you quit crying and so I just never knew what the hell to do. And so I hid in my closet a lot and I had this dresser in my closet and I would take all my clothes and I would pile them up on my dresser and hide in there and my mom would call that my "rat's nest." And it was the only place I felt safe. And I just became really terrified of the world. My mom just was so detached from anything real that it made it impossible to even process what was going on in our home. When my dad beat us my mom was never there and we'd come out and we'd be flipped out crying and she would just pretend like everything was fine. She'd put dinner on the table and we would just go on. I'm being sexually molested by my uncles because they were drunk

and she was sitting there watching it and she just put dinner on the table and everything's fine.

Tina's story is a perfect example of how her childhood world was "unmade" by her father and her uncle's behavior. Her story also reminds us of the previous chapters that concentrated more on childhood abuse and how girls are silenced; and it reiterates the sad condition of her mother's paralysis, one that provides no safety for the daughter's abuse. Her story illustrates how the oppressor's violence can "unmake" the reality of the people who live in the dwelling with him. Similarly, Teresa tells us about living with her dangerously abusive father:

> What went on in our family—not only was he abusive toward my mom— it was also towards the kids as well. My dad was the kind of person that it didn't matter what reasoning it was, whether it was right or wrong, it was his own, so you were punished for things—such as what he thought was important is not putting something, you know, right back into place, but even if you put that item back, you know, where you found it, it was either always a half an inch off—he was a perfectionist type of person. . . . But that was hard for me because I always—I became afraid of a lot and that's where the abuse was a lot, too. We knew that—it was a mind game, I guess you could say. We were always constantly thinking how he did it, how would he do it. Because we knew if we didn't do it his way we were going to be punished. . . .
>
> . . . I can *never* remember this man saying anything nice to any of us. There are so many episodes, it would take me forever to tell you all the things. One example would be, he would get, if he was sitting at a table, which we, you know, if that was what you want to call normal, what normal people do at nighttime to eat—but in a sense it was never normal because always when you sit down to eat—what you might say or think as a normal family dinner—it would end up in a dispute of him throwing tea or him throwing dishes. It was always something over anything and everything. So, it was just like you came to the table and you never knew how to act.

Can we imagine what life was like growing up in these childhood homes? The chaos and pain the girls describe in their early childhood years is then repeated in their abusive marriages. We hear a pattern here that will reemerge a bit later in their accounts with their husbands—a pattern of never, ever knowing how to act or what to do. They are damned if they do, and damned if they don't. Violence has no predictability, except its unpredictability. This is the true "unmaking" of a world. The world can make no sense, ever. The girls cannot know what will cause the violence. But they can rely on one thing: It will happen. Tina remembers:

> My father was the one who beat us. My father used to beat us with a belt and he would beat us for anything. If we didn't eat all of our dinner, if we spoke out of turn, if we embarrassed him. We were the most—everybody always said that my brother and I were the most well-behaved kids they had ever seen. And [laughing] there was a damn good reason for it. And when he was drunk, he was very cool because he was a very happy drunk. And if we would go somewhere at the beginning of the night and we would do something to screw up, he would tell us, "When we get home, you're getting a beating." If he got drunk by the end of the night, we didn't. If he didn't get drunk, we did. So alcohol was always my ally and when my dad was drunk I loved him and he was funny and he was fun and he was loving and he always had this glassy faraway look in his eyes that I just loved. And being so terrified of my mom and having my dad home drunk, my dad and I—he wasn't much at doing things but I could sit at his feet and he'd watch T.V. and I'd sit at his feet and I'd fetch beer for him and he would let me drink it with him and everything was fine. And so that, to me, was what life was about for me. And staying away from my mom when my dad would go back to sea—it was just horrible. And I just hated him to go away, and to me the beatings were so much better than being terrorized, because once my dad got all his rage out it was done, and my mom's rage was just never-ending. And it was always present and you never knew what was coming next. I was just a pretty terrified little kid.

We might agree that these fathers, and sometimes mothers as well, have managed to "unmake" the world of their families, but in truth, I would like to point out that they have also "made" their world. He has created for them a world of fear and chaos, pain and trembling. The children have no sense at all about what might be "normal," or what might exist in homes that are not like their own. Recall Tina's comment about her home: "My mom just was so detached from anything real that it made it impossible to even process what was going on in our home." Their world is one of always second-guessing him or her, of not knowing how to act, not knowing what to expect. It was a "mind game," she says, and only he knew the rules, only he could decide what would happen next. The entire family became afraid, and everyone in the family was constantly thinking about how they might try to please him, knowing at the same time that they never could. No matter how hard they tried, they would fail and suffer his wrath. This is the political "fiction of absolute power" Scarry is describing in her book. Pain and fear create the fiction that only the father, in many cases, has any power at all, and, through the use of fear tactics, physical abuse, rages of throwing things, and finding fault with everything the family does, this fiction becomes a reality for those trying to live in the same household with him.

Tina knows this creates in her a fear of everything and the desire to hide, and she uses language to depict this life: "I was just a pretty terrified little kid." Like so many of the women in this study, like the girls who wrap themselves in sheets hoping they can protect themselves from molesting fathers and uncles, like the girls who withdraw into themselves, hide in closets, make themselves numb, try to disappear, the effect of the abuse and violence is to cause the girls to fold in upon themselves. They recall that fixed position of defense, and one who hears their stories can easily see how their sense of "self" could not develop. The boundaries of the flesh—beaten, abused, and violated—form a kind of cage for the self to dwell. The boundaries of the skin constrict and pull inward, hoping to save the mind from suffering the same consequences the flesh endures. But this is never possible, and the mind, too, recoils as it becomes weary of the "mind-game," never knowing how to act, to stand, to be, to do. The wives and the children become like walking zombies, numb to the pain and the abuse, yet always alert to the constancy of the state of fear they must maintain to dodge the next blow. After a while they truly are numb, deflecting the blows by instinct but enduring them when they fall.

As long as the women and children are kept in this mode, there is no discourse available to them to talk about what is happening. Scarry says: "Pain is characterized by its 'unsharability'; it dismantles the victim's capacity for language and therefore the capacity to represent that pain to others."[3] A woman who is being beaten becomes immobile, which, of course, is the intent of the abuser. As long as she cannot speak the pain to others, she remains imprisoned in her own body of pain, and he is safe from her reprisals and the eyes of the world. And the fiction that becomes a reality moves with the children as they leave that house: They cannot learn in school; they cannot respond to the world around them, because that world has no real connection to the world they live in at home; they have no tools with which to gauge people's intentions outside the world he has created for them. They are extraordinarily vulnerable. His hold on their constructions of themselves is lasting and powerful as they move from being children there in the house of terrors into new houses full of the same terrors played out again and again.

Recognizing this as the context for the experiences of the girls in this study, I now want to draw attention to the stories that women are able to tell about the abuse and violence in their lives. Obviously, it is difficult for the narrators to find a language to describe what has happened to them. I encourage us to *hear* the women as they tell about some of the most vile experiences they have endured. I am aware that what they are able to tell is but a tiny portion of the full story of their lives lived in violence, and they often explicitly reminded me of that fact. I do not offer these graphic accounts for prurient interest. I offer them not to whet your appetite for more blood and pain, but, rather, to discover what language they are able to use, and to determine how they utilize words to describe the pain and the violence; in doing so, they find a language that assists them in their efforts to reconstruct themselves.

Through these acts of speech, the telling of their stories, through their voicing of the pain and violence, the women in this study are making one of several significant steps they must make to forge new constructions of themselves as they move beyond abusive relationships, into shelter, and beyond—into safe places to live. Scarry tells us the "task of the victim is to regain the power of self-representation by means of the imagination, which is the counterpart to pain and allows it to enter back into discourse and be represented."[4] Significantly, Scarry argues, it is through the use of language—through speech—that the self can be re-presented and reclaimed in new constructions. And, we might note, her use of "imagination" does not at all imply that an imaginative or "fictive" story is created, an untruth. Rather, the act of telling a story is a *creative act*, a kind of performance, that takes words and language beyond their mere rhetorical power and enables them to work for the narrator toward transformation and self-representation.

RAPE

Many of the women in this study were raped, either as children or as young adults. Without a doubt these were traumatic experiences and they shaped or at least influenced much of the rest of their lives, particularly in the ways in which they think about their own bodies and their self-worth. The women speak differently about childhood incest, abuse, and molestation by fathers and uncles, and their experiences of rape. For one thing, their accounts of rape are more fully developed as narratives than the very early experiences of being molested by family members, relatives, and neighbors. In fact, in terms of the narrative dimensions of this study, the rape stories offer a progression from the compressed childhood accounts and the later, more detailed accounts of violence in marriage or with partners.

I do think stories such as Delores's account of being molested by her babysitter's sons is a kind of transition story from violence in the private home to violence in a girl's wider sphere, but one where she had every right to feel and be safe. The babysitter's sons not only violated her right to safety, but the babysitter was equally abusive by telling Delores that she must never tell her mother or anyone else about the abuse, threatening that she will not continue to care for Delores and her siblings. In fact, the babysitter's "don't tell" stance is perhaps more devastating than the boys' actions against Delores, especially because it silences her and condemns her to further acts of abuse at these older boys' hands. Furthermore, Delores recalls the pain of not being able to tell her mother about the incidences. Her mother has not developed an open communication with Delores that would allow the girl to tell her mother what is happening, despite the babysitter's threats. Obviously, Delores feels the care of this babysitter is important to the family's status quo and opts not to tell her mother, probably because she is afraid to, but also because she fears she will be blamed if there is no other child care available to her mother. The weight of these complex decision-making moments for such young girls is excruciating to even imagine.

Tina's account of a rape she endured as a young girl is representative of some of these stories because it demonstrates the damage done when a girl encounters such brutality. Tina grew up in a terrifying household; her father brutally beat the children and her mother was too detached to do anything about it. By the age of twelve or thirteen, Tina was taking drugs and hanging out with tough boys. Her mother, too, often raged against the children, particularly when the father was away from the home. In her account of her childhood, Tina admitted she hid in the closet most of the time. Now, she tells about being a teenager and babysitting for a doctor's children. At first, through her use of language, we might forget her childhood traumas and how she had experienced pain and violence daily in her own home. She "sounds" fairly "normal" at first in her remarks about boys, but very quickly we learn why she will continue for the rest of her life to be "terrified of the world."

> And I tried to get this guy to notice me, whatever, and we had a pool at our house and I used that to get him—"We've got a pool. Come on over. We'll go swimming." And they would come over swimming and stuff and hanging out and it was pretty cool; we were just friends. But I started liking him a little bit more than that. And one day I was babysitting for this doctor's family and they, the boys, came over and I was just like— wow, you know, comin' over to where I was babysitting—this is so cool, you know. They were like eighteen years old, I guess. They were eighteen. This is so cool, you know. And they came in and [pause] it was a night I had forgotten—I had forgotten this night for a long time and I guess I had pushed it back in my mind, pushed it back and pushed it back. [Long pause] They very brutally raped me. And that's something I won't ever

forget. They sent the kids upstairs, tied my hands behind my back, tied my feet, gagged my mouth, stuck Coke bottles, mopsticks, broomhandles, whatever they could, stuck them all up inside me, made me put their dicks in my mouth, [pause] just, it was gross. [pause] It felt like they were there for hours and hours and hours and hours. And I know that it probably wasn't more than a half hour but it felt like it was forever. And I really felt like I was going to die. And one of the boys that was upstairs, he was coming downstairs and I'm lying there in the floor. He flipped. He called his mom and dad and I just thank God he was a doctor [speaks quietly, becoming inaudible]. And they whispered all kinds of things in my ear, like "You're not gonna tell" and "They won't believe you" and all like that. And I carried this for many years.

Without shame, Tina tells us she was interested in this older boy; she's even glad the boys are coming to visit her where she is babysitting, although it is clear she has never heard admonitions from her parents to guard her safety and the safety of her charges while babysitting. She thinks this will be a lark. But she was wrong. She has tried, in this doctor's home, to "make" a world different from her own home, but it is quickly "unmade" by the violence of the boys who violate it and her. She does not comment on the inappropriateness of the boys' behavior, yet we "hear" it in her story, implied when she says, again, "It was just so cool." Her story guides us to understand that it is about to become very, very "not cool." The boys "unmake" her imagined teenage world of crushes and boyfriends, babysitting and suburbia. She tells us she had forgotten this experience, this night of terror. She "pushed it back and pushed it back," yet she is willing, now, to dredge up horrible details and speak the violence. The ending of her story reminds me of Maxine Hong Kingston's story about her aunt, "No Name Woman," who shamed the family and was therefore disowned.[5] Kingston is told as a child never to speak the aunt's name or tell her story, but in the very act of writing the story about her aunt, she breaks the taboo of silence and tells the story anyway. Tina does a similar thing. She tells us the boys whisper in her ear, "You're not gonna tell" and "They won't believe you." Although she has carried this story, silently, for years—forgotten it, repressed it—today, on tape, she has told the story. She does not need to carry it any longer. She has broken the taboo of silence. She has spoken the violence and emerged on the other side.

Cathy's story about a teenage rape she endured is perhaps more typical, in that the details of the actual rape—that is, what he did to her sexually—are not as graphic as the rest of her story, which is rich in details and immediacy. She tells about the rape she endured at the hands, and the knife, of her brother's friend and the fear she has about the rape being "discovered" by her parents.

The details in this story are definitely "creative and imaginative," adding to the import of the telling of her story. She isolates specific images that stand out in her own mind as she tells a story that she can now formulate and even reflect upon, perhaps for the first time. It is very important to note that her most creative use of language occurs in the portions of the story that reveal her fear of her parents "finding out," not in the description of the rape itself. These more "imaginative" aspects of her story—like those about her fear of her parents—represent the aspects of her "self-construction" that are currently being worked through and being challenged through her narrative. The rape is still a kind of "unspeakable" moment that she is only able to share with her listener with a minimum of words. The creative and imaginative aspects of her storytelling are connected to those parts of the story she is more ready to deal with, such as her anger about her parents' response to her rape. The sexual aspects of the rape seem to be developed symbolically through the images of the blood on the bedspread and on her neck—blood she is desperate to erase. She begins her story much like Tina's, setting the stage:

> A storm had come up pretty sudden and there was a lot of wind, hail, lightning. It was really bad. And a knock came at the door. And I went to the door and it was Eddie Smith. And he was standing there with a suitcase in his hand and he said, "I was on my way to the bus station and this storm came up. Can I come in until it stops raining?" Well, I didn't even think twice about it. I opened the door and I let him in because I would have done that probably for anyone, short of Jack the Ripper or something.
>
> So anyway, of course that was against the rules; I wasn't supposed to have boys in the house when my parents were gone, or anyone in the house for that matter, but I let him in and he asked me if he could have a glass of water and I said yes and I went to the kitchen to get him a glass of water, and I heard this sound, and before I could react to it he brought a switchblade around in front of me holding it to my throat. And I dropped the glass of water in the sink and I was like, "What is this about?" And he let me know he wanted to have sex with me and I wasn't in a position to fight with him. He was holding a knife to my throat and so he basically pulled me, holding a knife to my throat, down the hallway to my parents' bedroom, and he nicked me several times in the process because I was trying to walk backwards and so was he, and it was kind of a clumsy thing. And he nicked my neck several times with the blade and we got back to the room and I was just pleading with him the whole time, "Please don't do this. Please don't do this. If you just leave now I won't say anything," and whatever, and it seemed to just make him angry.

So when we got to the bedroom he told me to take off my clothes and I was crying and pleading for him not to do this and he took the knife and swiped at me with it and he didn't cut me badly but he did catch my throat and cut it a little bit and I was very afraid. So I took off my clothes and he then proceeded to—he didn't remove his clothes—he just undid his pants and he then proceeded to have sex with me. While he was doing that, he was on top of me and he had his arm across my throat holding the knife next to my throat and so he nicked me several more times. He never did cut me badly; they were just nicks. And then when he was finished with what he wanted to do, he got up, and just about the time that he was getting ready to walk out of the room—I was just curled up on the bed crying—I heard a sound and I knew it was the car door, that my dad was home from work, and I was just terrified.

Her account is so vivid, we see her walk into the kitchen to get the young man a glass of water, trusting him as she did, letting him into her home; we hear the switchblade opening and the sound of the glass shatter as she drops it into the sink; we almost feel the sharp, little nicks of the knife on her throat, swallowing as she probably does in her fear. And after he rapes her, we share her fear—although we may not understand it—when she hears her father returning home, her panic as she hurries to cover up the evidence.

It is significant that the least descriptive portion of this experience is the rape itself. Language does not help her much when she is actually describing what Eddie does or how she feels about what he does. She says, "He let me know he wanted to have sex with me." As she relates her story, the imagery of his arm across her throat and the knife's sharp nicks on her skin are more accessible through language than what is being done to her most private parts.

This story is at least as much, or more, about Cathy's relationship with her parents, and how they will frame the reality of her being raped, than it is about the rape itself. She should be relieved that her father is returning home; she should be confident that he will rescue her from the rapist or go running after him when he realizes what has just happened to his daughter. But Cathy's story clearly reveals that this house holds nothing but fear for her. At the beginning of her narrative, when she acknowledges that she lets Eddie in, she also acknowledges that the whole thing is her fault—at least, she knows it will be construed as her fault by her parents—because she has broken a rule. But her careful use of language and storytelling here also convinces the listener to vindicate her of any wrongdoing. Her narrative itself condemns her callous parents, so she need not openly accuse them.

So when my dad came in, he said, "Who was in here?"

And I said, "Nobody. Why?" Because I knew I'd get in trouble for having someone in the house. And I was still shaking and I was just, you know, kind of in shock and very frightened. And I said, "Nobody. Why?"

And he said, "I heard somebody running down the steps when I got out of the car." And he took off out the front door, looking, I guess, for whoever had been in the house, and he didn't find anyone, and so he came back in and said, "I know I heard somebody."

I said, "Dad, I was downstairs. I came upstairs."

He said, "I thought I heard the back door close."

I said, "No, I was coming up the stairs."

And he said, "Okay." And he let it go at that.

But my mom came home from work probably an hour or so later, and I had been in the bathroom trying to—I had wiped the blood off my neck before my dad got home because there wasn't a lot of blood, just little drops and you really couldn't see the nicks too much. But by this time they were starting to show. They had turned red and whatever and I was trying to find my dad's styptic pencil, because I knew he used that when he shaved if he nicked himself. And I was trying to find it because they would still ooze, these little drops of blood, and I wanted them to stop bleeding. So I was in the bathroom trying to find that when my mom came home. Might not have even been an hour later.

But one thing I guess I had forgotten to do was straighten up the bed. My dad hadn't been in the bedroom yet, but the first thing my mom always did when she came in the house was put her purse in the bedroom and take her shoes off. So she walked straight to the bedroom, which was directly across the hall from the bathroom, where I was, and she called out to my dad and she said, "Were you—did you lay down when you got home from work?"

And he said, "No. Why?"

And she said, "Well, the bedspread's all messed up on the bed." And then she got to looking at it. It was a white chenille bedspread and there were drops of blood on the bedspread. And so she immediately called for me. And I went in there and she was very visibly upset and she wanted to know what that was about. And I broke down and started crying and told her what happened. Well, I hadn't really thought of it, but Eddie left without his suitcase, and so my parents found his suitcase stashed behind the living room couch. So I wonder, since he hid it behind the couch, if he actually came to our house for the purpose of raping me. I guess I'll never know the answer to that question.

But what ultimately happened was my parents made me—Eddie was nineteen years old, and I was only thirteen—and my parents called his parents and they came over to our house. And his parents basically had the attitude that, well, I should know better than to let people into the house when I'm there by myself. And, ultimately, I ended up having to apologize to his parents for having let him in the house and that kind of thing. There was never anything done about him raping me. My parents were very angry with me for having let him in the house and brought this embarrassment onto our family. And so I apologized to his parents for what I had done and that was that.

A devastating story of violence and silenced pain. The way Cathy tells her story suggests she has not yet totally accepted her own innocence and her parents' culpability. She guesses she forgot to straighten the bed and somehow conceal the bloodstains on the white bedspread. Somehow she should have known not to let him in, not to let him rape her; she realizes her parents would come in and blame her. But consciously or not, she is able to illuminate their abuse and expose the lie of the "fiction of power" they have established in their home, through the act of telling her story. Cathy is afraid of her parents for good reason; through her story, she shows their complicity through their abuse and domination over her. Other parts of Cathy's story support her emerging consciousness about how she lived in a household controlled by a father who has designated himself as absolute ruler. The power of his rage controls the universe inside the home. The mother is but a pawn in his perception of how the world is put together. Cathy might have thought at one time that the rule about not having boys in the house had been inscribed in order to protect her and keep her safe, but her evolving story does not support that assumption at all. Once he hears the story, Cathy's father is not at all concerned about the rape of his daughter, about her well-being, the trauma on her body and mind. Instead, he is angry with her—first, for allowing the young man into the house, never mind that they see the suitcase and hear her explanation that it was storming and he simply asked for some shelter and a glass of water, and second, for *embarrassing them* by *her actions!*

Meanwhile, the actions of Cathy's mother in this scenario are not fleshed out. She seems innocent when she asks her husband if he's already stretched out on the bed since arriving home. She is confused and concerned when she finds the blood spots on the coverlet. Cathy tells us, "And I went in there and she was very visibly upset and she wanted to know what that was about. And I broke down and started crying and told her what happened." Cathy starts crying and tells *her* what happened. There is a gap here in Cathy's narrative: Does her mother comfort her? Is the father's control so huge it fills all the rooms in the house? Does he storm out of the room, looking for the suitcase? Does he yell and scream at her as her mother quietly weeps? Cathy does not tell us that her mother is angry with her. It is her father's anger that captures her memory. But she does not seem surprised that they, together, require *her* to apologize to the boy's parents for her behavior.

She states matter-of-factly, in a numbed voice, that "there was never anything done about him raping me." And nothing is done to help her with the physical and emotional trauma of having just been raped at knifepoint by an acquaintance she had every reason to trust. She tells us she is humiliated, because her "parents were very angry with me for having let him in the house and brought this embarrassment onto our family." Cathy learns something about her parents in this narrative moment, and she learns something about herself. In telling her story, in locating language that will convey her own right to be above suspicion in this incident and to illuminate her parents' cruel and nonsupportive behavior, she is able to both "do" some self-construction work and implicate the collective abusers at the same time, all of them: Eddie, her parents, Eddie's parents, the police, and the society at large. We are appalled by this story. We know they were *all* culpable. She expands beyond the boundaries of her narrowly defined self through the telling of her story, as Scarry has suggested she might be able to do. And there are other ways in which this expansion of the self might be accomplished through speech.

LEAVING HOME

As is typical, according to the researchers who have studied the lives of young girls who are victims of incest and violence, Cathy's response to the abuse in her home was to leave:

> But anyway, when I was fourteen I decided that I didn't want to be there anymore—that I always had this sense that, even though I felt like there was something wrong with me that I was always being treated this way, something deeper in me always said, "It's not me; it's them," you know, because I know me, and I know that I'm a good person, and I know that I didn't do anything wrong. But why does everyone else think that I'm this bad person and whatever? And so when I was fourteen I just finally decided that it was time for me to prove to myself that I was the person that I believed that I was, not the person everyone—everyone meaning my family—was telling me that I was. And I ran away from home.

It is instructive at this point in Cathy's story to place this rape and her running away from home into perspective. The reader may recall other parts of Cathy's story, as well, when she tells of an uncle who abused her from the time she was three or four until she was fourteen, but she was careful to hide the bruises and not let her mother know. And she knew from a young age that her mother had not wanted her as a baby, had even checked into the cost of abortions, which were illegal at that time, but decided against it because of the high cost.

Other women tell similar stories. For example, when she was a girl, Cathy's brother terrorized her, putting her down the laundry chute, forcing her to stay in the basement for long, dark days. Is it any wonder that she, too, left home at fourteen? Most of the women in this study left home at a very young age. Getting pregnant and married was practically the only avenue for their escape. And most of them note the importance of this move away from home in their narratives, although all acknowledge that the move did little to improve their circumstances. Margaret and Delores both find young men to marry them to help them escape the nightmares in their own homes. Delores tells, in her life story, about being engaged to the son of a very rich and prosperous farmer who lived nearby. Her parents and his were eager to see the young people marry, but Delores never felt any excitement about marrying this young man and living the life of a farmwife.

I know I'm jumping around, but when I was about eighteen, I missed a period. And my periods started to come irregular. Well, I started to see a gynecologist and he asked me, "Could you be pregnant?" Well, I was a virgin, but I had kind of messed around with my boyfriend, and I had come into contact with his ejaculation, so I'm thinking, "Yes, it could be," because it *was* possible, even though there was no penetration. So, they took a test and it came out positive. So, I had to tell my dad I was pregnant and my boyfriend did, too. He was the one who told my dad, actually. So, my dad says, "There will have to be a wedding right away."

When my boyfriend left the house, I got down next to my dad's chair; I wanted to talk to him, but he pulled his arm back. I'd never seen my dad act this way. He pulled his arm back like he was going to hit me and said, "Get away from me, you—" and he didn't finish it, so I could fill it in with all kinds of negative words. But it seemed like my dad's and my relationship changed from that day—either my feelings, or it seemed like he reacted differently to me.

Well, it turns out, to make a long story short, I really wasn't pregnant. It was a false positive. And I didn't like—after that my boyfriend began acting really strange, too. I mean he just acted different toward me. His family acted differently towards me. My dad acted differently towards me. We continued to date but when I saw changes in people who were supposed to love me, it made me question even more what it was all about.

At this point, Delores was actually quite brave. She called off the wedding, even though the invitations had been sent. Her parents became even more frustrated with her and her father basically would not speak to her. So she moved out, moved to a different town, rented a dark, basement apartment, joined a Pentecostal church, and eventually met and married a Pentecostal man. But before this wedding, as well, she had misgivings and tried to call her mother to see if she could return home and not get married. Her parents did not bother to call her back; she married the man, who was abusive from the wedding night on. She began a life of violence and abuse.

Similarly, after her mother dies, Sherry moves quickly, at the age of eleven, into the home of an uncle (who eventually abuses her as well) and into a wild life of sex and older men:

> I got real promiscuous. The first abusive relationship I got into, I was thirteen. I was thirteen and the guy was twenty-two. He was the coolest thing in town. He had a Harley Davidson and a Green Demon and he was just so cool. He never really, his [abuse] wasn't—he wouldn't smack me in my face. He whipped my butt, you know, like a child, you know, that was his thing. But I thought I was in love [laughs].

Tina's story about her early childhood abuse, the neglect of her alcoholic mother, the abandonment of her father, and the sexual abuse she continually endured at the hands of her several uncles who moved in and out of her mother's house, reads like a contrived teenage novel, but her determination to escape is directly related to just how unstructured and chaotic her life at home was:

> So, I quit going to school. I just could not handle sitting in a classroom. Could not—I mean I was just so anxiety ridden I couldn't handle it. Met this woman. She's with this guy who physically abuses her on a regular basis. They get loaded all the time. She has one baby from him already. She's left him. She's living on the beach with this guy who's an alcoholic. He's really rich and living in a beach house. Do I want to come live with her? And I had been sexually abused by one of my teachers and I couldn't tell anybody. I was scared to tell anybody. And I tried to tell my mom and she said, "You're lying." So I just quit school. And my mom was fine with

that. She just didn't want to have to deal with the sexual abuse issue. So I said, "I'm not going back."

And get out they did. Nearly all the women in this study tell how they left home at a very young age, looking for an escape from the terror in their own homes. They had nowhere to go, though, and many were pregnant. They wake up, stunned, in abusive relationships with men who beat them, raped them, and silenced them exactly as their mothers, fathers, uncles, and brothers had done all the years of their lives. On what basis could they have expected anything else? Except for that brief flicker of a moment when they thought they were "in love," life looked pretty bleak.

In their stories, the women try to make sense of their relationships. Men would flatter them in order to gain their trust. The men in their narratives would "treat them like a queen," notice them, look at them, and listen to their stories about their lives. The pull of that promise would suck them in every time; they would be in too deep to escape before they realized what had happened to them. But they knew soon enough.

In her story, Margaret is the first to actually articulate what she calls her desire for the "American dream." This is repeated in many of the other stories as a kind of fairytale life the women envision for themselves with this "prince" of a man who pays attention to them in a way their parents never could. As Margaret says, "I just wanted to raise my child, you know, and have that American dream, having my husband go to work and you get to stay at home." Of course, in reality, they have moved from the frying pan into the fire.

> When I decided that I would have the baby, I decided to marry the father. So we did, and we got into subsidized housing, and I had a best friend in the same building. Unfortunately, they two had an affair. My husband had an affair with my best friend. It was Christmastime and things weren't going very well, you know. He smoked pot and he drank, and I didn't. It was really odd. We were *very* different. And what I saw in him, I don't know. You know, when I sit back and reflect on the two men—I've been married three times—and two of those men I don't understand what attracted me to them. I'm actually embarrassed to talk about it. So, I think that's where it all started.

In two of her marriages, Margaret faced brutal physical and emotional abuse. But she was always looking, she says, for her prince.

Teresa, whose father ruled the house with his fits of rage, also talks about how her relationship with her abuser began as a kind of "fairy tale" that went sour:

He was just, like I said, he was what you would call a prince, okay? He was a fairy tale that was going to close the doors to the madness that I grew up with. [Crying] He was going to be a hero and I would live happily ever after with this man. And that never happens, either, so that's why: Okay, that's my lost hope, so that's never going to happen. And I believe it's not. That fairy tale's gone. [Crying] But he had a way of making me want it everyday.

Janice Haaken reminds us of the dangers for women who "look back." She relates women's lives and experiences to Lot's wife, who dared to glance back and was instantly turned into a pillar of salt.[6] Can we challenge the efficacy of that story for women? The act of "looking back" is not an action that is likely to free her from her demons, but the act of remembering, of telling her story, can serve as an act of transformation. What we are seeing in these stories is perhaps a glimpse of how the self emerges through the narrative act. In the Bible, men, like Saul, get the opportunity to "see" something and through telling the story of that moment of illumination become a new person. As young girls, the women describe themselves largely as passive witnesses to the activities around them. They are shifting forms, unanchored, waifs, really, at first. To "look back" risks facing some of the most difficult parts of who they were and who they have become. But to look back and "tell about it" is an act toward new self-revelation and self-construction. They have accepted the challenge to look back and to tell it all. The result is a narrative construction of self.

Cathy is raped by her boyfriend's best friend and her parents force her to apologize to him and to his family. Delores thinks she is pregnant, even though she has never engaged in sexual intercourse, and her father turns against her, refusing to touch her ever again; when she tries to return home, her mother does not welcome her back. Marcie tells her mother that her stepfather is molesting her and forcing her to give him oral sex, only to have her mother beat her and call her a whore. In order to sort out their lives and their actions, the women telling their stories recall fathers who are abusive and mothers who at best are not supportive. They recall how they felt like they were hanging in the wind, grabbing at the first available rescue from a sense of void and invisibility.

When I tape recorded the stories of most of the women in this study, they were poised to leave the shelter. They have plans—some big, some tiny—but the important thing is, they have plans. Teresa, still new to this world away from her abuser, is still asking many of the same questions, but at the heart of her questions lie some of the answers, if she can only "hear" them through her searching, circular thinking. She still does not know whether to blame herself or her abusers. She wonders if she has a sign on her forehead that says "abuse me." But she has learned some very important lessons in her journey. Her musings bring us back, full circle, to the dangers of "telling" too much to the wrong people. Teresa, like many women who have been beaten and battered, told her new boyfriend about her former abuse. This act of speaking, unfortunately, traps women more often than it frees them. In effect, by telling, they open the door for the next abuser to assume that since she has been battered before, she can be beaten again.

> And I'll be so honest because the Lord upstairs knows I have trouble with faith. Because it seems like every time I get on a mission to do right, I don't understand why they get as destructive as they do. I know why they get destructive if I choose to let them be destructive, but I have a hard time understanding the "why me's" of abuse and why—like is it stamped here [motions to her forehead], I mean is it stamped here, you know, "abuse me"? I mean, why can't people just leave me alone, you know? I want to know why I keep doing the repeats all the time, you know. Is it me? Do I do these things to cause it? Sometimes I think, yeah, I do. And that's what I'm dealing with right now, because what landed me here, I, once again, got into a relationship. . . .
>
> But when I met this man, this was like walking into heaven and—[long pause; crying]—he was the most kind and considerate and very loving person I ever could have begun to imagine. It was me. I got to be involved in this. [Sobbing] And we had a good relationship for a long time, but he took advantage of that relationship; I once again made a mistake in telling my past, okay? Just things that I guess some people call standards, okay? Like this time, I thought, I'm not going make this mistake again. But as we grew closer together, I started to tell him more and more. He was the only man that knew that my daughter was born the way she was. He was the only man that knew that I had problems with alcohol and drugs. He was the only man that knew about my dad. He was the only man that ever knew I was sexually molested by my brothers. He knew everything about me [sobbing]. Just as if he was God. And I was absolutely trusting of him, that's how much I loved him, so I knew this was love, because, in my mind, I always thought—well, I didn't know really what love was.

Words fail her here. What did she think love was? The freedom to tell all, to be vulnerable, to reveal her secrets? And what happens if she does tell him? She cannot speak the unspeakable here because he has violated her, physically and emotionally. She is tortured by the fairy tale gone awry, by the man who loved her but who has broken her trust. She trusted him with her love and with her words. To learn, once again, that "telling all" is a dangerous act is more than she can bear.

But the transformative power of telling her story in a safe environment where damage will not follow is an important concept to pass on to these abused women. In the past, when they have spoken of pain and abuse about one abuser to a new boyfriend or lover, their speech has worked against them. They know well the dangers of making themselves vulnerable. On the one hand, as I have argued in this book, "naming" the violence and the perpetrator carries the possibility of reinscribing the "fiction of absolute power." This is why "telling her story" failed to help her when she revealed her abuse upon entering into a new relationship; her own story reinforced the political discourse that endorses male violence against women. On the other hand, speaking the violence to others beyond the abusive relationship(s) holds the potential to unveil those fictions of power that have attempted to silence the subject. The narrator recognizes, in that moment of using language to articulate the violence, of making pain "shareable," that her words, like a spotlight, illuminate his abuse, his inappropriate behaviors, and they shatter the illusion of his "absolute power" over her. Scarry suggested that speech holds the potential to "expand the self." In this case, it also carries the possibility of *exposing the abuser* and his abuse, as well as exposing the larger totality of abuse known collectively as *domestic violence.* As long as her act of speech can be both spoken out from her self, as well as internalized by her as an act of defiance and empowerment, she should be able to feel her self expand from the prison of damaged flesh into a new and freeing space. But I do not intend to romanticize this journey.

Although Teresa explains to me that she and her daughter are very, very close, she also explains why she must leave town on the brink of her daughter giving birth to her grandchild. She cannot stay. She must keep moving. She's moving to Tennessee with a friend. She is determined to start a new life. And through her telling of her story, she is beginning to frame the beginnings of that new life. Today she feels empowered.

> But I think that for my peace there are going to be things that I'm going to have to focus on. The more I read, the more research I do on a few things that we've talked about that I'm going to have to do, you know, and the one thing above all that I know I have to do, is research myself. I have got to spend the time to know—I can't even say that—not to know [pause] but to look inside this person and see all the many options that there probably already has been, see what's available to me. I'm just like a job working on the inside just dying to get out. . . .

. . . I mean I really am on a mission: I'm on a mission so powerful within myself that if I ever get there, if I live long enough to get there, it should be pretty good. I hope that, in time, that as some friends have said—one especially; she's gone—if you're up there, Tammy [her eyes lift up]—it will be an explosion. What you used to tell me. If I ever get to where I need to be, it will be dynamite!

Turning Points

6

Gonzales, La. (AP)—The pastor had just started reading a Bible lesson about being born again when the gunman kicked open the doors, fired twice into the ceiling and ordered everybody to hit the floor.

He then marched down the aisle, shooting between the benches as screaming parishioners scattered in horror. . . . Among the crowd, police said, were the man's wife and child.

"His little boy turned and said, 'Daddy.' That's when he shot. He hit his wife first and then the baby," [a witness reported]. . . .

. . . As he left, Holmes [the minister] heard him mumble something like, "That will show you."

. . . Investigators were still compiling the names of the victims, but the minister said the slain wife was Carla Miller.

. . . The Millers married about two years ago and [a cousin reported that] Carla Miller left her husband shortly after.

"It was just a domestic problem that turned into domestic violence," [Police Officer] Landry said.

Columbia Daily Tribune,
March 11, 1999

MOST OF THE WOMEN in this study married young and realized almost immediately that their marriage was a bad mistake and they were now in a binding relationship with a raging, abusive man. Their words can convey what the first years of their life away from home were like better than anything I could say. These are sad, sad stories of young lives in despair. We need to notice, however, that it is in the speaking of the violence that the women begin to emerge as beings *separate* from the violence. It is through the telling of their stories that the women begin to sort things out, to name and acknowledge the violence, and to reflect on their own sense of self and how it has and has not emerged for them. I believe they move from a place of negation and silence into a space of embodiment that is personally empowering. We know Tina and Sherry's stories fairly well by now, but we are barely prepared for the brutality of their first marriage experiences. Tina tells us:

> And I was with Kenny and six weeks later I was pregnant. I was seventeen and I didn't want to be married. And what I didn't know when I first started dating Kenny was that when Kenny got drunk—and I would see him drink—and he was okay sometimes. But when he got drunk. . . . And he got very very mean and I had never known a mean drunk. But he was a mean drunk. He was mean, mean, mean. And the night we got married and my Uncle Len was there and my brother was there and my mom was there and we got married. And it was the first time he had ever gone off on me. He went off on me. He was a terrorizer. He would just get in your face and he would throw stuff and he would break stuff and he just terrified me. And he would keep me in line by terrorizing me. He would terrorize me for hours on end. And that night we got married we went back to our room and he kept me up all night long just screaming and yelling at me. He wouldn't hit me. He would hit right here and he would hit right here [indicates abdomen with defensive gesture]. He would threaten to kill me and he would tell me that I was a whore and a slut and blah, blah, blah. And I believed him. And right before we got married, I believed that I was a whore and I believed that I was a slut and I believed all the things that he told me.

Sherry, too, became pregnant as a teenager and found herself in relationships with alcoholic and abusive men:

> And I had my first child; I was seventeen, pregnant when I was sixteen. The baby's dad was twenty-three and he was a drunk and he was abusive. He was just abusive to the point to where—his was more of an emotional, verbal type thing. But he was a drunk and for some reason there's something about drunks.
>
> I ended that one, and then I got with another guy and he was real, he was really physically abusive and emotional, verbal, that whole thing, but I would just stick around because I really loved this guy. I remember I was sixteen, seventeen at that time, and I really didn't think I'd ever find anything else. We lived in a small town at that time and it was just crazy.

Interestingly, these accounts about the women's teenage relationships and the beginnings of marital/partnership abuse are told in a kind of minimalist fashion. There are few details here. In recounting this portion of their young lives, separate from their homes and family, but newly attached to a stranger who is violent, the women are not yet able to speak the graphic violence in these stories. Their empowerment, their articulation of their "self," the turning point, has not been reached. They all seem to be in one kind of a "fog" or another, if not drug induced, then emotionally induced. They literally do not know what has "hit them," and it is this dazed confusion their stories convey. Yet, their new situations feel familiar, these new lives of chaos, yelling, abuse, rape, and beatings. Yes, it feels just like home.

Later in the women's stories, as they develop a narrative of abuse, they are better able to articulate what has happened to them. In recounting their adult abuse, many begin to speak the violence that finally propelled them out of the danger and into a safe shelter. When we listen carefully to women's narratives about violence, we are attempting to discern how the speaker *uses* language, silence, or both to communicate pain and violence. In listening to this violence being spoken, we should also be able to discern the emergence of a newly articulated self. Here I want to demonstrate how, as some of the women tell their stories, this process provides new avenues for understanding and identity formation. Language is utilized to bear witness to their lives. Women do find ways to articulate pain and violence, illustrating through their own stories that in the act of speaking the woman is able to begin the serious work of reconstructing her self and move beyond accepting her position as battered woman and passive victim. I am including several accounts of some of the women in order to demonstrate how they are able to talk about the violence, as well as to illustrate how they are then able to talk about their emerging self.

MARGARET'S STORIES OF VIOLENCE

After Margaret's first marriage, at fifteen, to a man who cheated on her and left her to fend for herself, she found herself back at home with two small babies, no money, no job, and wondering where she would ever find a man who might want to marry a nineteen-year-old girl with two small children. She met Roger and was impressed by his attentions to both her and the children. He seemed very mature and "together," a kind and generous man. Margaret "opens her heart to him" and tells him all about how Jerry had abandoned her and the children and didn't seem to care about them. And, of course, this new man, Roger, swore he would adopt her children and tells her he only wants to be with her and her children, forever. She was swept off her feet—at first. Then he moved in, became obsessive and possessive. Her instincts warned her not to marry him, but the pressure from her family and friends to go on with the wedding was overwhelming. Her own misgivings were silenced by their opinions about what she should do. They thought she was pretty lucky to find such a "good man" who wanted to marry her and was willing to take on the responsibilities of her two children. But when they marry, he quits his job, claiming he only wants to "be with her." Soon, she is working and finds herself supporting all of them; she also learns that Roger has a serious drinking problem she had not known about before. He is a chronic liar, too, and his abusive rages begin almost immediately. Margaret is reflective as she begins to recount how this abusive relationship evolved:

> So, I think it still has to do with that whole self-esteem thing. I had never gotten any growing up. I just went from one relationship to another without believing in myself and what I actually had to offer someone, so I went ahead with the wedding, and that is probably the worst mistake I have ever made. Because when we first got married he still had—he lied and he would tell the truth, and I never knew which was which. . . .
>
> . . . It just got to be a mess. Well, his temper got to be a lot more, really worse in this house, because I can remember him punching, like, the walls and in the door. He put a big hole in the door and the landlord found out about it and really, that was a mess.

Margaret worked in a convenience store, a low-paying job, but one with flexible hours. Roger would come into the store and "evil-eye" her while she was working; he was obsessively jealous and watched in a blind fury all of her interactions with her boss, her coworkers, and the customers. If she talked to any of them, it would set him off:

> Oh, he hated that. He would come in and throw his arms and his temper would just keep getting worse, and I can remember one time we were fighting in, like, a dining room that we didn't have any furniture in and he would get in my face. Well, at that time, I was just getting so sick of it I would get right back in his face and then he would pick me up and throw me across the room or something. Or he'd punch a wall and say, "Next time it will be you." And I just got so tired of that.

She got tired of his sexual abuse as well. She had already had two children and was trying to stabilize her birth control pills so that she would not get pregnant again. She began to withhold sex as a way to try to get him to "shape up," get a job, leave the house, and stop pestering her. But it backfired, and he forced himself on her.

Unfortunately, he got tired of waiting and didn't want to wait anymore. The whole entire time I kept saying "no" and tried to push him away. But he'd [say] like [using a deep, threatening voice], "You're my wife, you have to give me this." And I'm like [makes gesture and sound to indicate a cut throat] "okay," and so I kinda just laid limp, you know, and I ended up getting pregnant out of that, which was just—uggggh. I was never so angry! So, once again, I tried to put my heart back in it, tried to make things work. . . .

But then things kept getting worse. . . . And he would be at the bar all the time before he came home and it just escalated. He would yell at me and his was really more emotional abuse. He would yell and tell me how worthless I was, and what did he ever see in me? And it was so emotionally damaging to me that, you know, to begin with I didn't have any self-esteem, anyway.

Margaret's long marriage with Roger was a nightmare. As she continued to meet more people, Roger grew more obsessive, his drinking got worse, and the violence intensified.

Well, the more people I met, the worse it got. And he would go drinking and this was when it really escalated. I can remember incidents where [long pause] he would push me, and I remember one time that he pushed me over the couch, and I went down into the hallway into the bedroom and he followed me, pushed me on the bed, and I was screaming for him to get up because he was hurting me, and he was sitting on my hips with his hands on my wrists, holding them down and yelling at me and saying that he would beat me, or whatever, and so the only thing I thought of to protect myself was to spit on him, and I did. That was wrong. Because he smacked me really, really hard across the face. Then he got up. At least he got up and he left me alone. And then, he turned and he threw—we had one of those oscillating fans on a pole—and he threw that at me.

Margaret tells many stories like this about living with Roger. He abused her on a regular basis, keeping her life in chaos. She never knew what he would do next. He would push her out of the car on cold, winter nights and make her walk home. He would drink and hit her; he would scream and yell, throw things, and force her to have sex with him. But she still had trouble recognizing just how terrible her life really was; the turning point had not yet been reached. She tells about an incident when her sister was trying to help her get her son back, after Roger kept him following a visitation weekend:

My sister has never, ever been around anything like this. She only hears my stories. But it's different when you hear it and when you see it and when you're there when it happens. He got so angry, he grabbed my shoulders and pushed me up against my glass door and he grabbed my head and put it against the glass and started punching the glass around my head. Well, my sister heard that, and I was screaming, "Call the cops. Call the cops." And my sister came around the corner just as the glass broke and the glass went all over her and all over her baby, flew up the stair[s], I mean, glass went [over] just everything. And then he left and my sister was just freaking. She was screaming. She was freaking. And it was just a mess.

Margaret had been in the shelter several times when I met her. Speaking the truth of her own life of violence, though, is still difficult:

You know, it's funny, remembering, compared to all these other women I would see in the shelter, mine was not as bad as theirs but the more I would learn about emotional abuse, to me emotional is worse that the physical, but still it doesn't seem like it was ever that bad. Isn't that odd? And there's a lot of stuff I haven't said. I always remember just sitting in the bathroom and rocking and wanting the lights to stay out and not being social at all and never smiling. And that was never me. I was always outgoing and always athletic and always wanting to do things. It probably changed me.

Indeed. We might all agree that this life of violence "changed" her.

When I met Margaret, she had recently remarried for the third time. I tape recorded her story in the home that she and her husband were remodeling, a lovely two-story house facing a large parklike field in a quiet part of our town. The hardwood floors were warm, the furniture inviting. Margaret sat cross-legged on her sofa with her shoes off, her long hair still damp from the shower, a little sparkle in her eye. But by the time she had finished her story, huge tears were rolling down her face as she told me about the court custody case for her youngest son, which is still unsettled, and the charges of unpaid child support that had been rendered against her former husband. After a long pause, I asked her about her life today. Her chin went up, she wiped away her tears, and she said this:

I don't know if I'll ever feel totally safe, but I think I have come a long ways. I got my degree and I worked hard and I like who I am. When I look in the mirror, I like who I see. Yes, I have faults, like we all have faults, but I think my kids are very well behaved. I think I'm very lucky considering everything that they have gone through that I don't have some troublemakers and they are all three Christians, and they all—even though I don't see Bobbie very much, when he comes home, he's very loving. At first he's standoffish but, boy, once he gets used to being back here, he just totally just wants to sit on my lap the entire time, you know.

To me it feels like another lifetime. It doesn't even feel it's me that has gone through that. Because now I can sit back and see just how far I've come. It used to be just the mention of his name would just freak me out. I'm getting better at that. But you know, I really just can't stand him, and I struggle with that because being a Christian, I am supposed to forgive. But with him—[grimaces]—really, it would be so much better if he wasn't around. But Bobbie seems to be doing really well.

What does Margaret value today? Herself. She has gotten her degree; she has worked hard; *she likes who she is.* What powerful words: *"When I look in the mirror, I like who I see."* She measures her personal growth by the way she has moved beyond his ability to make her feel fear. She appraises her luck by the fact that her children are not troublemakers, that they feel safe enough to give and seek love. She feels like a new person—so different from the one who suffered so much, it feels like a different lifetime. She is no longer her old self, a fearful, victimized person, and, as much as it bothers her to say it, she can truly hate her abuser, now. She does hate him; she wishes he were gone—or dead. She says she knows she should forgive him, but it seems actually healthy that she can feel anger against him, now, for the first time. As a new and stronger person, she can despise him for the chaos he made her endure. Remarkably enough, her final marker for her new and improved life is that her son "seems to be doing real well."—perhaps because his mother is also "doing real well."

CATHY'S STORIES OF VIOLENCE

Cathy was not really aware of her boyfriend's violent streak early in their relationship, but as they became more serious he became more and more jealous and possessive. Looking back now, she believes she should have picked up on those early clues. Once, after work, she offered to take a male coworker to the room where he was staying. Her boyfriend saw them in the car together and stopped her on the road. She was casual about the incident and thought nothing about it until her boyfriend confronted her about it on the way back into town:

And he said, "I will be here waiting for you to come right back here." So I did. And he was so extremely angry that he got out of his car, jumped out of it, started kicking the hood of his car, dented the hood of his car, punching the windshield, and I laughed hysterically because I had never seen anyone in all of my life act like that. It was hilarious. A lot of it was nervousness, too, I mean, it scared me, made me nervous, plus I thought it was hilarious. I wondered what was wrong with him. You know, but it was just—well, he explained it to me that he just loved me so much and he could not stand to see another man around me. That it just drove him crazy, because if anybody ever hurt me . . . because I had already told him, you know, pretty much my history—the things that had happened as I was growing up—and he was just so terrified that someone would hurt me or whatever and that explained it away.

So it was all good. He basically put me up on a pedestal and treated me like a queen. One time he actually had to break a date because he had to work and he sent me two dozen—not one—but two dozen long-stemmed red roses to my work. We just—I don't know—we had this sort of fairytale thing going on and three months later we got married.

But their marriage was rocky; her husband was difficult to live with when he was there. Life was much easier when he was gone for long periods in the service. She is thankful for her two sons but notes with regret when the emotional abuse and jealousy began to turn into "something else."

[I]t became physical and he started getting physically violent with me. Before that he had run his fist through walls and things like that when he would get angry, but it sort of progressed from that to where he would punch the wall right next to my head or something very intimidating, and I've often thought, in retrospect, that I think maybe that's the reason or the way that abuse progresses. Originally when he would yell and scream and pound his fist on the table, that would intimidate me so badly I would back down. And then I sort of became immune to that and he would yell and scream and pound his fist on the table and I still didn't back down, so it took something more to intimidate me. And I've thought about it a lot but I think that's how it progresses. . . .

And one night—I have no idea why . . . but I do know that what I woke up to was him pulling me by the hair out of bed onto the floor and kicking me and just kicking me and kicking me. And I never experienced anything like that before and I was just in so much shock I couldn't believe what was happening to me, and when it first happened it was dark and I thought someone had broken into our house and was attacking me, because I was sound asleep. And I realized it was him and he was screaming and yelling but it was unintelligible—I have no idea—and I've had a lot of people say, "Did he drink?" No. He didn't drink. He was just mean. That was the first time I ever reported it.

The violence escalated even more after Cathy got an order of protection against her husband, banning him from the family home and from any contact with her and the children. That the violence increased is typical. Statistics indicate that this period of time, when a woman seeks an order of protection, or when she herself leaves the home, is the most dangerous time for the wife or partner of an abusive man.

> And he immediately started calling me and [saying], "How dare you have me thrown out of my house and propose to take my kids away from me. I'll see you in court, bitch," and whatever, whatever—[he said] he was going to do everything to me except draw and quarter me. He wore me down to the point where I dropped the ex parte. And at the time when I went to do it, I was asked if I was coerced into dropping it. Of course, I said, "No," because I knew they wouldn't drop it if I said yes. So, you know, duh: I said, "No," and so they dropped it, and he gave me to understand that [slowly, in low voice] *if I ever* got him thrown out of his house ever again that *there would be hell to pay;* he would kill me.
>
> So, as the pattern developed, it was about once every six months that he actually got physically violent with me.
>
> . . . .
>
> And never in front of the kids, never in front of anyone. Because they'd hear it, but never did they see him do that. But he was abusive toward our kids. He didn't beat them up, hit them with his fists, things like that, but he was very liberal with a belt when they misbehaved and always, always, always more so with our younger son than with the older son. A lot of times that, especially earlier, that's where our fights began. He would be so abusive toward Nathan and I would just go ballistic. I couldn't stand it. And [quietly pausing] . . . I never reported any of the abuse until we had been married about fourteen years, I guess.

Cathy tells story after story of being hit on the head by various objects, being beaten senseless, of striking back only to find her husband getting more and more violent. One of the worst nights she can remember she was able to tell in great detail.

> So this night we were arguing. What prompted him to do it, I don't know, but we had a breakfast nook in our house that was like a booth, you

know, a table with a booth against the wall. And he had thrown me down in the booth and he had the gun in his pocket and I didn't know this. And he pulled it out of his pocket and laid it on the table, and the way I was laying it was right in front of my face, and he got the bullets out and he stood there and loaded it, and he said, "I'm gonna kill you." And he held it to my head and cocked it.

And I was terrified and I said, "Ron, think of the boys." I said, "They're upstairs. They'll hear it." I said, "When they come downstairs, what are they gonna think?" I said, "What is that gonna do to them if they hear?" I mean, I was desperate. I was searching for anything and—I wasn't this calm, believe me—I said, "What is that going to do to them if they come downstairs and find their dad's in here with a gun having blown their mom's brains out? Come on. You don't want to do that."

But he was getting more and more agitated, and he said, "I might as well kill them and you and myself, too. I've ruined everybody's life." And he just went off and I was so terrified. I believed he was going to kill me. And I grabbed for the telephone. I thought it might be my last act but I grabbed for the phone to try to call the police. It was at the corner of the breakfast booth and he grabbed it from my hand and starting hitting me in the face with it. Finally I just managed to get underneath the table and he left the room. And I got up—my mouth was bleeding—he had hit my mouth several times with the receiver and my eye had already swollen up so where it was like nearly shut tight, but I was going toward the entryway—I was going to leave the house and I was completely hysterical. And I got to the entryway and I just collapsed. When I came to, he was standing over me screaming and yelling and just crazy, crazy, and telling me that I wasn't going anywhere, that I would die before I left the house and whatever.

At this point in this night of horrors, Cathy realizes that she is dangerously suicidal. She describes the urge to go get the gun and just finish her life as something that pushed her, against her will, toward pulling that trigger herself. In fact, the suicidal thoughts terrify her so much that she goes back into the bedroom where her violent and abusive husband is lying on the bed and wakens him to tell him how bad her suicidal thoughts are. Death, at this moment, was a scarier proposition that this raging maniac. True to form, though, he awakens only to be furious with her and begins to yell again. But her actions diffuse the situation. He is no longer yelling that he's going to kill her and, apparently, her suicidal thoughts are thwarted for the time being. Somehow the danger passes for the night and they agree to go to counseling the next day. The counseling sessions go badly, however, and soon she has thrown him out of the house again and changes the locks on the doors. After several weeks, he calls her and begs and pleads, cries for her to allow him to come back so they can "talk." She acquiesces but quickly realizes it is a bad mistake. He reaches for a favorite framed poster of hers and proceeds to bash her over the head with it:

And he took it off the wall and broke it over my head, pushed me down our basement stairs, and then drug me back up by the hair. Chunks of my hair came out on the way, so he kept having to grab different spots. And, basically, he got me in our main floor bathroom and had me up against the wall. The towel bar was in my back. And he had me by the throat up against the wall and he brought his fist back and he said, "I'm gonna bash your face in, you bitch."

And I closed my eyes because I knew what was coming and then— everything that I'm going to tell you happened in a split second—all of a sudden, every Oprah Winfrey show, every magazine and newspaper article that I had read, everything that I had ever heard about domestic violence all just came rushing back to me. I saw myself being carried out of the house in a body bag and the thought went through my mind—and I don't think it originated with me, I don't know where it came from, but the thought went through my mind: "Does he have to kill you before you realize that this man is dangerous?" And for the first time, I saw the day that he jumped on top of his car and kicked it, and all of that right up to that moment, as one big picture instead of a bunch of little isolated segments. It was one big picture. It was this big [gestures widely with both arms], you know, and it was progressing and it was going kill me. And it was the first time I ever saw that. And all that happened like this fast [snaps fingers] because he had brought his fist back and said, "I'm gonna bash your face in, bitch." And he meant it; he was going to. I know this for an absolute fact.

And the next thing I heard was our oldest son's voice saying, "Oh, no, you don't, Dad." And I opened my eyes, and for the first time my son had his dad by the wrists, and he had his fist brought back and he said, "You will not hit my mom again."

And his dad turned around, pushed his sleeve up, and raised his fist to our son, and I jumped between them. I said [slowly, enunciating each word], "You will not hit my son." And he backed off.

And I just turned around and I said, "Matt, go in the other room."

And he said, "No, Mom, I'm not going to let him do anything else to you."

I said, "He's not going to do anything else to me. Go in the other room."

And he [Ron] looked at me and said, "I love the way you've turned our kids against me. I left them with you to nurture them and mother them and you turned them against me like this." And Matt hollered at his dad, "Mom didn't do it, Dad. *You* turned us against you."

And he turned around and grabbed me and just literally threw me into the bathtub and walked out.

It may appear that her husband got the last "word" in this bitter story of violence and confrontation, but perhaps the most significant portion of Cathy's story is the moment of revelation, the turning point, when she seems to watch his fist in slow motion heading for her face. She gets the "big picture." She puts all of the information she has ever heard or read together with that long-ago picture of him bashing his car in a fit of raging jealousy. She hears Oprah's voice in her own head asking the question: "Does he have to kill you before you realize that this man is dangerous?" Fortunately, her own epiphany coincides with her older son's intervention. Together they face down the father who is out of control. He throws her into the bathtub in a last-minute fit of desperation, but we know he is defeated as he leaves the room.

Cathy leaves this abusive husband several times; they go into counseling but he rages at the therapists and wrecks their counseling center. She finally knows she must get away for good, but the dangers are plentiful. She recalls another time when she tried to escape, but he found her, pulled a knife, and forced her to go back home with him. She managed to get an order of protection against him and he moved out of their house. But she knew she was not safe.

Cathy's life seemed to go from bad to worse. Because the police and the prosecutor would not help her, she turned to a computer friend she had met on the Internet. He and his druggie friends helped her escape from her abusive husband and protected her for a time. She became involved in their crazy, chaotic lifestyle and quickly found herself sexually involved with this new friend, who is the same age as her older son. No sooner than they had become intimate, however, he began to beat and abuse her, severely. She felt she was going crazy. She knew, again, that she had to escape if she was going to live. This is the point in her story where I met Cathy. She had come into the shelter to escape this violent young man; her frail body was battered and bruised, her hair was thin, and her eyes were vacant. And she was still in court battling it out with her former husband. In group meetings at the shelter, I heard her speak of violence and pain unlike anything I had ever heard before, and sometimes she would mix up the stories of the abuse of her husband with the stories about this more recent abuser. It was all of a piece, it seemed, in her mind. Violence and destruction. Always. And more violence and destruction.

But I watched a kind of miracle evolve while Cathy lived in the shelter. She asked for shampoo, eventually a brush, some new underwear, a razor. Over time, her hair grew out a bit and she began to color and shape it. She had a pretty, wispy kind of face, and she knew how to apply her makeup well. She would dig through the shelter donations, looking for a neat pair of size-four jeans and a "new" pair of boots. She got a job. She and another resident became tight friends. They began to make plans to move into an apartment together across town where the trees were really lush and pretty. Cathy began to circulate flyers in the shelter. I would type them up for her. She created an organization that would help women help themselves, she said. "We have to stick together," her flyers announced. "We cannot let them take everything we've got, our bodies, our minds, our possessions, our money." She called for meetings in the back rooms. She believed women could help themselves and each other. It was a joy to see her enthusiasm for moving beyond the role of victim. When, at the end of telling me her life story, I asked Cathy how she was feeling today, these were her final words. They are incredibly telling, and they demonstrate how this woman has moved beyond the violence into her new self.

I learned a lot over the last four years about myself. And [long pause]—I kind of agree with the sign in the office that says, "She who waits for a knight in shining armor gets to clean up after the horse." I'm pretty cynical now—well, maybe I'm not cynical, I'm just defensive. I'm pretty defensive. But I know that I'm never going to let anybody walk on me like that again. And, so, you know, I just don't know how long it's going to take. You know, the counselors I've talked to say I'll probably never be completely over it; I mean, it'll always be there. But, I know it will get better, it'll get a little bit easier, I'll get stronger. But until I am, I'm just not going to put a hell of a lot of pressure on myself. I'm going to give myself permission to kind of take it easy, and I'll take it easy on myself, because as hard as the men in my life have been on me, I've been ten times harder on myself. And—that's what I was talking about in group tonight—just learning how to take it easy on myself and giving myself permission to be me, hurt and wounded, but free.

And my roommate, I love her to death and you know, she is like, the best therapy for me. And we sit and we talk and we just, like, I don't know—if you've ever heard her talk about it, but there are so many parallels in our lives that it's unbelievable. I mean, it can't be coincidences. And—it's really strange. I never would have thought just meeting her that we would have anything in common. But we do. And—I think we're really good for each other and we really affirm each other a lot. And there is no "why did you do this, why didn't you do that?" You know, we just get along. So, that's my story and I'm sticking to it.

I have included this rather lengthy portion of Cathy's story because I believe it clearly demonstrates how women coming into shelter and speaking the violence that has dominated their lives emerge to connect with their self in a way they have never done before. Cathy is able to articulate the positive things that are now happening to her, and they include a safe space, a place to be at peace, a place to "just be me." It includes a place shared with other people who do not abuse her and violate her mind and body, who can talk with her openly about what has happened to her and to them. She finds the similarities in their experiences comforting because she no longer has to feel like the lone victim. She has found companionship here, but she has also discovered friendship, a new concept for her. She and another resident have become good, close friends. They can talk and talk, a new experience for both of them. She is astonished to find someone who can "affirm" her decisions, who does not question, blame, or accuse her. And they are making plans, now, to move into a place together, trusting that the friendship they have developed can grow and continue into a new life.

I was delighted to hear her final words: "That's my story and I'm sticking to it." This is the language of confidence, strident even in its tone, a bit confrontational. Cathy has made some decisions about herself, about who she is, and who she might become. She is making new decisions about her life, about her education, her career, and who she is willing to live with. I have seen Cathy since she left the shelter and she is constantly battling the demons that still haunt her. Sometimes her journey is two steps forward, one back. But she is doing it and that's the important thing to remember. She is out there; she is alive; and she knows who she is, wounds and all.

SHERRY'S STORIES OF VIOLENCE

After her mother died and she was able to leave her abusive stepfather, Sherry moved into the household of an abusive uncle, who beat his wife and the children, and seemed overprotective of Sherry. It is only when she begins to pay attention to boys that her uncle openly takes notice, forbidding her to see the tough, party-type, motorcycle guys she is attracted to. Sherry makes little comment about her uncle's obvious jealousy, although she does note that he was telling her things like "you're just pretty, I don't want you to get hurt or anything." He beats up her boyfriends when they appear, responding to their attentions to Sherry in inappropriate and violent ways. She does not explicitly say that she leaves his lecherous implications and violent behavior to move quickly into a sexual relationship with someone else and move out of his house, but in one smooth rhetorical move she admits that the first "love" of hers, at thirteen, is also her first abusive relationship with a nonfamily member.

Her description of this first lover's abuse is brief and is accompanied by a short, nervous laugh as she tells me what he would do to her: "He never really, his [abuse] wasn't [terrible]—he wouldn't smack me in my face. He whipped my butt, you know, like a child." Sherry cannot actually *name* what this man does to her. I have inserted *abuse* for what she leaves blank. She reveals here that she has a preconception of what abuse is—for example, smacking her in the face—but he doesn't do that exactly. What he does is equally abusive, but she is not able to reconcile his acts of abuse and her feelings about him. She does reflect upon the fascination and attraction she has with tough, older men but finds no answers to the question and leaves it hanging with "I don't know why." It is the older men to whom she is attracted, and we are perhaps not as surprised as she is to learn that he treats her like an incorrigible child, spanking her as a father might do. She laughs nervously, again, when she reveals that her response to his abuse is that she "thought she was in love." Love, then, for her is associated with dominance and abusive behavior. She laughs nervously when she recalls the sensations of power she enjoys with younger men, boys, really, her own age, whom she could so easily control and who treated her "like a queen." The patterns of abuse and domination have already taken their toll in her young life. Significantly, Sherry compresses the next several years of her life of battering and abuse into a few sentences:

> And I had my first child; I was seventeen, pregnant when I was sixteen. The baby's dad was twenty-three and he was a drunk and he was abusive. He was just abusive to the point to where—his was more of an emotional, verbal type thing. But he was a drunk and for some reason there's something about drunks.
>
> I ended that one, and then I got with another guy and he was real, he was really physically abusive and emotional, verbal, that whole thing, but I would just stick around because I really loved this guy. I remember I was sixteen, seventeen at that time, and I really didn't think I'd ever find anything else. We lived in a small town at that time and it was just crazy.
>
> And then that ended. He moved away.

Following a succession of bad relationships, her time with her child's father, who was twenty-three, became extremely abusive. She hints at how terribly abusive and violent this relationship became, but in this account she cannot find language to portray that pain and violence. What she offers is a skeleton of the reality of horrors she must have endured at this time. She tells us only that he was "a drunk and he was abusive" and then diverts her description of his abuse to commenting that she believed she was in love and would never find anything better. Her only reflective comment is "it was just crazy." Several months of her life are then compressed into the next two short sentences that manage to hide all the concern, fear, and anger she must have felt at that time and perhaps she still carries today: "And then that ended. He moved away."

So, at seventeen, and seemingly eons of time and numerous abusive relationships later, Sherry returns, with her small child, to the abusive uncle's house where her aunt has "left" her family, mentally if not physically, by trying to commit suicide and succeeding only in damaging her brain beyond repair. As Sherry tries to describe what living with this uncle is like after his wife is no longer really "there," language again fails to help her actually describe the pain.

> So, I went back home, and my uncle George, I just thought he was the greatest thing in the world, you know, 'cause we could just sit down and we could just talk about anything, you know, at times. And then there was times when he would just knock the shit out of us. He choked me to where I couldn't breathe one time because I was twenty minutes late coming home. He would never—when I was younger—he never called me a bitch, slut, whore, but he'd tell me I dress like a whore, acted like a whore, talked like a whore, the only thing left was to be a whore, you know. And when I started getting boyfriends he'd beat them up, young, young guys, you know.

How does Sherry use language here to communicate pain? She doesn't. We perhaps hear her indignation—"he would just knock the shit out of us" and "he choked me to where I couldn't breathe one time because I was twenty minutes late coming home." But we have here an example of the failure of language to convey pain. What does "knock the shit out of us" convey? How are these words employed to communicate how the flesh and bones of these children responded to the fists and other instruments of torture inflicted upon them by this wretched uncle? "He would just knock the shit out of us" must suffice because this speaker cannot locate language that can do justice to these significant moments in her young life. Somehow the use of the word "just" adds a dimension of credibility to the account. The word conveys constancy, truth, and deadpan reality: "He would *just* knock the shit out of us." And her terrorizing experience at his hand, when he chokes her to the point she cannot breathe, is not elaborated either. No graphic details here, nothing about how her throat ached or how her lungs felt or how his large hands felt on her neck— it was, after all, beyond description. Again, this account of pain and abuse is related in the monotone voice of resignation. She is relating the "facts" as she remembers them. Her voice and her words might be ever so slightly accusatory, only implying that it was absurd that he choked her breathless just because she was twenty minutes late. This account can be aligned with Teresa's in documenting the reign of terror men constructed for their households. In essence, her uncle is a violent, raging man who beats every living being in the home and drives his wife to a suicide attempt. And he eventually forces Sherry to leave because of the physical and sexual violence she has to endure living there.

It is not until she begins to recall how he violates her sexual space that she is able to use language that can, hopefully, begin to free her from the stage of numbed immobility and toward self-construction. As she tells this story, her narrative loops back again to pick up some threads of the earlier times and she somehow manages to articulate a bit more about what living with abuse and violence was like for her in her mother's house. Her move beyond being the paralyzed little girl who is only an onlooker, a witness to her own fate, is indicated as she fleshes out her story, moving beyond the simple sentences:

> So, I went wild after Uncle George did that and just started getting real crazy and started drinking real heavy. And I told him that night, I just got up and I told him, I think it's just the alcohol talking. And I got up and left the room. He started trying to touch me and stuff and I left; that was just sick to me. After that I left and I didn't go back.

Although it does not take long before Sherry finds herself in yet another abusive relationship, the language she uses to describe this marriage seems to pull her ever so slightly out of her vulnerable, passive victim role.

> And I messed around at a party and I got pregnant again, in the back seat of a Chevy [laughs], you know, and I was drunk and everything, and I had a little boy. I got married three weeks after he was born, to a guy named Dale. Dale seemed like a really nice guy, you know, he took care of the baby and everything, but he was a drunk and real abusive. He had a real [temper]—it was bad—I would have to say that was my worst abusive relationship I've ever been into. He broke my ribs and everything and his big thing was—there was him and then there was the part he called "the other guy." . . . "[T]he other guy" hated me.
> . . . Dale was a construction worker and so we built a house. And I burned his toast one morning and he bulldozed our house, because I burned his toast [laughs nervously]. It took us three years, and it was just me and him only building this house, it took three years. And in twenty minutes it was bulldozed and we hadn't even had it standing up for six months.

And he used to beat up his dad. And I found out that he had been married prior to our marriage and he was real abusive to her. And then he got to where—he got mean with my kids. He eventually went to prison for attempted murder on me and both my kids. He did four months and got out. And it's been—it was '89, '90, the last part of '89, it went so far—I tried to get away from him. It got to the point that I literally stole a car, drove to the police station, threw the keys at them, and told them I stole a car: "Dale's coming, put me in jail." And the cop—it's in a small town—he just kinda laughed and said, "Sherry, it's going to be okay." I'd called him a million and one times. And Dale slid up in front of the police station in a truck, and I literally punched the cop to get thrown in jail. They would not put me in jail to protect me from Dale. And as I'm going up the steps, 'cause I started running up the steps, I just wanted to get someplace safe, Dale was right behind me. He busted right through the policemen in the office and they charged him on attempted murder on me and the kids and he did four months and got out.

In what Sherry defines as her most "abusive relationship," it is constructive to isolate the language she uses to describe what happened to her during this violent marriage. She describes Dale as having a bad temper, but actually when she said it into the tape recorder, I couldn't quite understand the exact word she used so, I have inserted *temper* in brackets because she implies that it is his temper she is describing when he bulldozes the house when she burns his toast, or when he barges past the policemen to get to her and hurt her. Perhaps she didn't even really finish that thought, just sliding into "no word" when she got to the end of that sentence about him having just a really bad—. It is unclear if she voices "temper" or some other word here, and her grasping for words indicates how language is failing her in her attempt to explain what living with this abusive, brutal man was like. The rest of this account in the police station implies that his behavior in the police station contributed to his prosecution and spending time in jail for "attempted murder." Without being strident, Sherry's account does make her husband look like a raging bull and the police department is revealed as slow and unresponsive to her very serious needs. Clearly, he should have spent more time in prison for such an offense, but Sherry's narrative intent here is not to critique the judicial system but rather to relate in the only way she can just how insanely abusive this man, Dale, was. Perhaps by going to the police station, or at least framing the story in this way, she is shifting the view of Dale away from her own fear and concern. She had called the policeman "a million and one times" she says, but to no avail. The "cop" laughs at her and condescendingly tells her: "Sherry, it's going to be okay." Of course, she knows it is not going to be "okay"; the only way they may ever believe her is if they see Dale in full force. Apparently, it worked, briefly.

In this account she is *never* explicit about the actual violence. She only paints a wider picture of her abuser. He "beat up his dad"; he had been "real abusive" to his first wife; and he "got mean with my kids." The only language she can use comes in the form of "it got to the point that . . . ," a grossly inadequate articulation of what was apparently years of battering, abuse, terror, and pain.

After this story of her marriage to Dale, Sherry becomes reflective for the first time in her narrative. Dale is in prison, soon to be released, but the period of time away from him and the abuse provides a space for her, a turning point, to think about herself in a successive line of abused women and it provides a way for her to redirect her life:

> And the thing that bothered me was that everywhere I turned, 'cause I finally figured it out, is during my marriage to Dale I remember everything with my mom, you know, all the men and stuff. And she used to get the shit beat out of her, but she'd still take men. She thought it was—I don't know what she thought; I thought she was crazy. And then with my aunt Susan, seeing all the stuff she'd gone through, and then all my little here-and-there relationships. And my big thing was always, I was always, I never, ever let any of them dump me. There was only one that ever dumped me up to this point and that was the guy that I just thought was God. And I would always dump them. It was like a rush, you know. But I was sitting here, while Dale was in jail, really trying to get my shit together and think about all that. And he got out in four months. So, I just—

We need to "hear" her thoughts here; she is trying to sort out the connections between the abuse endured by her mother and her aunt and her own abuse at the hands of the men she loves or, alternatively, manipulates. It occurs to her that with the younger men (as she mentioned earlier in her story), she can always walk away from them. She gets a "rush" from breaking their hearts. But with the men she comes to know and love, her own sense of control disappears. In this reflective moment, she does not really figure anything out, but she is, as she says, thinking about "all that." This is a pivotal moment for her, but she is definitely not out of the woods. The next stage in her life is a terrible struggle. She gives away her two children, one to her grandparents, one for adoption. For a while her son comes back to live with her, but he must fend for himself when he lives with her because she is usually drunk during this time and he must witness her "getting my ass kicked" repeatedly by the various men who stay with her off and on. Eventually, he chooses to leave her again to go back to his grandfather. She has another child by another abusive man. She eventually leaves him but is, by now, completely destitute:

> I finally got away from him and I went to a homeless shelter, away from all of my family, you know, I decided I want to clean my act up and get a real life and I want to be a mom and everything.
>
> And that's when I met Ernie, the reason I'm here—it was in the homeless shelter. He was a security guard, yeah [laughs]—he was there to protect people [laughs again].

Sherry's description of Ernie fits the standard "cycle of violence" mold. At first he appears to be wonderful, nice, and polite; he treats her like a queen. But, she admits, he was also abusive, "from day one." In retrospect, she can identify the abuse as verbal and emotional. She came to recognize his concerns as not loving but controlling, telling her what to wear, where to go, when, and with whom.

> The next thing I know he's drinking a little bottle of wine, no big deal, and he quit his job. And that's when he started getting physical and stuff. He didn't ever hit me as hard as Dale; he never broke a rib or anything. But he would slap me and things like that, and that was crazy. And I went ahead and stayed with him—I left him twice and then he settled down a little bit and tried to straighten up and then I would go back and things would be good for a while, and after the third time I left, when I went back it got really physical, to the point that I would run and hide. And I don't know why I'd go back, 'cause I'd feel sorry for him, you know. . . . Then I had Justin. But a month before Justin was born, Ernie got high with some men and he was way off, really high, and he put a gun to my stomach. And I told him, I was tired, [that] I didn't give a shit, which was stupid, now when I think about it. And I told him, "If you weren't high, I'd be afraid, but since you're stoned I really don't care, you won't remember any of this tomorrow anyway."
>
> And then he had Lori, she was three—no, she was two at the time, and he had her playing with a loaded automatic weapon and there was nothing I could do, you know, I just had to sit there. So I left, and after I had Justin, we got back together, you know, I just had his baby and blah, blah, blah, blah, you know, and that's when he got really physical, was after I had Justin. To the point where he would come home drunk and just knock the shit out of me for no reason. . . .
>
> And he finally—I got to where I was working two jobs. I worked two jobs to stay out of the house, and I didn't get to see my kids and stuff. And

he come in one night and just sit down at the table and he said, "I think I'm going to kill you." And I'm like [laughs] really [shocked]—you know I'm like, I'm just sitting there reading, and he just walks in the door and he told me he thought he was going to kill me. And I remember I looked up at him and I said, "Why?" And he said, "I don't know." And I said, "Well, when?" [laughs], you know. And he told me, "I don't know." He said, "I think you need to leave," and I called this place [the shelter] and that's how I got here.

During the time I knew Sherry in the shelter, she was still in communication with her abuser, especially on account of her children. He tried to "clean up his act" so that she would go back home with him. But, somehow, I did not think she ever would. The language she was beginning to use was new language for her. She began to articulate the thesis of this book: Through the speaking of the violence, the articulation of her abuse, she was emerging on the other side a new person.

Yeah. You know, Dale called me last night—I finally told him—he called last night to tell me where he was going [laughs], where he was going! When we was together he never would do that; he would just go out the door, you know. Now, we're living miles away and—he's quit drinking, he's quit smoking cigarettes, he jogs. Looks awesome. And I told him last night, you know, I see all these things you did. You quit your drinking, quit getting high, all this stuff, and I'm happy for you. But you didn't give a shit enough to do it when I was with you and I know this is just another game and I've been away long enough and lived with real abused women who are real with theirselves and serious about breaking the violence, the cycle, to where I can see it now. I can see what he's doing to pull me back in, you know. He's being—I'm getting my life together so he's going to try to get his together. And now I can see it. I can see those red flags. And the whole thing is like, the whole thing makes sense, everything that he did to make me happy was just that little piece of me he just happened to latch onto. But I have all that in me I can pull out myself and you know I think I can do that.

The only thing I think keeping me back—I can say I don't want my kids to grow up being abusers and abused and that is a big part of it, 'cause I don't want that for my children. I love them and I don't want them to have a life like that. But if I'm saying I'm doing it for somebody else it's never going to work. This is for me, because I don't deserve that. It's like I want to go to school. I've got all these dreams, you know. I want to be self-sufficient, and here's the kicker, I *have* been self-sufficient, I've just supported somebody else. I had to be. I think I could handle the work and support my family part. But it's like I need to build my own self-confidence and slowly but surely I'm achieving that. The only thing I think is going [to help]—and I know people here have heard me say here—wisdom and knowledge are the only things I seek. I don't want pity. I don't want empathy. I want education.

Before, I've never tried to get educated. I knew "run from the abuser." And after you've been gone for a few hours, then "run right back." I never took time to get an education. I just want to know everything there is to know about an abuser. And everything I need to know, I can just look back and see the men I've been with. And it's all about wisdom and knowledge and keeping your focus, because if you lose your focus on you and your future, you're going to go back into theirs. And that's stupid; I don't want to do that.

Like Margaret and Cathy, Sherry's words are brave and they ring true. She knows she still has a long way to go, but she knows about the self-confidence she is trying to build. She knows she is developing a new sense of herself that is a far cry from the woman who was only a victim, always running away only to run back again, into "his" reality rather than "hers." She has looked back, faced the turning point, and chosen a new future.

JANIE'S STORIES OF VIOLENCE

Janie's life story included three marriages, all of them bad. But the first and the last of these were the most abusive. Her second husband was manic-depressive and confused her more than abused her; eventually he just left, never to be seen again. The story of her first husband is rather typical in some respects. They had a long marriage and a son together. For years, it appeared her marriage was rocky at times and her husband could be moody, but there is, in her story, a definite turning point when she recognizes her life with this husband became scary and dangerous.

But then all of a sudden it got very, very good or very, very awful. There was no in-between. He would leave for work in the morning and somebody might cut him off in traffic and that would just shoot his whole day. I mean, you know, he might come home, he might not. He had never physically abused me until we were married about three years and he, we were at these people's house at a party and everything was going fine, I mean, we weren't arguing or anything and everyone was drinking and stuff and I said, "Don't you"—you know, we were sitting on the couch—and I said, "Don't you think it's getting time we ought to go home?" And he said, "Yeah." And then all of a sudden he stood up and he got in my face and he started calling me all kinds of names, he started hitting me, he beat me clear through the house, into the bathroom, knocked me through shower glass doors. I got away from him and there was a man that was a fairly large-sized guy was passed out with his head down on the table and I literally lifted him up in between us. My nose was bleeding, my face was all bloody and everything and so they got him, they all came to, and they got him away from me by holding him. And I got into the car, my car, and left. Well, these assholes [laughs] did nothing but bring him straight to the house and then we were there by ourselves.

My son was up the street at a girlfriend's house spending the night and the minute he walked into the house and he saw me he just went into a total rage and he started beating me. He knocked me almost through a wall. He got me down on the bed and started choking me and somehow I got my legs in between us and I kicked him off. He was drunk enough and I was sober by that time. He tried to throw me through the kitchen window, tried to knock my head through that. Anyway, I got away from him and got out of the house and I run up the street to my girlfriend's and he run after me and he caught me out in her front yard and threw me down and started choking me and was, kept saying, you know, "I'm going to kill you," you know, and I screamed or whatever and she heard enough of a commotion when she opened the door he got up and run and she pulled me into the house and she called the police.

Janie generally feels that the police have helped her when this husband was mean and abusive. In this particular case, she enjoyed telling about what happened later that night when a female police officer came to answer her friend's 911 call. But the effects of his battering are vividly clear some ten years after this incident happened.

And I told them I just want some things out of the house for the night and so we went down to the house and the woman policeman—there was a man and a woman—and the woman policeman, she was very large, she was like six-two and big and muscular, and when we walked into the house he didn't see them at first, he saw me and he started to get up off the couch and he was almost growling, and she walked around me and she looked at him and she said, "I pray," she said, "you get up off that couch." She said, "I pray you do." And he sat back down.

And so, I went and got my things and I lived with Susan, I guess, oh, for two or three months and he wanted, he stayed down in the house. We were just a few houses apart but I told everyone I had been in a car accident and, I mean, both my eyes were black. He had cracked my nose. My sinuses were all messed up. I went to the hospital and, you know, they just, they had to do some rework to the sinuses. But anyway, he ended up—he had hit me so hard he broke his hand. He was in a cast several months because he broke all of the bones in his fingers. That's how hard he hit me.

Eventually, in counseling, her therapist told her how much he felt her life was in danger, and she acted accordingly, completely escaping from this husband who was intent upon hurting her.

Dr. Samuels told me once, at one session, he said, "You need to get out of here. There's going to come a day," he said, "when either he's going to kill you or you're going to have to kill him to defend yourself." And, he said, "the farther you get away from him," he said, "the better off it's going to be."

When I first met Janie it was during group meetings at the shelter. She had begun to come in on a regular basis. We learned by bits and pieces that she was involved in a good deal of courtroom drama with her husband, several years her junior, who had tried to kill her. I did not know this earlier part of her life story until the day she told it on the tape. When we hear both stories in conjunction, we are astounded by the stamina of this woman. When I first met her, I thought that Janie was in her early sixties. However, she was only forty-three; after we heard her full story in the group meetings, the stress in her face became truly understandable. Here is the way she told her story on tape:

He started giving me the drugs the day before—this is the gun incident, the last one. He started giving me drugs the day before. I ended up in the emergency room having no recollection of being there; I have no idea how I got there. I guess I was also over at the lab, too, but I don't remember that and the toxicology and the drug, the blood test showed up negative! But I have no memory of any of that, in fact, I even went over at twelve o-clock at night over at the hospital and made the emergency room produce the paperwork. I was that sure that I was not there. But when I came home, the one thing that convinced me that I was there, I had the tape recorder going and he got a call from his, from his boss at the hospital, and she said, "Your wife is in the emergency room and they say she has a baby aspirin bottle" with his name on it "and it has Xanaxes in it." And he told her they were mine and I was doing that to try and get him into trouble. Now, why anyone let me leave there with that I don't know; I know enough to know that is illegal. A baby bottle with Xanax in it, somebody should have been asking me or somebody some questions, but they let me leave with those. But I have no idea how I got home, no memory of it.

The next morning, when I woke up at five o'clock, that's the next thing that I remember, he was gone. He had my car, and for some reason I called my son, and I guess he'd been on the phone with them all night and other people that I talked to. He was just, you know, he drank a whole bottle of rum. He drank a twelve-pack of beer. No telling how many drugs and crap he took. And when he walked in the door he said, "We need to talk." And I said, "Okay." So, I starts toward the table and he got up and he said, "Sit down." So, when I sat down, like our bedroom is to the back of me. And he said, "Wait a minute. I need to go get my cigarettes. I'll be right back."

And so, I heard him walking towards me and I could see him kinda out of my peripheral vision, and I started to turn around and all of a sudden the gun hit my head and pushed it back around. And he opened the pill bottle up and threw them on the table and he said, "I give you one of two choices. I will either blow your fucking brains all over the kitchen or you take the pills."

And I sat there for a moment, and strange things came to me. You always wonder what you'll think, what you're going to think about when your life's passing before you, but I know that the grief process is important and I know that having an open casket is important, I mean, for the family members to be able to view the body and to be able to grieve. And I thought, if he blows my head off, blows my brains out, they won't be able to open the casket and the kids won't be able to view the body. If I take the pills they'll be able to, and so they'll be able to grieve better. That's what went through my mind, I swear.

And, after I took the pills—he made me chase the first bunch with whiskey, and I can't stand whiskey, don't like the smell of it, don't like the taste of it, and I started gagging. And he saw then that I was probably going to throw up before he could get them down me, and so he gave me a glass of water and so the second batch he let me take with water. And then he gave me some paper and started instructing me on how to write my suicide note. And it starts off pretty good, you know, and everything, and about the middle of it, I'm writing it myself, I mean, you know, cause I'm feeling that this is probably the end. And at the end of it it doesn't make a whole lot of sense and the writing just kinda goes down off the page, you know, you can just tell that I'm getting out of it.

And at first when I started coming to, I remember him, for some reason, having me on the couch, pouring whiskey down my throat, and when I came home after the hospital—I was in intensive care for two days—I thought now there's going to be a whiskey smell on this couch or something, 'cause I wasn't going to want to lay my head down on that, you know. And all of a sudden, finally, memories, when I got back into the house, started coming back a little. He put me on the couch, after this all happened, he laid me on the couch. And the police, somehow—I don't even remember calling 911, I don't remember. But the police told me, when they asked me what happened, I told them my husband held a gun to my head and forced me to take pills. But there's been nothing done to him about it.

He checked into the mental hospital that same day. They couldn't touch him, couldn't even talk to him. After eight days, the caseworker, or whatever, called the prosecutor's office to see if there were any charges against him and they said no, so that's when he came out. But they tell me that my memory is not good enough. Then when I do get memory back, they treat me like I'm adding to the story, like I'm starting to make things up now. And it's not that. I don't even remember a whole lot about being in the hospital for two days. I remember them pumping my stomach, but I wouldn't have had enough mind about me to make something like that up. But nobody seems to look at that, you know. I had to go get all the toxicology reports. I found all kinds of drug paraphernalia, other drugs, things he had stolen, and took them out to the police. Nothing was done. Nothing's going to be done. They're not going to do anything.

It is heartbreaking to hear Janie telling her story and hear the despair in her voice. I don't know exactly what she can and cannot recall. Her latest husband had access to drugs and alcohol and brought them home on a regular basis. He had enough pills to kill her, she knows that. Her memories of what he made her do, and the suicide note he forced her to write, seem clear enough evidence that he forced her to take the pills and drink the alcohol. And she knows he demanded she do this while he had a cocked gun to her head. Her complete frustration and anger with the "system" that will not help her prosecute him bleeds through the fabric of her story. But her frustration takes a different turn by the end of her story. Janie's voice changes a bit and acquires a new, defiant tone. Her strength is different from most of the women in this study, yet I found myself applauding her gutsy conclusion:

Yes. I dropped the ex parte after all that happened. Because he violated his twice, and I thought if this doesn't mean any more to them than that, the hell with it. And to be honest with you I felt like if I didn't have it, the ex parte, that there might be more of a chance that he would come after me, and I'll be damned if I let the son of a bitch get the drop on me again. I will kill him. And that's why I dropped it. I was hoping he would come after me.

DELORES'S STORIES OF VIOLENCE

We may recall Delores's story about how difficult her mother was when she was growing up, how hard it was to please her. We recall, as well, how the babysitter's sons molested her when she was very small and the babysitter warned her not to tell anyone or she would not take care of the children anymore. Delores's family rejected her when she thought she might be pregnant, and in desperation she left her home rather than marry the well-to-do farmer her family expected her to marry. She moves to a different town entirely, rents a basement room, and works in a fur factory in the hot sticky southern heat. We hear in her story about the influences of Pentecostal religion and how drawn she was to their austere dress and the "holiness" values. She meets her first husband in this church, and in her story, we begin to see the abuse unfold. Knowing her childhood story helps us immensely in terms of putting his domination of her into perspective.

> We would ride around in his truck a lot and then, after things developed, we started petting. Or, let's say he initiated petting and I enjoyed it even though I didn't really feel right about it, not being married, but I still enjoyed it. But after we were finished, he would say, "You know, I really think that Satan is influencing you in letting me do this, and you need to pray about this because you are the woman and you really have the control." So, every time that we would pet, then I would have to get on my knees and ask God to forgive me and he—I was very—well, at that time I was very vulnerable and I wasn't spiritually mature. I really wasn't able to use good judgment because I did not have a very large frame of reference where scriptures are concerned. But I had a heart where I wanted to know and I wanted to do the right thing. And Steven had a really strong personality as far as his beliefs, his spiritual beliefs, and was very domineering in that respect. And he would say things to me like, "Well, maybe you have been chosen as a vessel of dishonor. Maybe God chooses people to be vessels of honor and maybe you are one of dishonor." He would put just this little twist on scripture. But I began to think of myself as, maybe, not so good.

Early on in this sick relationship, Delores senses that Steven is trouble. She calls her mother and asks if she can return home. Her mother wavers in her answer, saying she'll have to discuss it with her husband, Delores's father, who is quite disgusted with her now; they never call her back. She felt she had no alternative but to go ahead and marry Steven, against her better judgment. His true sadistic nature emerges almost immediately.

I got married in April in 1974 and then, July 4, we were playing, throwing water on each other, in our house, and I slipped on the linoleum and broke my leg. And it was the most excruciating pain I have ever felt. And I went into shock. I got sick to my stomach and I was shaking and cold. And Steven wouldn't call a doctor. The minister taught against going to the doctor. So, I laid there, I kid you not, for an hour before I could move. He did give me a blanket and that did help, you know, my chills, my shivers. And he sat on the couch and watched me. And finally, I pulled myself across the room. The kitchen was closer but the phone was up on the wall and I couldn't reach it. So, I pulled myself across the dining room, across the living room, into our bedroom, to where there was a phone on the nightstand. So, I was going to call my mom or dad or someone. He waits, then he walks across the room, picks up the phone just as I was about to reach for it, and moved it where I couldn't reach it. And I'd been begging him all this time, "Please call someone, please call someone, my leg's broken, it's broken." Well, it wasn't through the skin, so you really couldn't tell it, but I just knew it was. And the thing was, he smiled at me, when I tried—when he took the phone away—when I tried to get it.

[Long pause] It went from bad to worse. I spent like three days in the hospital because my leg was so swollen by the time I got there. And it may have just continued to swell because I didn't have any ice to put on it or anything. So, they kept me there three days, didn't want me walking around on it.

And there was another time. Steven was really, really *sick*. But I didn't know it because I was sick, too. I didn't have enough self-esteem to know that all this was crazy and I really began to doubt myself. And the church was so—the minister—I would have to say she was sick, too.

And then, we got into an argument one day—it was Thanksgiving and we had a long drive to his family's house. So, we were driving up the drive and his little sister's dog, who always ran to me. His sister had several dogs, but this one always ran to meet the car, the truck, whenever anyone pulled up. Steve gunned it and ran over the dog because he was mad at me. And it didn't die instantly. It just flopped around for a while. Then, I remember, I was just horrified because, you know, he runs over the dog,

I look in the back and there's this dog—because he's mad at *me?* And this is his little sister's dog, who's twelve or thirteen at the time. That dog had been in the family for years. And it got to where things were—he had a lot of accidents and I would be the one to get hurt.

It was always like he was trying to make me feel guilty, for everything! Like on my wedding night, I started my period, unfortunately, and I didn't want to have sex, but he did. And he was totally inconsiderate of my feelings. So, I started to develop an aversion—you know, he was the first person that I'd ever had intercourse with, you know, and I just built up an aversion toward him—

[Q: Did he actually rape you?]

No, no, he didn't rape me. He was just very pushy, you know, [saying] "I don't care if you're in your period. This is our wedding night." And I didn't want to say no, I did, well, I didn't actually say "No," but I said, you know, "I'd really rather wait," you know. And I felt really humiliated, since I had never had sex with him before and all this. I remember crying the morning after. I went to breakfast and I was crying. And he said, "Why are you crying?" And, as a rule, I'm not the kind of person that will say just what people want to hear, but I knew I was trapped and I knew this was for life, at least that's what I believed, and I said, "Well, I'm crying because I am so happy." But I knew I had just made one of the worst mistakes—I was trapped. I didn't have anywhere to go. I didn't have the means to support myself. I was so sick of that sewing factory.

Delores endures this marriage for several years and bears two children with this man. He continues to be sadistic and even in marriage forces her down onto her knees after "causing him to lust after her" and leading him into sexual relations. Getting away from Steve proved to be a long and difficult process that continues to haunt her even today. It obviously taints all of her subsequent interactions with men.

Much later in her story, long after leaving her first husband and getting a new job in a prison facility, she tells the story of being attracted to a male physician who worked at the prison. He invited her out for dinner but at the last minute invites her to his motel room instead. Hesitantly, she agrees to go and gingerly steps into his room. His shirt is unbuttoned; he offers her wine. When she sits on the bed, he literally attacks her. The language she uses in this account echoes much of the language we have heard women using throughout this book. She is terrorized; she is numb; she removes herself from the situation and can only do exactly what he tells her to do.

He ended up raping me, just raping me. But it's strange, it's so strange, even then I did not realize what was happening and I kept thinking he was going to stop. And he's a doctor. I think his position made it more difficult for me to fight back in a way that would be violent, to hit him or anything like that, which would have meant my job and everything I'd worked for. So, he rapes me, multiple times. And I went into shock. And the funny thing is I couldn't even call it that. I couldn't even in my mind put the proper label on it. I remember getting completely numb. I wondered if he was going to kill me. I really felt like I was going to die that night, for a few moments. There had been a few rape-murders in the area, and he'd ask me if I'd told anyone where I was at. So, it's so funny the things that go through your mind when that is happening. It was like my mind went up in a corner, you know, I was there. I was numb but my focus was on the corner of the room. And I was thinking about the rape-murders that had occurred, and I wondered if he was the one that had done them. And, he even got up and went to the bathroom, and the different times, the things he did, he would go to the bathroom and wash himself off and I could not move. And later, in being questioned, people said, "Well, why didn't you run out of the room?" Well, I couldn't, but no one could understand that. And I remember thinking, "When he comes back is he going to kill me. Is he going to strangle me like those other women had been strangled?" Actually, I doubt if he was the one—but the other murders had involved strangling. And even with that thought in my mind, wondering if he was going to do that, I still couldn't get up and run. He told me that if I ever told anyone that he would deny it. I actually stayed there all night long. I wanted to pretend that this was perfectly normal, you know, that this was just bad sex, so that I could continue to function normally.

Later in Delores's narrative, after gathering up her strength and actually bringing a harassment suit against the physician, she tells how she ended up marrying one of the prison guards, partly to protect herself from the abusive, domineering, male culture among the prison staff. Yet the influence of this macho community on her husband to keep her "in her place" results in making her life even more miserable than it ever has been. She says her "Corrections experience" was the worst of her life. We can understand why when we hear her descriptions of what it was like.

My husband, who had had drinking problems at one time, had stopped drinking because of our marriage and because he was trying to do better. They started accusing him of being "pussy-whipped" and [they told him] if he didn't go home and put me in my place he was always going to have problems with me. So, these guys in Corrections—it didn't take much, but he was responsible for himself. But he did start drinking again. He came home and he beat me up.

For me, Corrections was not a good place. I already had the reputation of being someone who had filed harassment complaints against the guys. I complained about a dirty Kotex they had put up on the wall near my workspace. My complaint against the Kotex was very threatening for them. They wanted my husband, on their behalf—and he was a sergeant—to put me in my place, which he tried to do. It was so bad—I had my good job that I had taken away from me. I was put back down in with the doctor who had raped me. It was just—[shivers and grimaces, at a loss for words]

The flashbacks I have are because it was connected to Corrections. The abuse he afflicted on me was part of my Corrections experience. He would bang my head against the floor. He made me sit in a chair while he dumped beer and cola on my head. Made me say, "I'm the squaw, you're the chief." And so, it was another experience of someone dominating me and telling me I had no worth, and me being in a position to survive, I had to go ahead and do what he said.

But not for long. When Delores gave me her life story on tape, she had already been in the shelter and had moved on. She is now living beyond the sheltered life, renting a place of her own with her two girls, and she is in therapy with one of the counselors at the shelter. I felt a sense of quiet peace as she sat in the overstuffed chair across from me in that pleasant office; I knew she felt safe there, because she visited every week. She got away from that last abusive man and she has experienced a couple of nonabusive relationships since, one with a woman. She is concerned about her children. But her summary words are appropriate for this discussion of moving through the violence into a new beginning. She tried to sort out her feelings about how the doctor's rape and her marriage to the penal officer had shaken her beliefs and her spirituality. She was beginning to realize that she must trust herself, above all.

Yes, I felt abandoned by God and I don't know if that was just my own self, my feelings, about why these terrible things happened. But I felt that in my own intuitions, I felt that I had been warned about him. I knew from the day I met him, I had been warned, stay away from him! We have to learn to trust our intuitions. You know as a child I was always taught, I learned, not to face people, not to make any waves, to please, to be invisible. But I don't feel that I ever want to be vulnerable to a man again and let him have power over my life.

I control my own life now. And that's what I hope that my daughters can see. And I'm at a point now where I'm very pressed to give my time now to my daughters' psychological needs. And they need me, they both tell me that. They have gone through so much. But they are too mouthy. You know, I didn't want them to feel like I did, so I think I went too far the other way, and they are too mouthy [laughs]. They are not at all afraid of losing my love.

What a beautifully articulated tribute to her new self. Here is a woman who recognizes at the end of the recounting of a long and arduous life, full of rape and violence, abuse beyond the imagination to fathom, sitting here talking about the importance for her daughters to speak, to be "too mouthy." For they know something she never knew, that speaking will never damage her love for them. What a tremendously significant gift.

When we examine the women's narratives in this light, hearing the pain and violence juxtaposed with the emergence of a new self, Scarry's argument is convincing, for she claims that in the act of speaking, through the projection of the *voice,* the "self" is expanding the *boundaries of its own flesh.* When we speak, we must project; words go forth out of our mouths and, in that act, make us larger than we were before we spoke. Self-representation through speech, says Scarry, "becomes the final source of self-expression. So long as one is speaking, the self extends out beyond the boundaries of the body, occupies a space much larger than the body."[1] I would further argue that the more imaginative and creative, the more articulated the narratives can become, the more "work" is being accomplished through language in terms of the speaker's development of a more positive self-construction.

As long as women are living in violent relationships, experiencing pain and the politics of domination by another, they cannot possibly speak, even to develop their selves. But when they do emerge in spaces away from the violence and experience the act of speaking the violence, the story played out on their bodies by the men who batter them has a *new plot.* Through speech, the women are able to move from the role of passive victim to that of an active self, telling some of what has happened to them and expanding the construction of their selves through the act of speaking. We must remember at all times that this act of speaking is an entirely new and different experience for the women who have just emerged from lives of violence. The very act of speaking the pain to others, and admitting it out loud to herself, is uncharted territory.

To illustrate the power narrative holds for women who attempt to enter these dangerous waters, I want to return to the end of Sherry's life story. Her story had been focused on her silenced childhood, her self-destructive teenage years, and her narrative of one abusive relationship after another. When she finished her narrative, I asked her if she had ever in her life had a job she enjoyed or had a passion for something, or if she remembered doing something well and feeling proud of it. Her answer is in the form of a story, a story that holds the potential to break our hearts and teach us well at the very same moment. Her story demonstrates the way we make connections between violence and our physical bodies, between the aspects of our lives we believe we can control and those we feel we cannot. But her story also demonstrates how significant it is for Sherry to see herself as an embodied person, separate from the violence, a body that does not want to die.

Yeah, I'm a housekeeper by trade, believe it or not. And I was real good at it and I worked in hospitals. My one area where I work, I'm real good at my work. I worked in a hospital once and they gave me a block of rooms. I did really good in my own area so they gave me my own area. I did really good, I stayed up and I was real particular about it. I even got a letter of recommendation because I had to clean the morgue. Because—oh, this is really interesting. I had this belief because I was with Dale at the time—and at home you could look around and there was always—I could clean up after a fight, but there was always a speck of blood somewhere on my walls and I hated that. I hated that. And I had to clean the morgue; that was part of my area. Well, there was the autopsy table with all the blood. And I had this belief that if I could get all the blood off of that autopsy table that the abuse in my home would stop. I don't know how I associated that. But the morgue was brick, painted brick, you know, it's got those little holes. I would go through with a toothbrush and a toothpick, a wooden toothpick, trying to get the blood out of the little holes [laughs]. Now, when I look back at it, it was crazy, but the whole time I was working in the morgue, cleaning the blood, it was somebody else's blood I was cleaning, it wasn't mine. So, that was a comfort. So, the whole time I was doing it—I would replay all those years, my aunt Susan, and my mom, just everything. And my morgue was spotless. It was absolutely spotless. . . .

. . . I got to go in on the autopsies, and what was really weird, there was a woman that they dragged her out of a pond. She'd been in a pond for three months. And it was a mysterious death. Well, after they got her all cleaned up and everything, turns out she got beat to death. And her ex-boyfriend was prosecuted for her death. And I followed that story because I saw that woman come into the morgue and it was weird watching the trial and reading about it in the paper. And I kept picturing that woman laying on the table and stuff. That always bothered me.

When I got transferred over to the other hospital in surgery, we'd get people in there, women and children, I mean, a bunch for lots of different kinds of surgery. But every now and then we'd, I'd get to go in on a woman who had just, had been—just beat to hell. And they would have to go in and like remove her spleen and shit, where she got beat. And it was one thing, it was weird seeing a dead body that got beat and then a woman go through all that shit in surgery from being beat, it was weird. When it was me going through all that pain and stuff, that was one thing, but to actually sit and watch these other women go through it—it would—it was never going to happen to me. And it did.

Sherry knows the woman on the table is not her. She knows the dead body dragged from the lake is also not her. Logically she knows that cleaning the blood off the brick morgue walls with a toothbrush, just like cleaning her own blood off the walls of her house, will not stop the violence. She nevertheless wants to make some sort of connection between her actions and the violence. She never wanted to acknowledge the probability of her own death at the hands of her abusers; yet by the end of her story, she is able to make that imaginative leap—from their dead bodies to her live one. As she cleaned the blood, it became not only the blood of the dead woman in the morgue, but it also became the blood of her aunt Susan, her mother, and herself. She didn't think it could happen to her, but it did happen to her. The difference is that she is here to tell about it. That is her saving grace. Her voice and her ability to imagine the worst, to look back, to turn, and then seek a different reality. She has cleaned the blood off the walls for the last time.

Conclusion COMING HOME TO SHELTER
TO SAVE OUR SELVES

> We are volcanoes. When we women offer our experience as our truth,
> all the maps change. There are new mountains. That's what I want—to hear
> you erupting. You Mount St. Helenses who don't know the power in you—I
> want to hear you. . . . If we don't tell our truth, who will?
>
> Ursula K. Le Guin

EARLY IN THIS BOOK I explained that I had begun this work suspecting that
the "cycles of violence" narrative that all professionals in the field and even the
victims of domestic violence know well needed to be revised, or, at the very
least, revisited in terms of how violence is approached from the point of view
of the woman who is being battered. The cycle of violence pattern that focuses
on the predictable details of *his* abusive behavior, and *her* responses to that
violence, has both assisted and possibly hindered our attempts to understand
and deal with the issue of male violence against women. I have suggested that
it is possible for such a neat schema to become a kind of master narrative—
one that could possibly work against the rights and the healing of women
who live with violent men. In light of the work I have done for this book,
I would like to come back to that concept now, in conclusion, but expand
upon those earlier thoughts based on what we have learned from listening
to women tell their own stories. Furthermore, I would like to explore what I
believe can happen for all of us—readers and listeners alike—if we begin to
examine our own lives as we move toward safety and healing, strength, and
independence.

Janice Haaken has suggested that we must identify within women's stories
a "complex subjectivity." In *Pillar of Salt,* she compares women's narratives
with the Biblical story of Lot's wife, who dared to look back and was turned
into a pillar of salt, but notes that she hopes for contemporary women a better
resolution to their dilemma. The first act in reconfiguring Lot's wife's story
might be to note that Lot's wife does not even have a name. We need to name
this woman and, in so doing, breathe new life into her body. This book, devoted
to the hearing of women's stories, offers an affirmation of Haaken's claims that
women should dare to look back, remember, and tell their stories as an act

of defiance and transformation. I agree with Haaken that it is possible that "important truths reside at the periphery of what is most readily noticeable." We have gone to the margins in these pages and we have listened well. We have heard here the kinds of remembering that women actually do in their recounting of a life. We see how they have bravely looked back, have marked turning points in their experiences, and have forged a narrative that traces deeds done and actions taken through a new lens, rather than talking about memory as a fixed entity. Haaken calls this the process of "transformative re-membering"; this "refers to the recollection of an event that serves as a psychological marker from an early to a later form of self-knowledge." In that way, "the motivational and active dimensions of mind are in the foreground." For the women in this study, the term "transformational re-membering" is appropriate, offering them, as Haaken says, "a new vantage point from which to view the past." She continues: "The activity of remembering stands at the threshold between body and mind like a translator." Put another way, her thinking and mine coalesce: "transformative re-membering refers to the creative use of the past in *redefining the self*."[1]

I remember a small, half-page flyer that was circulating in the shelter for a time, typed out by a resident on the office typewriter. I do not know if it was her own composition or if she had read it somewhere, but the version she typed was certainly her own re-composition. It read:

> ACCEPT yourself as a whole person COMPLETE! If you feel incomplete, you feel as if you are half a woman and will look for half a man to make you whole. If you're not connecting with him, or he leaves you, you will again feel like half a woman, so ACCEPT yourself as a whole complete individual, because THAT IS WHAT YOU ARE!

Certainly, those of us who know the "cycles of violence" narrative well can see evidence of the identified "cycles of violence," the noted "red flags" of his behavior in the stories in this book. Yet, as observant and caring readers, we can also see that the patterns of the "cycles of violence" prototype as narrated in the domestic violence literature do not constitute the driving force of the narratives of the women in this study. There is so much more we can learn from listening to the women's stories about how their lives have been fragmented and splintered apart by the abuse inflicted upon them even from birth, but also how they are able to move beyond the role of victim and toward empowerment and transformation. We are all Lot's wife's *daughters*. Many of us are unnamed, beaten down, muted, silenced, and fearful of looking back, but we are invited to speak, and in that speaking we are able to free ourselves from the perils of being immobilized, paralyzed, and silenced.

One of the more interesting things that has happened while I have been working on this book has been the response I get from women I have talked to about the research and about the difficulty of the writing. More often than not, a friend or colleague would tell me they find this work interesting—and, then, she might launch into a rather reflective mode in which she would reveal some fascinating and surprising details about her own life and her mother's life. One of my best older friends began to talk about the abuse of her own husband, beginning at first to talk about what I would term emotional abuse, only to move beyond that to actual accounts of how her husband would pin her against the wall or throw things in rages or strike her when she "acted out." Professional women, colleagues, neighbors, students responded to the work with stories of their own. One of my walking friends, also several years older than myself, spent long hours on our walks exploring how this work pertained to her own life. Unsolicited, she talked at length about the emotional abuse of her own mother but was able to reflect upon her mother's emotional neglect because she could relate that pattern of behavior to what she knew about the life of her mother's mother. A younger walking friend revealed the secrets of her own unraveling marriage and the abuse of her minister husband. Women in high places, and low, began to tell me their stories.

My students would tell their mother's stories of pain and abuse in my women's studies classes, once they knew about the book I was writing; my graduate students would tell story after story about their mothers, their sisters, and their best friends—many locked into abusive marriages with no way out. A counselor who works with battered women asked me, after reading the entire manuscript, if she could tell me *her story.* She was convinced by the arguments here that the act of telling our stories is significant in and of itself.

As women, what we do in this act of speaking—and the act of listening—is to acknowledge that *we are there* in the "gap" in our knowledge of what domestic violence is and how it operates in women's lives to unmake their worlds. The woman telling the story is the woman being beaten; she is the speaking woman; she is the escaping woman. Blanchot may be right in claiming that perhaps what we cannot see in the rupture is the essence of *the disaster,* but what we may be able to discern is the essence of *her* disaster. We can see and hear her telling her story. This may not illuminate or capture the totality of the monster we call domestic violence, but it does acknowledge, honor, and respect the reality of the life she has lived in violence and that she has now named and left in a brave and terrifying moment of pure audacity. She dared to tell all and she dared to leave. Her speaking of the violence expands her beyond the borders of her once negated self. She moves in expansion with the words she speaks; she becomes as big and as wide as her words can carry. She takes up both physical and auditory space. If she can scream and yell with Sandra Cisneros's "woman hollering," as she crosses the creek, escaping in a truck driven by a woman, then she can grow that much larger.[2] And not only does she expand when she speaks the violence, she also exposes her abuser in this act as well. She most definitely names him, identifies him as the violent one, and makes him accountable.

We must tell our stories—in order to understand where we have been and where we are going, in order to heal, in order to see the larger patterns that are emerging as we listen to our stories, our mothers' stories, and their mothers' stories. It is in the collective telling of all our stories together that we will expose the essence of the monster called domestic violence. In speaking loudly the abuse, the violence, the damage done to our minds and bodies, our united voices must reach a crescendo that will translate, eventually, into political clout and a stance of *no tolerance* for abuse, ever, to another woman by a man.

Alice Walker reminds us to go "in search of our mothers' gardens" to find evidence of the beauty they were able to create in their otherwise barren lives, and Virginia Woolf says we tell our own stories backward through our mother's and our grandmother's stories.[3] When we do this kind of remembering work to bring our mother's stories into the present, there is, on the one hand, a sense of joy and nostalgia for the recognition of lives we perhaps never really knew. But there is another side to this work, a darker side, that also reminds us that we are, indeed, our mother's daughters. And for many of our mothers, their gardens were not enough to heal their wounds or enable them to be strong enough to help themselves or us. I was not prepared to discover in the stories from women living in violence a persistent pattern of disconnection from their mothers, or to uncover the brutal reality that many of our mothers, and their mothers before them, suffered abuse as well. The stories of the women in this book can eventually lead us to uncover the truth of our own mother's stories in addition to our own. I believe this link is an important part of this work.

As I grew more involved with the stories from the women in the shelter and spent long, tedious hours transcribing the tapes of the women who had agreed to tell me *their* life stories and the stories of abuse they had endured, my mother's story and her mother's story began to haunt me, as did my own. I heard their stories and my own in the stories of the women on the tapes; I heard my words in theirs; their stories, my mother's stories, my stories sometimes swirled together in my mind during long walks on the trail near my house, as I tried to sift through all the transcriptions. In the air in front of my eyes, I would actually watch my mother's and grandmother's stories, and my own, weave in and out of the ones I had collected and listened to repeatedly on the tapes. The act of telling our stories lays bare what I think is at the very heart of how women come to find themselves in abusive relationships, and why they think they cannot extricate themselves from the partners who abuse them. In truth, I had never once, before doing the research and writing for this book, thought of my grandmothers and my mother as women trapped in abusive and damaging marriages—nor had I ever admitted to the violence in my own. But in doing this kind of work, we acknowledge the power of narrative with which we speak ourselves into being.

My own story is as complex as all the other stories told in the pages of this book. But the full story of my own, or my mother's, life of abuse has not yet been told. Even though my father is dead, my mother cannot tell her story; and even though it has been nearly twenty years since I left my first husband and his own angry violence, I am not yet able to tell that story. The moment of my escape has been captured in the poem I included at the beginning of this book. But that was a turning point in my life. I could not yet "look back," but I recognized the pivotal power of that moment of escape.

What I *am* able to recall without pain was the day I left the house where I lived with my husband and son. I moved into town, to a house where several other women lived. They offered me the only space left in their yellow clapboard house on the corner, a closet they emptied out for me to sleep in. They also listened. I brought a foam pad to sleep on and a few clothes and my bicycle. I knew not one thing about any network of safe houses or shelters for women like myself, scared and alone. In the Midwest in 1978 I doubt if there were many places available. But I would not have looked for them anyway, not knowing at all, then, how to name what was happening to me. What I remember best was the next morning, when I rode my bike to my graduate class: I soared. I remember the wind in my face, the bump on the railroad tracks, the blue sky, and the total sense of exhilaration. It was like nothing I have experienced before or since. It was pure, unconfused, freedom. And like the women in Sandra Cisneros's story, I do believe I yelled out loud, a salute to myself. In a way, writing this book has become the way for me to begin looking back.

Unfortunately, abuse and violence permeates the lives of many women, both in the United States and globally. How that abuse gets played out in different homes, behind closed doors, is both different and yet surprisingly similar. What the abuse does to us as women is devastating—whether it comes in the form of verbal abuse, badgering, and willful negation of our worth, or whether it includes the use of fists, knives, and cocked guns to our heads in violent acts of domination and torture. My story and my mother's story are not the same as Sherry's or Margaret's, Tina's or Marcie's, and they are not the same as yours or your mother's, your grandmother's, your aunt's, your sister's, your best friend's. But the response to this book should be a powerful moment of recognition and acknowledgment, a moment when you know for certain that the stories in this book *could be* the stories of some of the women you know well, including yourself. I have come to believe in the thesis of this book: To tell our stories is to re-create our selves. The power of narrative comes in the act of telling our stories, breaking the silence, narrating a life, constructing a self.

Fortunately, some of our stories are success stories, stories of escape, re-creation, transformation, with good and happy endings. But the staff members who work in the shelter where the women who speak in these pages lived and told their stories know, as I do, that not all the stories of the women who come through our doors end up being "success stories." Some of the women have to leave many times before they finally escape for good; some have to go back into drug and alcohol rehab centers; some struggle for years, never quite getting their "selves" put back together again. But the positive endings of the stories in this book are just as real as the stories of near successes and of failures. The hope and the determination that is in evidence at the conclusion of the stories I have tape recorded for this research attest to the inherent strength of women and the power of narrative to help them as they attempt to construct their newly emergent selves.

All the women in this book are works in progress, as indeed we all are. Their journey, and mine, and yours, have crossed paths in the writing of this book, in the listening and the telling into self. They need to hear our stories, and we need to hear theirs: Strength in numbers. Fighting the good fight. Yelling at the top of our lungs as we cross the border. Carrying our sisters across in pick-up trucks and in our arms. The prize is our selves and our daughters' selves and their daughters' selves—a worthy goal by any standard.

Some of the Stories

THE STORIES I CONTINUALLY hear in the shelter are protected stories—told in the safety of the office, the kitchen, the living room, the support group, the smoking porch. I cannot tape record those stories for good reason. The safety of the women in the shelter is of paramount importance, and I would protect their right to privacy with my life. In some ways, working in the shelter on a daily basis is doing just that—protecting the women and their stories with our very lives.

Only parts of those stories told in their natural context within the shelter appear in this book, disembodied, unnamed or with pseudonyms, to protect the innocent, the women in hiding. These four life stories transcribed here, then, are not the same as the spontaneous stories that are told in the spaces of the shelter. They were solicited by me from the shelter residents and from various women who come to the shelter's weekly support group (these include women who are still living in abusive relationships and some who have escaped and now live apart from their abusers).

All of the participants who trusted me with their stories on tape did so voluntarily and with the full understanding that I was intending to use their tape recorded stories for a book about violence in women's lives.

Sherry's Story

WELL, I'LL START. My earliest memory is, I was, I'm going to call it three, and—this is a screwed-up first memory—I witnessed my father get murdered by my uncle. This is my earliest memory. My mom was a drinker and so was my dad. And they got into it one night and my uncle came in and shot my dad. From there I moved to an apartment and I got a new dad. He was a drinker like Mom, too. And he was abusive. Mom, God rest her soul, she slept around a lot. She was just a good-time party girl, I guess.

And then when I was in kindergarten, first grade, she got cancer and we moved from the city to a small town and we had long years of cancer, and through that time she still had lots of boyfriends, lots of parties. My stepdad was still there and there was all kinds of boyfriends. But my stepdad molested me when I was seven. And then Mom died and I was eleven. But from seven to eleven we went back and forth with my grandma and my uncle and all our relatives. She was up here in a hospital. After Mom died we went and lived with my uncle back in the city. And that's where most of my memories are. He was abusive to his wife. There was me and my brother and my sister. We moved in with him and he had at the time two kids.

And he was drunk and abusive and my Aunt Susan was a real—what I call a real lady. You know she'd do anything for us, you know, she was just wonderful. And he just always beat the hell out of her. Then we left the city and moved back into the country and he was still mean to her. And that's when I started getting onto drugs—but years before that—see here's where it gets confusing—

When Mom was sick, I started getting into—I made friends in town, we lived out in the country and I started—I think my drug use has to do with my abuse. The first time I ever did any drugs I was like seven and I took "tea"?— which is like a base of heroin and cocaine mixed. And I was the youngest of the crowd. It was my sister-in-law, it was her friends, her age, she was three years older than me. And then I started drinking. It wasn't like I turned into a seven-year-old alcoholic or nothing, but every weekend we would go in and I was always the funny one to get drunk, I would always throw up first. I was seven. And then I started getting high. Then we moved up to the city and Mom died when I was eleven. The drinking and the getting high went on through

162

that period. But Mom was on liquid morphine and my sister, she was three years older than us, and she was trying to keep up with me and my brother and raise the family and she started giving us Mom's liquid morphine, you know, to put us to sleep. Not a whole lot, she wasn't trying to kill us or nothing.

Anyway, Mom dies and we moved back to the city and my uncle, he's drunk and abusive. He used to let us sniff gas. He thought that was the coolest thing in the world to do and get high on the stuff. He was really stupid. That went on and then I started getting interested in boys and my big thing was like, I'd always have to have the party guy. You know, the cool, tattooed, long-hair, skull-earring-type guy, you know [laughs]. I got real promiscuous. The first abusive relationship I got into, I was thirteen. I was thirteen and the guy was twenty-two. He was the coolest thing in town. He had a Harley Davidson and a Green Demon and he was just so cool. He never really, his [abuse] wasn't—he wouldn't smack me in my face. He whipped my butt, you know, like a child, you know, that was his thing. But I thought I was in love [laughs]. People started finding out about us and my uncle never did anything, he just kept an eye on me, made sure I didn't go back around him.

I got into relationships like that and for some reason I've always been attracted to older men, I don't know why. I had a relationship with one younger guy, actually two. And they were just so easy to control, that was like just such a rush because they thought I was Queen Sheba [laughs]. And I had my first child; I was seventeen, pregnant when I was sixteen. The baby's dad was twenty-three and he was a drunk and he was abusive. He was just abusive to the point to where—his was more of an emotional, verbal type thing. But he was a drunk and for some reason there's something about drunks.

I ended that one, and then I got with another guy and he was real, he was really physically abusive and emotional, verbal, that whole thing, but I would just stick around because I really loved this guy. I remember I was sixteen, seventeen at that time, and I really didn't think I'd ever find anything else. We lived in a small town at that time and it was just crazy.

And then that ended. He moved away. I don't really remember where he moved to or what happened to him. I had the baby and I went back home and my aunt, that my uncle beat up on all the time, she tried to commit suicide. She got on a Yamaha 100 dirt bike and ran into a tree in front of the funeral parlor at eighty miles an hour trying to commit suicide. And the one thing she did, she has a head injury, she has the mentality of a seven year old now. The most ironic thing was it took that for my uncle not to be abusive anymore. Yeah [laughs], that was stupid. And I realized then why Aunt Susan had done this and, you know, I remember all those years of seeing him beat her and stuff and I thought, that sucks. The kids knew why she did it; she would say, I'm tired, just so tired. The sad thing was that she left them. She had an eleven-year-old boy, a seven-year-old boy, and a two-year-old boy, left them. But the abuse got to where she just couldn't take it. So, I went back home, and my uncle George, I just thought he was the greatest thing in the world, you know, 'cause we could just sit down and we could just talk about anything, you know, at times. And then there was times when he would just knock the shit out of us. He choked me to where I couldn't breathe one time because I was twenty minutes late coming home. He would never—when I was younger—he never called me a bitch, slut, whore, but he'd tell me I dress like a whore, acted like a whore, talked like a whore, the only thing left was to be a whore, you know. And when I started getting boyfriends he'd beat them up, young, young guys, you know.

There was one time when I was twelve, yes I was twelve, and I had a boyfriend whose name was Chad, and Uncle George broke a broomstick over his neck because he kissed me. And I thought that was—I couldn't understand that, you know. But Uncle George was just telling me, "You're just pretty, I don't want you to get hurt or anything." And after Aunt Susan got hurt, I came back home with Reggie, my baby, when Aunt Susan got hurt and I was trying to help around the house and take care of the kids and stuff. And Uncle George got drunk one night and told me that he wanted to be "with" me, sexually, and I thought that was real perverse, because this is the man that raised me; my mother had entrusted him to take care of us and stuff. And he told me he was attracted to my other cousins, my other female cousins, and we were all blond haired and blue eyed. And I thought that was kinda—[pauses, grimaces]—so I started sorta watching how he was and I told them about my stepdad, who lived there with us in the city. I told them how he had molested me and they never believed me. And when my mom found out about it, when I was younger, she never once, never once—I told a friend of mine, and she told her mother, who told my mother—my mother never once took me to the doctor, never once asked me about it, and I thought that was really [weird]; and my stepdad still stayed around. She kicked him out, but he'd still come back and stuff and she wasn't even around home. That was really sick. But then anyway—my family never believed, my uncle never believed that he had molested me.

So, I went wild after Uncle George did that and just started getting real crazy and started drinking real heavy. And I told him that night, I just got up and I told him, I think it's just the alcohol talking. And I got up and left the room. He started trying to touch me and stuff and I left; that was just sick to me. After that I left and I didn't go back. But I started drinking real heavy and doing whatever drugs I possibly could. I was eighteen at the time that I'm talking about. And my mother, we had inherited some money from my mom, we inherited ten thousand dollars. So, I took my money and I moved away, got me a trailer and stuff, moved away from all of my family.

And I messed around at a party and I got pregnant again, in the back seat of a Chevy [laughs], you know, and I was drunk and everything, and I had a little boy. I got married three weeks after he was born, to a guy named Dale. Dale seemed like a really nice guy, you know, he took care of the baby and everything, but he was a drunk and real abusive. He had a real [temper]—it was bad—I would have to say that was my worst abusive relationship I've ever been into. He broke my ribs and everything and his big thing was—there was him and then there was the part he called "the other guy." And "the other guy" was like his protector and it was like a whole different personality. And I've got pictures to where you can actually see the difference in the way he holds his jaws and his stance and everything. And Dale was wonderful, I love Dale to this day. But "the other guy" hated me.

We built a house. Dale was a construction worker and so we built a house. And I burned his toast one morning and he bulldozed our house, because I burned his toast [laughs nervously]. It took us three years, and it was just me and him only building this house, it took three years. And in twenty minutes it was bulldozed and we hadn't even had it standing up for six months.

And he used to beat up his dad. And I found out that he had been married prior to our marriage and he was real abusive to her. And then he got to where—he got mean with my kids. He eventually went to prison for attempted murder on me and both my kids. He did four months and got out. And it's been—it was '89, '90, the last part of '89, it went so far—I tried to get away from him. It got to the point that I literally stole a car, drove to the police station, threw the keys at them, and told them I stole a car: "Dale's coming, put me in jail." And the cop—it's in a small town—he just kinda laughed and said, "Sherry, it's going to be okay." I'd called him a million and one times. And Dale slid up in front of the police station in a truck, and I literally punched the cop to get thrown in jail. They would not put me in jail to protect me from Dale. And as I'm going up the steps, 'cause I started running up the steps, I just wanted to get someplace safe, Dale was right behind me. He busted right through the policemen in the office and they charged him on attempted murder on me and the kids and he did four months and got out.

And the thing that bothered me was that everywhere I turned, 'cause I finally figured out, is during my marriage to Dale I remember everything with my mom, you know, all the men and stuff. And she used to get the shit beat out of her, but she'd still take men. She thought it was—I don't know what she thought; I thought she was crazy. And then with my aunt Susan, seeing all the stuff she'd gone through, and all my little here-and-there relationships. And my big thing was always, I was always, I never, ever let any of them dump me. There was only one that ever dumped me up to this point and that was the guy that I just thought was God. And I would always dump them. It was like a rush, you know. But I was sitting here, while Dale was in jail, really trying to get my shit together and think about all that. And he got out in four months. So, I just—

I gave my oldest son to my grandparents to raise and then the little boy I had, I gave him up for adoption to a family I had met. He was put into protective custody because Dale really hurt him and that's how I met the family and it was a really good family. So I gave him up. So, there I am with no kids, so it's time to party again. And I'm back into the relationships and stuff and it was just one right after the other. And none of them lasted, but the whole time I just stayed drunk, just real stupidly drunk. And my older son came to stay with me again and it got to the point—and at this time he was five, five years old, he knew how to scramble eggs on a gas stove, he could cook rolls in the oven, and he knew what "350" was on the oven, you know, he was real self-sufficient there at five. And he saw me with all the different boyfriends and getting my ass kicked and he didn't want to live with me any more, so he told me he wanted to go back to his grandparents. So I let him and then I moved to a different city; I was trying to get myself together and stuff and just got into [a bad relationship]—for about two years it wasn't a physical [abusive] relationship, but it was abusive. I was just bouncing, just partying, and then I got with Lori's dad and I got pregnant with Lori. Me and him, we never stayed together; it was an off-and-on thing and he was abusive. I finally got away from him and I went to a homeless shelter, away from all of my family, you know, I decided I wanted to clean my act up and get a real life, and I wanted to be a mom and everything.

And that's when I met Ernie, the reason I'm here—it was in the homeless shelter. He was a security guard, yeah [laughs]—he was there to protect people [laughs again]. He was in the AA program and stuff like that. Real clean-cut guy, real nice, polite, mannerly, you know. And I got with him and his abuse started, it was—it was just from day one. He was the one—he would—it actually didn't start out physical. He put me up on cloud nine. I was the most important person in the world. There was none other than me, you know, and he would protect me and if somebody looked at me wrong, he was in their face, you know. And that was nice. And then it got to where he would tell me, like if I put on a pair of shorts, he'd say, you know why don't you wear those other shorts, they look better. And I thought, well that's cool, he's paying attention to how I dress, you know. And he didn't want me drinking, and he was really good to the baby, and so I thought that was cool, someone cared.

The next thing I know he's drinking a little bottle of wine, no big deal, and he quit his job. And that's when he started getting physical and stuff. He didn't ever hit me as hard as Dale; he never broke a rib or anything. But he would slap me and things like that, and that was crazy. And I went ahead and stayed with him—I left him twice and then he settled down a little bit and tried to straighten up and then I would go back and things would be good for a while, and after the third time I left, when I went back it got really physical, to the point that I would run and hide. And I don't know why I'd go back, 'cause I'd feel sorry for him, you know. He would tell me he didn't mean to do it, and I always called him and let him know the baby was okay but that was always just a lousy excuse, just calling to let you know your daughter's fine—it wasn't even his daughter. And then I got to messing around with methamphetamines with him and we went on a big getting-high thing for like seven months, we were high and then I got pregnant with Justin and I stayed clean all through my pregnancy with Justin. And Ernie, he wouldn't work or anything like that. I did all the work. I worked at a motel; I worked. Then I had Justin. But a month before Justin was born, Ernie got high with some men and he was way off, really high, and he put a gun to my stomach. And I told him, I was tired, [that] I didn't give a shit, which was stupid, now when I think about it. And I told him, "If you weren't high I'd be afraid, but since you're stoned I really don't care, you won't remember any of this tomorrow anyway."

And then he had Lori, she was three—no, she was two at the time, and he had her playing with a loaded automatic weapon and there was nothing I could do, you know, I just had to sit there. So I left, and after I had Justin, we got back together, you know, I just had his baby and blah, blah, blah, blah, you know, and that's when he got really physical, was after I had Justin. To the point where he would come home drunk and just knock the shit out of me for no reason. He had an imagination that wouldn't stop. He would see some guy walking down the street and he might think, well, Sherry thinks he's cute. The next thing, you know, [he's saying] I've slept with this man, I've been doing it for a hundred years, and that's just the way it is, you know. And with him, I didn't try to do the power/control thing. I worked, I supported him. I would stand up against my family for him, because my family kept telling me to get away from him. But I always thought they were real scum anyway, so if there was someone they didn't like I was going to go for it, you know [laughs].

And he finally—I got to where I was working two jobs. I worked two jobs to stay out of the house, and I didn't get to see my kids and stuff. And he come in one night and just sit down at the table and he said, "I think I'm going to kill you." And I'm like [laughs] really [shocked]—you know I'm like, I'm just sitting there reading, and he just walks in the door and he told me he thought he was going to kill me. And I remember I looked up at him and I said, "Why?" And he said, "I don't know." And I said, "Well, when?" [laughs], you know. And he told me, "I don't know." He said, "I think you need to leave," and I called this place [the shelter] and that's how I got here.

[Q: Why did he tell you he was going to kill you?]

If a man is sober and calmly tells you he's going to kill you, you'd better believe him and you'd better get away, 'cause he's probably going to do it.

And now, this is how stupid it is. Now, I mean, I can picture myself being away from all men for a hundred years and I'm actually content with it, you know, I'm okay with that. I don't have to be with somebody, but I still contact him, not to go back home to him. I'm secure in the fact that I don't want to be back home to him. But just the fact that I don't ever want to be with another man to kick my ass, to cuss me, that I have to support and stuff. But yet, I've grown so used to having that that I cannot get away from it. And it's not that I don't want to—I really do—but what is life beyond that? I don't know. And that's a scary prospect when you don't know what it is, right? It's like, what do you do now? [Laughs] So—

[Q: Are there any stories, now, that you want to go back and pick up?]

A lot of the reason why I got into abusive relationships is like my *family*-family—I think family is a big support system and if your family doesn't support you, then nobody is ever going to. And I know when my mom didn't ever ask me about what had happened, you know, that really—I remember that bothered me, you know. So, I knew my mom really didn't give a shit, you know. And if your mother doesn't care, then who in the world is really going to care? You're not going to have that. And then when I finally—it takes a lot to tell somebody that you've been molested, you know, when you haven't dealt with it yet, and then when my family didn't believe me, that bothered me. But when I was pregnant with Lori, my stepdad who molested me, literally laid on the kitchen floor Christmas night, drunk, and I never told Lori's dad, but my stepdad, drunk, jacked off, and he told the whole story, the whole thing, with my little brother standing there, who I had never told. And here's the sick part: My family welcomes him into their home more so than me. I'm the outsider, I'm the jackass. They never told me you're bad and you're nasty, but I know when they look at me, they look at me differently. But when they see my stepdad, well, his excuse is 'cause he was drunk, you know. And growing up, I remember when I was little, Mom would like all those men who were drunk. So, as long as they were drunk and did it, that was their excuse, 'cause they were drunk, they didn't know. And like all the stupid shit I did, like sleeping with all those men I had and getting my ass kicked, it was okay because they were drunk. And I really believe that the alcohol part had a lot to do with it and the self-esteem. Because I don't think a child is born with self-esteem. I think it's up to the parents and the people who love that child to build that self-esteem and make them strong and make them—you know. A child is not born with self-value, self-worth, you know, that's something that is taught to them. And if you don't have that, you just—you're just not going to go anywhere.

With all of my abusers, when I would try—because it wasn't like I wanted to get my ass kicked—when I'd try hard, it was like the more I tried, the worse the abuse got. So, I learned if I just shut my mouth, go to work, and do what I was supposed to do, I wouldn't get my ass kicked. And, you know, there were also a few occasions where I wouldn't have to do nothing, you know, it was just a lucky night [laughs], it was my lucky night, and I didn't have to work for that ass beating, you know, it just happened [laughs sarcastically].

What bothers me is that my kids have seen it. And you know it started a cycle in them. If you're raised in a family of violence, you're going to bring up a family of violence. Now, I'm wanting to move away. I've left all my family. I've cut every member of my family off. They know there's a boundary. You can talk to me on the phone, but don't ever come towards me again because they didn't believe in me. I was always the wild one. I could do anything. I was the heartbreaker; I could break any man's heart. And I would tell them up front. I was honest about it, you know; "I'm going to chew you up and spit you out." And it was a challenge and it was fun. And anything for a challenge, just to make myself look good. And it was being with older men and being able to be with a man and get your ass kicked and still stay with that man. To me, that was—that made me strong. That was the power. Because I could take it, you know. I stood it well, you know, and that is all that mattered. I stood it well. And you're taught that loyalty, you know, which is stupid. It's like, this time around, since I've left this time, I've put more distance between us. And I've come real to life with myself and just say, that's it, now I've got kids that are going to grow up—I've got two boys and a girl and the way it lies now, statistically, my children, my boys, are more apt to grow up abusing women and my daughter is more apt to be abused and accept it. That's going to be normal for them. In their minds that's normal. And that's sick. That's sick. I don't think my cycle would have stopped until I got with some real people. I've been in some other shelters, but here—you've got to meet someone who is real tired of being abused before, and meet someone who really cares about you as a human being, before you can realize that you don't deserve that. My family, they had all gone through it, you know, they would abuse one another and their spouses, the husbands and wives would always—and that was normal. It's just the way it was. And my grandparents, they cared and they didn't want me to marry, to marry into abusive marriages and stuff like that, but their thing was more of, "Let her do it and learn," because there was nothing they could do. They could have talked until they was blue in the face and they would have never made me stop it.

[Q: Do you think you can stop the cycle of violence for your kids now?]

Yeah. You know, Dale called me last night—I finally told him—he called last night to tell me where he was going [laughs], where he was going! When we was together he never would do that; he would just go out the door, you know. Now, we're living miles away and—he's quit drinking, he's quit smoking cigarettes, he jogs. Looks awesome. And I told him last night, you know, I see all these things you did. You quit your drinking, quit getting high, all this stuff, and I'm happy for you. But you didn't give a shit enough to do it when I was with you and I know this is just another game and I've been away long enough and lived with real abused women who are real with theirselves and serious about breaking the violence, the cycle, to where I can see it now. I can see what he's doing to pull me back in, you know. He's being—I'm getting my life together so he's going to try to get his together. And now I can see it. I can see those red flags. And the whole thing is like, the whole thing makes sense, everything that he did to make me happy was just that little piece of me he just happened to latch onto. But I have all that in me I can pull out myself and you know I think I can do that.

The only thing I think keeping me back—I can say I don't want my kids to grow up being abusers and abused and that is a big part of it, 'cause I don't want that for my children. I love them and I don't want them to have a life like that. But if I'm saying I'm doing it for somebody else it's never going to work. This is for me, because I don't deserve that. It's like I want to go to school. I've got all these dreams, you know. I want to be self-sufficient, and here's the kicker, I *have* been self-sufficient, I've just supported somebody else. I had to be. I think I could handle the work and support my family part. But it's like I need to build my own self-confidence and slowly but surely I'm achieving that. The only thing I think is going [to help]—and I know people here have heard me say—wisdom and knowledge are the only things I seek. I don't want pity. I don't want empathy. I want education.

Before, I've never tried to get educated. I knew "run from the abuser." And after you've been gone for a few hours, then "run right back." I never took time to get an education. I just want to know everything there is to know about an abuser. And everything I need to know, I can just look back and see the men I've been with. And it's all about wisdom and knowledge and keeping your focus, because if you lose your focus on you and your future, you're going to go back into theirs. And that's stupid; I don't want to do that.

[Q: Were there ever any jobs that you liked or that you had potential for, but never got to explore?]

Yeah, I'm a housekeeper by trade, believe it or not. And I was real good at it and I worked in hospitals. My one area where I work, I'm real good at my work. I worked in a hospital once and they gave me a block of rooms. I did really good in my own area so they gave me my own area. I did really good, I stayed up and I was real particular about it. I even got a letter of recommendation because I had to clean the morgue. Because—oh, this is really interesting. I had this belief because I was with Dale at the time—and at home you could look around and there was always—I could clean up after a fight, but there was always a speck of blood somewhere on my walls and I hated that. I hated that. And I had to clean the morgue; that was part of my area. Well, there was the autopsy table with all the blood. And I had this belief that if I could get all the blood off of that autopsy table that the abuse in my home would stop. I don't know how I associated that. But the morgue was brick, painted brick, you know, it's got those little holes. I would go through with a toothbrush and a toothpick, a wooden toothpick, trying to get the blood out of the little holes [laughs]. Now, when I look back at it, it was crazy, but the whole time I was working in the morgue, cleaning the blood, it was somebody else's blood I was cleaning, it wasn't mine. So, that was a comfort. So, the whole time I was doing it—I would replay all those years, my aunt Susan, and my mom, just everything. And my morgue was spotless. It was absolutely spotless. And I did such a good job that another hospital in the area checked around wanting a housekeeper for surgery, and I guess my boss was a friend of this guy at the other hospital. He said if you want to use her to train your people, you know, I'll send her over. Because we had a rotation because they were all affiliated. So, I got to go over there in surgery and clean. The coolest part about it—I found it real relaxing. I got to go in on surgeries, right?

Also, going back to the other hospital, I got to go in on the autopsies, and what was really weird, there was a woman that they dragged her out of a pond. She'd been in a pond for three months. And it was a mysterious death. Well, after they got her all cleaned up and everything, turns out she got beat to death. And her ex-boyfriend was prosecuted for her death. And I followed that story because I saw that woman come into the morgue and it was weird watching the trial and reading about it in the paper. And I kept picturing that woman laying on the table and stuff. That always bothered me.

When I got transferred over to the other hospital in surgery, we'd get people in there, women and children, I mean, a bunch for lots of different kinds of surgery. But every now and then we'd, I'd get to go in on a woman who had just, had been—just beat to hell. And they would have to go in and like remove her spleen and shit, where she got beat. And it was one thing, it was weird seeing a dead body that got beat, and then a woman go through all that shit in surgery from being beat, it was weird. When it was me going through all that pain and stuff, that was one thing, but to actually sit and watch these other women go through it—it would—it was never going to happen to me. And it did.

I've got a scar here, right underneath my chin here [gestures to show scar]. My first husband, I fixed him dinner one night, and I don't know why our fights were always over dinner—I must be a bad cook, man [laughs]. We had pork chops one night, and his pork chops had to be broiled first so they'd stay tender and garlic, 'cause garlic was a health food. And then fried in canola oil—that was a "have-to." And I don't know what happened, but he bit his meat and he said, "This tastes like shit." And the only thing I said was, "I did it just like I've done it every night." And this "other guy" came out of him—that's what he said, it was "the other guy"—and put a knife through my chin, trying to cut my tongue out so I couldn't back talk him anymore. I don't know.

Trying to understand an abuser is beyond anything I'll be able to do. You can't understand them. But it's weird how they can make an excuse for everything they do. And sometimes it really makes sense to us. Something as weird as "the other guy." And Dale had him down to a T, had him down to a T. And he didn't have a split personality, you know, there was no split personality. There was no paranoid schizophrenia, nothing. This was something he created himself to cover the abuse. And it literally fooled me. They are that creative, you know. That's creative. There are people [who] say, "I got drunk," or "I had a bad day," oh, hell no, "it was another person coming out of me" [laughs]. But they are convincing. He convinced me that it was another part of him—you know, his "protector." You know, it's stupid, now—but during the abuse, that was an excuse for it.

I haven't met an abuser yet that enjoyed doing the abuse, that did not feel, or did not claim to feel remorse afterwards. Yet, they'll do it again and again and again. I don't know about that, you know; if I feel bad for doing something, I'm not going to do it again. Of course, that's me. But, I've seen Dale, I've seen several men, sit and cry for what they've done and tell me they were sorry and all of that, and then it would happen again. And it's gotten to the point where *sorry*'s just a word; it has no meaning. I don't believe in the word *sorry*. It's just a word. It has no meaning at all. If they were sorry and if they felt real remorse, they would do something about it, you know.

With Dale, that knife was the final thing. And I remember Aunt Susan hitting that tree, and it was just like, I was ready to commit suicide. I was tired and I didn't want to do that, but I sure as hell didn't want him to kill me *for* me [laughs]. If I'm going to go out, I want to do it myself, thank you. But yeah, it got scary. And my oldest son, he got to witness it. And he was old enough to scream and know that I was hurt. And there was one time I remember I kept trying to tell him, "Go to the bedroom—go to the bedroom," and he wouldn't listen to me and he just stood there, and I remember just laying there and looking up at him and I'll never forget the expression in his eyes. I won't ever forget that look. But he couldn't look away, you know, it was like he couldn't look away. I don't want him to grow up and think that's right. And I don't want him to ever see it happen again.

My personal belief is that in order to stay with an abuser, you literally become an abuser, in one way, shape, or form. Because I know, being abused,

I've learned how to use those tactics on other people, and I think that's where the whole cycle begins. And I know if I don't stop it then I'm going to be just as good at it as all those abusive men, every one of them. I've picked up so many traits from them. And I think of all the traits in them that I hated. And it was sick the day I found myself doing it, or having those thoughts, being able to rationalize why I did things that I did. To where I was hurting people and I'd think I really didn't want to do that, but where's the next one. I think with alcohol and drugs, you know, you've got to hit your bottom. I think it's the same thing with an abused woman, you've really got to hit bottom, and there's a mirror on the bottom where you've got to look at yourself before you say enough's enough. And it hurt, because everything I thought I was and wanted to be, I wasn't. That's the most lowest feeling that I've ever felt in my life. That was the worst.

Margaret's Story

YOU KNOW I REALLY don't remember a whole lot about my childhood. I think that's really odd, because when I talk to other people they can tell me incidents that happened in their childhood, and I'll sit back and I'll think and I just don't remember. I don't remember having a happy childhood.

I think that we had a really good home. I loved my parents to death, and they were the best parents ever. But growing up, I don't think I ever found "happiness," and I think I struggle with that today because I tend to become more depressed or get in a "funk" mood. I think that has a lot to do with when I was growing up, and I don't remember a whole lot of it. So, about my childhood, I don't remember a lot, and that bothers me a lot when I can't remember it. I know that we went on family vacations and that was a lot of fun. I was the youngest of three children; I had two older sisters. And I can't understand why I can't remember more. My parents always let my friends come over.

I don't think I got a whole lot of self-esteem growing up at all. I remember when I got a job in a convenience store as a manager, my mother was very skeptical that I could actually run that store and handle the money. She's never really given me the "open door." You know how today, I'll tell my kids, "The sky's the limit; go for it—I'll support you." I didn't ever get that. That might be one of the reasons I got pregnant at the age of fifteen. I wanted to get out of there.

She was always there. She always helped get me and my husband out of trouble. She would give us the money for rent. I lived on Aid to Families and Dependent Children for a while. When I was married the first time, at the age of fifteen, my parents were very supportive. They asked if I would have an abortion, but I said I wouldn't. My mom had my brother when she was fifteen. When I decided that I would have the baby, I decided to marry the father. So we did, and we got into subsidized housing, and I had a best friend in the same building. Unfortunately, they two had an affair. My husband had an affair with my best friend. It was Christmastime and things weren't going very well, you know. He smoked pot and he drank, and I didn't. It was really odd. We were *very* different. And what I saw in him, I don't know. You know, when I sit back and reflect on the two men—I've been married three times—and two of those men I don't understand what attracted me to them. I'm actually embarrassed to talk about it. So, I think that's where it all started. It started with a lack of self-esteem. I really think if I had believed in myself more, was in touch with myself more, liked myself more—I think I used sex as a tool to get guys to like me, especially him. Actually, I even tried to get pregnant. It didn't just happen. I really was out to get my parents.

I got married on [a] Tuesday; my birthday was three days before. I was fifteen. And it was fine, but obviously I didn't give him what he needed because he went elsewhere. And we didn't have anything in common. And we got to doing different things. I just wanted to raise my child, you know, and have that American dream, having my husband go to work and you get to stay at home. That's what I was looking for, and obviously I didn't get it. And when it was Christmastime and I found out that he was having an affair with my best friend, and I'd been confiding in her, letting her know how I feel, how things were going, how I wasn't feeling very good about us in bed. She lived right above me but on the other side of the building. So I would go out of my apartment and go up the stairs, and hers would be the first apartment on the right. And I started realizing that around one o'clock in the morning, I would hear footsteps, boots that sounded like my husband's boots, and I finally started to spy on them and found out that he was living with her, and that was really devastating.

Later I found out that he'd also had another affair with one of my best friends before this one, that he eventually married, and the only reason I found out about that one was that Susie felt really guilty and had to come to me and tell me what she'd done. So, it was like I had two friends in the world and both of them had been sleeping with my husband. Well, at that point, I was like, "forget it." So, unfortunately, I was pregnant again with Jerry's child, and I tried to hold on to him but I knew he wasn't happy.

I moved back home, pregnant, nineteen years old, and I had a two-year-old and a new baby. And he would never come, would never ever come to see them. When I was going to the hospital to have the child, he didn't, he wouldn't even come. He had this new wife or girlfriend. He didn't want to have anything to do with me or the children. And Keith was at this time best friends with Ryan, who was her son. So, leaving was not only leaving the only daddy he knew, he was also leaving his best friend that he had. So, that was really hard.

There I was, alone with two kids, and I'm thinking: *Who* in the world would want a nineteen-year-old girl with two kids? I kept thinking: Where in the world would I ever find anybody? And I was on welfare and I hated that. I hated getting aid. I would have conflicts with my mother about raising the kids, because I wanted to do it one way and she had her own thoughts, and we were living in her home. So, I struggled with that constantly. Do I stand up to my mom, or do I let her try to raise them, you know, what do I do about it? She was a big help; we fought a lot, but she helped me quite a lot, too.

I finally got to move into a subsidized apartment with Keith and Craig and I met a man named Roger. And Roger was very, very nice. But he was one of those types—reflecting back—he was a con artist, a full-fledged con artist. He had a full-time job and he had a house on the river that he shared with two roommates. And he worked in communications and he really seemed to have everything together. And I met him through a friend of mine and he fell in love with my children before he fell in love with me, and I thought, oh, who would accept two kids as his own? Who would ever do that? And I opened up my heart to him, being reluctant, because I had just been burned, and I told him how I felt, and how Jerry had pretty much deserted his children, and how he wouldn't come to see them or send them presents, and how awful I thought that was, and how awful it was that just anybody could bring any children into the world and not take the responsibility for them. That was just baffling to me. And he promised me that he wanted to do right by them. If we got married, he would adopt the children, and it was like a dream that he came out of nowhere. He swept my parents off their feet, just everybody loved him and thought he was the best and would treat me like a queen and he just had everything going for him.

Well, I decided to marry him and I said that. Well, then things started to change. He started to pretty much live with me and I didn't like that much. I'd tell him, "You need to go back to your own home," because he wasn't on the lease and I might get kicked out of my apartment. But he really wouldn't go. He just kind of stayed there and he started drinking, then a little bit more, and that didn't go very well, and then he lost his job because he was so obsessed with me, just wanting to be with me, that he no longer had a job, and his attitude started to change a little bit, and this was all before we got married. But I felt so committed; we already had all the wedding invitations sent out, my best friend was flying out to be in the wedding, and I just felt too scared to say, "We have to stop," that it's gone too far and it's not going to work out. To this day I don't know why I couldn't call it off. I remember on the night of the rehearsal dinner I was in the bathroom crying 'cause I had ran out of the church, and my best friend came in and pretty much said, "You've got to marry him—you've bought this dress, we've bought the cake and everything, and everyone is here and everyone's in town and you can't back out; you're just having cold feet."

So, I think it still has to do with that whole self-esteem thing. I had never gotten any growing up. I just went from one relationship to another without believing in myself and what I actually had to offer someone, so I went ahead with the wedding, and that is probably the worst mistake I have ever made.

Because when we first got married he still had—he lied and he would tell the truth, and I never knew which was which. Like he lost his job and then he started working in St. Louis, and that lasted for about three months, and then he came home. And he would have hundreds of dollar bills laying around, and once in a while, Jerry would come to see Keith and Craig and then he would make sure the money was flaunted on the table. He wanted to show Jerry that he could take care of us. And then the kids would cry and didn't want to go with him [Jerry], but I felt like they needed to go with him, to get to know who their real dad was. Eventually that fizzled away and Jerry never came to see them anymore, didn't call, and didn't want to have anything to do with them.

This seems like another lifetime. This doesn't even feel like it happened to me. When he quit the job in St. Louis, he came home, then he went to Chicago and stayed with my sister; she had an apartment up there. At this time we still lived in Pottersville, in Ohio, then we moved into an old farmhouse in a neighboring state that was really run down and needed a lot of work. I'm trying to think what job he had when we moved out there. I still don't think he had a job then, but I couldn't live in that housing division anymore when I got married, because you always have to show what you make to prove you are qualified for that housing. So we moved out there hoping he would find a job, but he didn't, and so I went and got a job at Wal-Mart and I was pregnant with my third child.

But before that, before I began to work at Wal-Mart, Roger had previously tried to find other jobs but was unsuccessful, and then he got all involved in this food pantry thing. He just got so involved in it, I can't think of a better word to use. I guess right before that time he'd moved to Chicago and was trying to have a, get a job there. I forget the name of the company where he said that he worked. I worked at Breaktime and was their shipping manager and at least it had income coming in. Because ever since we got married, he hasn't supported me at all. We lived on food stamps and ADC for a while, and I got so sick of that. I just hated that. So, I got a job and he would watch the children, or I had a cousin who would watch the children. But he got this job in Chicago and we were so excited, I thought "great," 'cause my sister lived in Chicago, and now I could live close to her. Well, he rented an apartment and I quit my job and we went up there, and you know what? We could never find the apartment that he rented, nor did he ever have a job. He took it that far, and probably to this day he would probably tell you that he had a job in Chicago, and yet when we—I still don't know how that really played out in my mind, because at this point I started not to trust him. He had a boat and a Jeep, but that was repossessed from our house and it was done in the middle in the night and he gave me the story that his friends came, they were coming to take it, and we would get it back later; and things would come up missing, or I thought I'd paid a bill, and then it would get shut off and just—the lies kept going around.

One night he said he was in a car accident and he had, like four hundred dollars on him, and he paid it to the person that got in the car accident that he hit, but yet there was nothing, no scratches on the Jeep, you know; one lie led into another and so I started to kind of "eagle-eye" him and kinda watch and ask more and more questions. But the more questions I asked, the more attitude I got. And I finally said, "I want out," that this was not the way it was going, and I wasn't going to live my life that way, and that he needed to find a job; and by this time he was so involved with the food pantry that the lady that ran it thought that I was an awful person because I didn't want my husband to work there anymore. But she didn't understand that he wasn't bringing in any money, and it's not that that isn't important, but that is a necessity to pay the bills.

And I found that I was pregnant; and that pregnancy was a total mistake, and actually I didn't even have sex with him until one night he forced me to have sex with him and that was the night I conceived and so I—I would take the pill like, three or four times, and then I'd miss one day, and I'd make it up the next day, and you know, I wasn't having sex until he got his life back on track; that was one thing I wasn't going to do. Because I didn't want to end up getting pregnant. I was having problems anyway with the birth control after having Craig before I got pregnant with Bobbie, so they were changing the dosage on that, too, so between that and not even wanting to have sex, I just kinda played with the pill.

Unfortunately, he got tired of waiting and didn't want to wait anymore. The whole entire time I kept saying "no" and tried to push him away. But he'd [say] like [using a deep, threatening voice], "You're my wife, you have to give me this." And I'm like [makes gesture and sound to indicate a cut throat] "okay," and so I kinda just laid limp, you know, and I ended up getting pregnant out of that, which was just—uggggh. I was never so angry! So, once again, I tried to put my heart back in it, tried to make things work.

By this time, I was working at Wal-Mart and I was five months pregnant, and nobody knew I was pregnant; that's the only reason I got the job. When I probably turned about seven months pregnant, I started really showing, and people began to ask questions, and I 'fessed up and said I was pregnant, and after a while, they were like, they didn't really want me to work there, but there wasn't much they could do about it. They felt kinda really lousy that they hired me. After that I got a job at a convenience store that Roger started working at part-time, and Roger was working there, and I found out that he was taking money from there, and—ugh!—that was a burden to hold. But at the time, I thought, well, it's bringing some extra money. I don't really like the idea, but

I got tired because I had to do the bill-collector stuff, and they were always after me and things were being shut off and my car was going to get taken, you know, and Roger had a tendency to spend more than what he would make. He would buy a brand new Chevy truck, and then I'd [be] like, "How can you do this? How can anybody sell you a truck?" But you know, I'd [help him]—why would I co-sign on it? Why would I sign for the truck also, you know? I don't know. And I still think about times, like why would I do things.

But one part of my relationship—he got a job with a painting company and he made a lot of money there for about a year, and he spent a lot of money on me at Christmas, and he said, "This is to make up for all the times," you know, "that I wasn't bringing in any money." At this point in time, we moved to a new home, a nicer home. The house before that we lived in, the landlord was friends of my family, and it really kept going back to my mom that we weren't paying our rent, and we were like five months behind and they were kicking us out, and my parents paid the rent, and we had a lot of financial problems, and a lot of—he still, like, lied to me all the time, and he would go out and he would drink, and sometimes he wouldn't come home, and sometimes he would come home and he wasn't very nice . . .

But when he got that job at the painting place he seemed to change a little bit. He seemed to be able to hold the job and be nice and bring in money, and that helped a lot, and we got to move into this other house, which was really nice—and the landlord dropped the rent down so we could afford it, and it was just awesome. And we moved in there the same time I had Bobbie, which was in November. And after Bobbie was born—oh, I should back up for a second—

After I got married to Roger I let him adopt Keith and Craig. So, they both have his name, and their name before was Jerry's. And so, for a while when our relationship seemed to go well, then Roger adopted them. So, then, I had Bobbie, and at first I didn't want to have a whole lot to do with him. Roger took care of him a lot. I was sick. I had my tubes tied during that time and—no, back up . . .

When I had Bobbie, I just seemed to become more kinda depressed a little bit, but Roger took care of Bobbie more than I did, I would have to say. And things were going really well until he lost his job, which seemed to be a [again, gesture like cut throat] pattern. He did that all the time: He'd get a job, things were going really well, then boom, he got into a fight and you know he'd come home and he'd lost it. It just got to be a mess. Well, his temper got to be a lot more, really worse in this house, because I can remember him punching, like, the walls and in the door. He put a big hole in the door, and the landlord found out about it and really, that was a mess. And Roger would tell me that they gave us permission to remodel, like, the upstairs bathroom. And so, like

Roger did because he worked in that business, and they didn't give permission. And when they came in to just take a look, they were shocked and I would say, "I thought that you gave permission . . ." I always felt like I was in the middle—between the world and my husband—and I didn't want to support him anymore. By this time—I just got so fed up with it and I didn't support him like I should have. When you are married to a husband, you know [you're supposed to support him], but I got so tired of the lies, and I didn't know when it was lies, when it was the truth, you know.

So when I got this job at this convenience store as the manager, of course I couldn't manage Roger. He did not think that I could be his boss, and so he would have to quit that part-time job, although he would come in there and evil-eye me because this was the most popular place that people would come in and out of and guys would come in and talk to me. Oh, he hated that. He would come in and throw his arms and his temper would just keep getting worse, and I can remember one time we were fighting in, like, a dining room that we didn't have any furniture in and he would get in my face. Well, at that time, I was just getting so sick of it I would get right back in his face and then he would pick me up and throw me across the room or something. Or he'd punch a wall and say, "Next time it will be you." And I just got so tired of that. And I got tired of him not wanting to help with the kids. He was drinking so much that I decided, okay, I'm done with it. I've tried.

I saw a minister, a pastor used to come into town, and I would say, "Would you mind, would you talk to us?" And we would go and talk; we went and talked to this guy, and there was one thing that he said that bothers me still today. He says, "One of you is trying and the other one's not trying at all, and I'm not going to tell you which one is who." So, when we left there, he's like, "See, you're not trying. You're not trying. You're not supporting me, you're not giving me the support I need and you're not trying." So, I'm, like, argh! That didn't help at all, you know, I don't know why this minister wouldn't just say who's not trying, because I really thought, "Roger's not trying here," and I've given every effort that I could to support him, but yet he kept giving me the mistrust, you know. He would tell me something, and later I'd find out it's not true, and he thought it was awful that I'd snooped around and I'm like, "I wouldn't have to do that if you would just be on the up-and-up with me."

So, I finally decided that I'd had enough. And he helped me find an apartment and everything and helped me start moving in. And when I started moving in, he said, "Well, the kids are just going to stay with me. So, you can have your time alone. He made me feel like it was me that had all these problems and that he had it together. I still don't know, to this day can't tell you how he can manipulate me and how he can make me believe things that weren't true. But before I moved out, I mean I had my stuff in there, but I really wasn't living there, the kids came to me and said, you know, "Mommy, we don't want you to move out, we want you to stay here with us. Please don't leave us." And I'm like, "I'm not leaving you guys," you know. And so I never moved out. I lost the money on the deposit and moved back and ever since then he knew that he had the kids to play against me. He'd played with me before with the kids but at that time it was pretty obvious. There's a lot of subtle things that had happened—

But then things kept getting worse. And then once he lost that job, then I was supporting us. I was working two jobs and I had gone back to school full-time—so I was working full-time, working part-time as an aerobics instructor, also going to school full-time. And the more education I got, the more Roger started to get furious. The more friends I made, the more he got furious and the more he didn't trust me and, you know, if he'd come into the store and saw me talking with a man, oh, my, that was the end of the world. And it got really, really bad. He got so possessive. I couldn't even go out to lunch with a mutual friend, a guy friend. There was no way. I was not allowed to do that. And he would be at the bar all the time before he came home and it just escalated. He would yell at me and his was really more emotional abuse. He would yell and tell me how worthless I was, and what did he ever see in me? And it was so emotionally damaging to me that, you know, to begin with I didn't have any self-esteem, anyway.

Now this was my second marriage that was going bad, and I kept thinking: "What's wrong with me? What's wrong with me?" And he was starting to turn our mutual friends against me, and it got really, really bad. And there was two times that I went to a women's shelter. I went there because [long pause] the emotional abuse was getting so bad that I would catch myself just sitting and rocking and not wanting to be involved in anything. And to this day I don't know what took me to the women's shelter. I still couldn't tell you what exactly, why I went there. And when I was there, I saw all these people being physically abused, and I thought, gosh, mine is not bad. Mine is just telling me how awful I am, and I can't really remember what took me there. I must have . . . I think there's a lot of things I've blocked, because it's just so vague; that they taught me about the cycle, about how it starts emotional and how it keeps going, and I thought, "That was really neat," and I learned a lot from that visit.

Then, when I would go back to him, things weren't getting any better, and I was trying to communicate with him more, and he finally, through his dad, got a job in Kansas City and we were going to move. And this was the big decision I had. Was I going to move with him, or was I going to stay and try to support the three children by myself. Well, after talking with the priest, and after going to the women's shelter and talking with them—*they* said, up and down, don't go, because what he's doing is taking you away from your family, the friends that you know, the security that you know. 'Cause now he can't stand it that you're—I'm becoming more educated than he was and, you know, I'm not this country girl anymore, and I'm not listening to the right kind of music anymore, and, you know, I wasn't wearing the clothes that I should wear. And they were telling me, "Don't go. He's taking you to a place where you don't know anyone—just him—and you're going to have to depend on him," and not to go. Well, gosh, it was my second marriage. I didn't want it to fail. I felt like a failure. I felt like I wasn't giving it my whole 100 percent, so I went. I went with him, packed up everything, and I thought, okay, we couldn't do it in one place, let's see if we can make the marriage work in another, because we're away from all the problems, everything that happened—you know, we're blaming it on everybody.

So, we moved. And at first it was fine, it worked and all because I just stayed at home. But then, I started working at the same place he started working at, and I was working in the front office and got to meet and got to know some of the guys that worked there, and I started teaching aerobics there, and I started going to school. Well, the more people I met, the worse it got. And he would go drinking and this was when it really escalated. I can remember incidents where [long pause] he would push me, and I remember one time that he pushed me over the couch, and I went down into the hallway into the bedroom and he followed me, pushed me on the bed, and I was screaming for him to get up because he was hurting me, and he was sitting on my hips with his hands on my wrists, holding them down and yelling at me and saying that he would beat me, or whatever, and so the only thing I thought of to protect myself was to spit on him, and I did. That was wrong. Because he smacked me really, really hard across the face. Then he got up. At least he got up and he left me alone. And then, he turned and he threw—we had one of those oscillating fans on a pole—and he threw that at me.

The more he drank, the worse temper he got, and I remember one time that we were going to go home for Christmas, come back to my parents' house, that was a five-hour drive and we were supposed to leave right after he got off work, which was at four, and he didn't get home until, like, six, and he was drunk as could be, and the kids was wanting to go and I was wanting to go, and it just escalated, and finally we got in the car to go, and on our way home he pulled over and said, "Get out." I said, "I'm not getting out." And he says, "Just get out. I'm so sick of you. Just get out." And the kids were screaming, "No, Mommy, don't get out," you know. And Roger was trying to push me out of the car in the middle of nowhere. And finally he—I begged and pleaded, you know, I begged and pleaded for me to stay.

You know, it's funny, remembering, compared to all these other women I would see in the shelter, mine was not as bad as theirs but the more I would learn about emotional abuse, to me emotional is worse than the physical, but still it doesn't seem like it was ever that bad. Isn't that odd? And there's a lot of stuff I haven't said. I always remember just sitting in the bathroom and rocking and wanting the lights to stay out and not being social at all and never smiling. And that was never me. I was always outgoing and always athletic and always wanting to do things. It probably changed me.

He would make the kids do everything for him and that was driving me nuts: "Keith, go get me a beer; Craig, go change the T.V. station; go do this; did you pick up that; did you clean this; did you do that?" And I'm like, "These kids are *not* your slaves. You get up and you go and you do stuff and you help." And he would never help around the house, you know. He'd come home and he'd sit in the bathroom for two hours and whatever, and come out and sit on the couch, and that's all he'd want to do—that and have sex. That's all he ever wanted to do. And I just got so tired of that. And the more I started to stand up to him, the worse it got.

One time [long pause]—there are so many little things, they're not really little things but, you know, that have happened—he [long pause]—I had to have surgery. I had cancer of the cervix, but it wasn't that severe, but I already had three kids and no marriages were ever working, and I was just like, just take out my uterus. I was always having female problems anyway, and so I got the doctor to do that [a note of contentment in her voice]. So, I went in and I had surgery and my parents came up. And by this time, my parents hated coming to visit. They wouldn't come, because Roger and them didn't get along, because whenever I had a problem I'd call them, or I'd call my sister in Chicago, and so they knew about everything that had gone on, and all the lies, and everything that he's done, which it's hard to remember all the details [long pause], that's one thing I always tried to forget. But I went in and I had surgery and when I came out, when they were done with surgery, they had left a sponge inside of me and so they did that, they went in and had the surgery, vaginal, but they left this sponge inside of me, so they had to cut me in my stomach to get the sponge out, because when they started to unpack me, it started to bleed and they didn't want me to hemorrhage, so they cut me to get the sponge out. Well, I don't handle abdominal stuff very well because my stomach was so toned, because I exercised all the time, that it really, really hurt. I don't know if people "untoned" go through the same thing, I don't know, but I just know I don't handle incisions on the abdomen very well.

So, I went home, and this garbage has piled up at my home. I'd been in the hospital, like, four days, okay, and this garbage is just heaping. And after my surgery my mom took my kids home with her, because she wasn't going to stay at that house with Roger, there was just no way. "No one would come out alive" is pretty much how she put it. She respected me for trying to make it work, but she felt that I had really gone too far with it. But at that time I was, like, "Stay out of my life. Let me run it. Let me take charge of it, and I'll deal with it." Her way to deal with it is to just pick up the kids and go. So, when I got home, Roger's brother was staying with us—which was no problem, he was a nice kid—and I had just gotten home and Roger had gone to work, and so we were both there and doing whatever. And I said, "Why don't we call and see how much a trash dumpster would be to get all this trash out of here, it's just not healthy." And so I did. And so, when he got home that day, I told him about it, and oh, my gosh, you would think I had just committed adultery. He was so angry. He yelled. He was like right here in my face and pointing his fingers at me, you know. And I had just had surgery, and I had this towel over me and I'm just crying, holding the towel, and sitting on the corner of the couch—couch—I can remember this just like it was just yesterday—rocking and listening to him yell, and anymore the words, the words just—you never heard the words, you just heard the voice. And his brother left, he went outside, he didn't want to be a part of it. He [Roger] threw this fan at me and it was just awful. So, as soon as he left, out into the yard to cool off, I crawled—I literally crawled—crawled to the phone. I picked it up. I called my sister in Chicago and I said, "In one hour you call here, and you make up whatever excuse possible to come get me. I don't care what you do. Don't let him say no. You get in your car and you come get me tonight." And she goes, "Are you okay?" I say, "For right now, I am, but you need to come get me." And she did. In exactly one hour the phone rang and it was her and Roger had come in right before that and had said, "What are you doing?" He was like a totally different person. "Get up. What are you doing?" Like he had never did that to me. And he said [deep, threatening voice], "You just sit there rocking, not saying anything—what's wrong with you?" And I'd be, like, "Were you just not here. Did you just not experience what I experienced. Am I like losing it? What is going on?" I mean, this emotional abuse had been building for a long time. [Crying]

And my sister called, and I'm not supposed to drive or ride in a car. I mean I had just had major surgery and so she came and got me. I even told her when she came and got me, she said, "So, are we going to spend the night here?" And I said, "No way. Let's just get in your car and let's go." It was a three-hour drive. And she had just had this baby, she had her little baby with her, and he was only about three months old. And he started crying and fussing and everything and so, I had to end up driving back to Chicago while she took care of her child. And I stayed in Chicago four or five days and I let her take care of me. And Roger, he never knew anything about that, like he—and I still to this day, I've never ever brought it up because I really didn't want to talk about it, but isn't it odd that your wife would leave after just having surgery, you know? He got to go out and play, I'm sure. He didn't have the kids there or anything.

After that, and after him telling me to get out of the car at Christmas and things like that, it wasn't happy in my home, and I didn't want my kids to grow up like that. I had gone to the women's shelter in one state at this time again and they had said I was getting around to that abusive part, where he's going to start hitting me. And I didn't want that. I didn't want the kids to be around that. So, I called my parents and I was going to run away. They were going to come get me in the middle of the night, pack everything, and then just totally disappear. But the more I thought about that, the more I thought, no, that's hiding. That's not facing what I need to face, and my parents were like, "No, come, because it's getting really bad," you know. Now he was accusing me of having an affair with his best friend and it was—and it just seemed like every time he accused *me* of something—*he* did it! I'm [thinking] like, you accuse *me* of having an affair; who are *you* having an affair with? Not that I even cared, you know. Don't keep blaming me. But I felt like I was a chicken to get out like that, to just disappear. So, I didn't. I called my parents and I called it off. They already had the truck and they were going to come get me. And she was like, "Oh, what are you doing." She says, "I don't want to wake up one morning and read that you are dead in the newspaper." I said, "Well, Mom, I'll get out. I'll get out and we'll get out now."

And so I went up to him: "I want a divorce." And, whoops, that didn't go over too well. He was like—[long pause] it was like he wasn't as bad as he had been. And for three months we lived together, except we were separated. But he was more loving and more caring and more understanding and more wanting to help me do things, wash dishes. And I'm like, "You ain't changing my mind. You're not doing this to me again." Because before, I was going to leave him, and he got a job and things were going to work out, and they did work out pretty well for a short time, and then it went right back to what he used to be, like he has always done.

So, I finally found out there was an apartment complex right around the corner, and the back part of it was subsidized housing, and I couldn't afford anything on my own. So, I went there and I explained to them that it was an emergency, and I needed to get out, and they got me out of there. So, I got my own apartment, and my sister came down and helped me move stuff after Roger and I had fought fierce over who was going to get what out of this house. So—and he wasn't going to help us move out. At that time, he knew I wasn't changing my mind and he went back to drinking and cussing at me and everything. So, at that time, I was going to school, too, and there was two guys, I can't even tell you their names or whatever, I just asked them, "Could you please come and help me move my refrigerator and my washer and dryer?"

And they did. So we got all my stuff moved to the apartment and all the kids' things were moved to the apartment. And he lost the house because he couldn't afford the rent and he wasn't going to go to work anymore. Actually, by this time, he quit his job because he really thought I was having an affair with his best friend and he couldn't stand it and he quit. So, he didn't have a job again!

And I got into this apartment and everything was set and so through the divorce things were kinda okay, but things would happen—like, he would take the kids and not bring them back. Or, he was supposed to come and get the kids but never came and got them. Or, showed up drunk, and there was one time he showed up drunk and my sister was there and me and her were going to go out and have a nice dinner and the kids didn't want to go. But I said, "Just go. Go with him. All of you go." When he got there he saw that my sister was there and my sister is, you know, the Christian you look up to, the religious person. And he's like [deep, threatening voice], "Oh, yeah, like you and your sister are going to go to bars and pick up guys." And I'm like, "What are you talking about? Do you not know who this is? You know her more than I know her." And it just escalated, and he took the kids and he put them into his little red Escort and he sped out really fast. And I'm looking at that car, thinking, "Oh, God, why did I let them go?" He's drunk. He didn't have anyplace to live. He would live in a warehouse or he'd spend the week at a friend's house when he was supposed to have the kids. I mean, there was nothing stable about the kids visiting their dad. Sometimes he would, sometimes he wouldn't. And when they did go, they would be locked up in this warehouse. I didn't find that out until later, that they would stay in this warehouse all day while he worked at the bar, and at night when they wanted to eat, they would come and set in the kitchen in this bar and eat! And then they'd go back to this warehouse. Well, the kids thought it was cool because it was a big room, you know, they could do whatever they wanted. I about fell out of my skin when I found out about it.

So, that night I let them go and Julie and Jesse had come, Jesse is her little baby, a knock came at the door and when I opened the door, there was Roger with Craig in one hand and Keith in the other and their hands around his neck, and he opens the door and he pushes the two kids through the door, and he said, "Take them. I don't want them. They only want you; they don't want to be with me." And, I said, "Roger, that's fine. Let me have Bobbie, too." "No, you're not getting Bobbie and you'll never see Bobbie again." And I said, "Roger, come on." And so, he was really, really mad. I'd never, ever seen Roger as mad as he was that night. And so, I followed him out the door, saying, "Roger,"—I kept grabbing his arm—"Roger, you can't leave with Bobbie," and I could see Bobbie crying in the Escort, and I say, "Come on, Bobbie." And he'd say, "No, Bobbie, you stay in that car. You stay in that car."

And the kid is only like two, you know, two or three, and Keith and Craig are inside and my sister is inside, and my sister has never, ever been around anything like this. She only hears my stories. But it's different when you hear it, and when you see it and when you're there when it happens. He got so angry, he grabbed my shoulders and pushed me up against my glass door and he grabbed my head and put it against the glass and started punching the glass around my head. Well, my sister heard that, and I was screaming, "Call the cops! Call the cops!" And my sister came around the corner just as the glass broke and the glass went all over her and all over her baby, flew up the stair[s], I mean, glass went [over] just everything. And then he left and my sister was just freaking. She was screaming. She was freaking. And it was just a mess. And I told her to call the cops and she's like, "No. Stay inside." And I'm like, "No, I've got to go get Bobbie," you know.

And when I tried to get back outside—I got to back up here—'cause when the glass broke, Roger let go of me and started beelining to the car, and I went in because this was very traumatizing for my sister, but this was something that I was used to, you know. Yeah, it was traumatizing, but not at all like she was taking it, and I got to the point where I almost smacked her to get her to—you know: "Hello. Don't freak out like that. I need you to call and I need you to take care of Keith and Craig," because Craig was hiding behind a chair and I don't even remember where Keith was—oh, Keith was *right there,* right there with my sister, because he's always been the nosy one, wants to know what's going on. So, he was right there. So, I ran out to get Bobbie, but Roger was leaving; he ran right over the curbs, over the grass, and off he went. And I thought, oh my gosh, he's right, I'll never see Bobbie again. So I called the cops and I filled out an ex parte. A lot of good that is!

[In] about an hour the phone rang and it was Roger. And he says, "If you ever want to see Bobbie again, you meet me" in this parking lot that was abandoned. It was deserted. I knew where this parking lot was. He says, "If you ever want to see Bobbie, you'll come meet me alone." And I say, "Roger, I'm not going to come meet you in that parking lot." I said, "If you want to talk, let's go to a public place and we'll talk and you can give me back Bobbie then." And he says, "No. If you want to meet me, I'll be there, and if you're not there, you'll never see Bobbie again." And that is the hardest thing I've ever done in my life, is say, "Okay." And I hung up the phone. [Crying.] But I knew he'd kill me. I mean, that was really, really hard.

But my sister got so upset that she called her husband and he came down from Chicago and stayed with us that night and the next morning before anyone was even up the phone rang and it was Roger. And he says, "Bobbie is awake. He's crying for you to come get him. You come alone. You don't bring anybody with you. You just come get him." And I say, "Okay." So, I woke up my brother-in-law and I said, "I'm supposed to go there by myself to get Bobbie, but I'm not that stupid." And my sister and her husband have always, they have always been my safety blanket. Roger has always acted on the up-and-up when they were around. This was the first time, they [had seen this]—and so, I *knew* it was *really, really* bad. If he could do that in front of my sister, then they were not [any] longer my safety blanket.

So, I took my brother-in-law with me and he drove and I said, "You stay in the car; park the car to where you can see inside the kitchen window and the living room window and whatever you do—don't lose sight of me. Okay?" And he said, "Okay." And I said, "Don't come in. Whatever you do, stay out in the car." So I went in and I opened the door and he let me in and he immediately shut the door and locked it behind me. And my heart just started racing and Bobbie was laying asleep in the floor. And he just needed to talk to me, I guess. So, he said what was on his mind and about half an hour later he went over and unlocked the door and said, "Pick up Bobbie" and to leave.

And I still couldn't tell you what he said to me that day. I was so scared that I didn't listen to a word that he said. [Laughs] I'm like, the minute he locked that door I froze. And I stayed in front of the window. And he'd say, "Come over here and sit beside me." And I'd say, "No, I'm fine." And he finally let me stand where I wanted to stand. And he tried to give me a hard time about having my brother-in-law drive. And I just said I was in no shape to drive, you know. And he's just staying out in the car and he would look for cops and there's no problem. Because the night before, the cops tried to find Roger and we tried to get Bobbie from Roger and that just all exploded. That didn't work out at all. The cops didn't want to go get him, and Roger, if he saw the cops, he just went berserk, but I got Bobbie the next day.

After that, Roger didn't have a whole lot to do with any of us. Well, I can't say that, because he would still have the kids every once in a while and like I would come home, and I remember one night, I had a black friend that we had class together, and we went out to eat, and so we came back to my apartment to study for a test that we had. And Roger was there, sitting on my doorstep, drunker than could be. Drunker than a skunk. And all the kids were upstairs in bed sleeping. "How'd you get in," I said to him. And he said, "You left the door unlocked." "I don't leave my door unlocked." And he says, "Well you did this time." So, I called the cops and then once they found out I was with a black guy, ohhhhh, Roger yelled at him so much. I said to him, "Rex, just get back in your car and go." He said, "I can't just leave you." And I said, "That's okay, I'm used to this. Just go. You don't need this—" and Roger was chasing this car down the street and it was just awful, so embarrassing. So, by the time the cops got there, it was—they still won't do anything to him and just told him to leave. [He was violating an ex parte.]

But back then my lawyer says it wasn't worth having an ex parte, that it wouldn't do me any good anyway. It wasn't going to be bulletproof, he said, so why bother. And by this time, I understood where he was coming from. I'd already paid my lawyer three hundred dollars, and by the time the whole divorce came through, my lawyer hated him so much he just did it all free. He just wanted this guy to pay. You know, he put him in jail a couple of times for not paying child support.

Roger would take the kids and not bring them back, and I would have to go get them in another state and bring them back. It was one thing after another. I could sit here and talk all day about all the things that have happened. And finally, it was Christmastime, and Roger was the manager at a bar, and it was Roger's year to have the kids for Christmas and I said, "Fine, you can have them. You can take them when you are off from work, come get them," or whatever.

And at that time I was dating this guy named Mark, and Mark and I were pretty close, and Mark would go to wrestling practice with Keith and teach him how to do things. Until—one day, Roger showed up there and went out on the mat and yelled at Keith, "Keith, that is not your father. He has no right being here. He's not taking care of you. I'm your father." Ugggh. It was just humiliating and then he came up to me and I was trying to not even talk to him, to ignore him, and that made it worse. And nobody, all these parents, like fifty parents in this gym, not one person tried to help. Everybody was just like looking away. But a lot of that kind of stuff would happen.

At Christmas, this was the time he was going to have them and he knew that I was having Christmas with the kids on Christmas eve. So, after I had Christmas—he knew what time, he knew all the plans—he called me and said, "I'm not going to pick up the kids for Christmas." And I went, "What? There's no way that I'm going to have these kids tomorrow morning, on Christmas morning, when Santa Claus is supposed to have been here and there's nothing for them. There's no way. You come over here and you get them." And he says, "No, I've bought some stuff for them and you just come over and get it." And I'm like, ohhh, I was so mad. So, I went over to his work, parked in the back and I got out, and he brought me a slingshot, maybe a sleeping bag and one other thing. I'm like—"What is this? I'm sorry, but Roger, I'm not going to do this." And it escalated to where he was yelling and pushing me and I got back into my car and he started to punch my window and he said, "I'm going to break it, if you don't roll it down." So I roll it down a little bit and he grabbed my head and tried to pull me through my car window, and finally I just screamed so loud that the manager came out and the cops were called. And I said to the cops, "He's supposed to come get those kids tonight. When he's off work he's coming to get them." And he did! So, I was glad for that. Although that scene wasn't good.

It's like—I just never knew what to do because I was always the one who had to make excuses. They would go in and have Christmas with Roger's parents and Roger would never have any money. So Keith's birthday was in November, and Keith always saved his money so that when Christmas time rolled around, Keith would give all his money that he saved to Roger so all of them could buy and get Christmas presents. And I used to get *sooo* angry. I'd tell Keith, "Don't give that to your dad." "But Dad said he would pay me back." But, you know, Roger's never paid a kid back. This past summer Craig actually worked for him, and Roger owes him $178, and he's never gotten the money, and that was before Roger left town.

It had gotten so bad that I think he knew in order for us, for me to stay alive, 'cause at this time he had threatened twice that his life would be a lot better if I wasn't in it. And I considered that a threat. And he finally left, and he left for a year and a half. Life was peaceful until one Christmas morning again, he calls. And I said, "Sure, you can come see them." But it's just the same old–same old, you know.

This last time, Roger has done a lot to these kids and especially through this custody thing with my younger son, Bobbie. Roger, in all of this, he has called, he's found Keith and Craig's real dad. He called him and said that I was abusing the children and that it was about time *he* came back into Keith and Craig's life, and that Keith and Craig were asking for him and that he was going to set all of them up. And when I caught wind of that—and the only reason I caught wind of that was because he gave my first husband my pager number, and he paged me 911 from North Carolina and I called and I was like, "Who is this? What are you calling me on 911 for?" "Well, I hear you're abusing my children." "What are you talking about?" "Well, I've been in contact with Roger for several months now and he's telling me all this stuff that you've been going through and that now the kids want to meet me because you are not much of a mother." And I'm like, *"What?"*

Actually, you know, Jerry believed me more than he believed Roger. And I have a deposition of that. But you know, it's really cruel. And the judge here thought it was very cruel and took it in front of one of the commissioners asking for a child protection order and she would not grant that at all. She is just worthless. The kids would go there and Roger would tell them to pack their bags and find their own way home, a four-hour drive, and yell at the top of his lungs because Craig would barricade himself in the bathroom, in the shower, and could still hear every word that Roger was saying. The only way I got the ex parte is that I lied on the stand, you know. Things really got bad. But yet I always tried to keep my feelings out it.

So, one summer Bobbie asked if he could go live there for a while, and I said sure, let's try it and see what would happen, you know. Roger would go in spells and I thought we could try it, but the minute I let Bobbie go, which is the stupidest thing I've ever done in my life, Roger would never let me see him. I would call over there and he's never there. Of course Bobbie would never call me, and I would ask for him for a weekend and the only way I could get Bobbie is if Keith and Craig would go there, but Keith and Craig didn't want to go there. And, you know, I'm not going to force them to go there, but Bobbie wanted to come to see me, but Roger could never see that. And I said, "Well, the kids can come there." So, these two would have to go there before I would ever get Bobbie. He was supposed to come one Christmas, but it was Thanksgiving time because that's when I had Christmas with my parents.

And we met halfway and that was really bad. Roger got there and he said that we were two hours late because everything visitation-wise always went through the child. I would always try to talk to Roger but it would never go well, and a couple of times I would hang up on Roger because if it wasn't his way it was no way. So sometimes I would say, "Just forget it," you know. I just got so, yuck, I just didn't want to deal with it anymore. And I was sorry that Bobbie was getting the worst of it, but I didn't know what else to do. I'd just say, "Bobbie, I love you and I'll be thinking about you on Thanksgiving and I'll call you." And that's pretty much all it's been. And then Roger would call back a couple of hours later and say, "Bobbie's really crying and he really wants you to come." So, I'd say, "Well, let's see if we can work this out"; I'm going to go back and see if we can work it out. And it always had to be on his terms.

Well, we met, and he said that we were two hours late and he was telling Bobbie that we were probably dead on the side of the road, or that Bobbie's not important anymore, that we're not coming to get him. So, he, Roger was really upset by the time we got there and Bobbie come out running and he hugged me and everything. He asked if Craig could get out of the truck, and I asked why, and he said, "Well, I have a birthday present for him. I want to give it to him." And I said, "Well," you know, "let's exchange the child and let us go." And he didn't like that response. And I felt like we were a half hour late, and I started to apologize for being a half hour late, because the exit that he told us to get off of was not there, so we had to go all the way down and turn around and come all the way back and get off on this exit. And it just escalated so bad that he threw Bobbie back in the van and took off and said, "Bobbie's not coming with you," and Bobbie's crying, begging his dad, "Please let me go with Mom—please let me go with Mom."

And we had to promise to bring Bobbie back, otherwise Bobbie wasn't going with us. And that incident is how I got my ex partes, because he got really close to me and moved my hand and pushed me and pushed the kids and the whole thing. And I had to promise to bring him back, and that was another mistake; I should have never taken him back, but I did. So, I lost custody of him and I still have problems seeing him. I lost custody of him. It happened in that other state. If commissioner Smith would ever had guts enough to stand up to the judge over there to bring him back over here. And the judge over there, after everything's said and done, said really it should have been done here.

Next week, Roger has a criminal felony charge of nonpayment of child support. He is over fifty thousand dollars behind and he could serve up to seven years in prison, if the judge decides to do that. Who knows what that judge will choose to do. And I'll have to petition the court to have Bobbie move back here. See, I'm supposed to get Bobbie this Friday, too, but let's see if I get him. He lives more than a four-hour drive from here. I'm going to drive and we're supposed to meet half-way.

And ever since this custody thing ended, Roger has not once called if Keith and Craig are there. He doesn't even hardly call them. And they know they are adopted but they don't understand that that's different. Like they'll say, "What's so different about Bobbie?" I always just say, "I don't know," because nobody knows that Keith and Craig were adopted by Roger, and for me really there isn't any difference. Like in court, Roger would try to show that these two were just adopted, but that Roger and Bobbie have this special bond that nobody else shares and that Bobbie doesn't miss his mom or his brothers, any of us, doesn't miss Stuart [Margaret's third husband].

He's eleven now, and my lawyer kept saying, "Don't put the kids on the stand, 'cause that will make the judge look bad upon you for putting the kids through that." And I didn't want to put my kids through that. It infuriated me one time that Roger called Keith to ask to testify against me in the court here, that he's never seen Roger hit me or yell at me or abuse me. He wanted Keith to get up on the stand and say that. And I'm like, Keith, if you don't want to—if you want to do it you may do it—but if you don't want to do it, don't do it. To where it got so bad that every time Roger would call here, he would just bust out crying. Keith tried to bring back a game that I had bought, just a game, and he wanted to bring it back, and he made this boy cry over a game. It is just—ahhh, the abuse that he puts those kids through. They don't even want to go there. They want to go there during the summer to the fair because they enjoy that, but they don't want to go there to see him, and Craig still thinks that if he goes there that he'll get paid for what he did last year in July. It's just one bad thing after another. And I don't know just what to say, or where to start, or what to talk about, because it is just all so bad.

[Q: What is your life like now?]

Well, actually, I think—I still have a lot of problems, and my husband lets me know that, my husband that I'm married to now. He's very supportive, but I think I do hold a lot of garbage that I need to get rid of. Actually, I'm very well. I'm a very positive person, or I try to be positive; that's hard for me to be a positive person, anymore, it's very hard [laughs nervously]. And I try to smile and I try to be light-hearted. Each day I work on that, to get better. But that's hard. And then when I hear, when I go to group, which is really hard for me, especially if they really talk about what happened to them, it's hard for me. And when I hear some of their stories I am thinking, "Mine's been nothing [crying and laughing] compared to what some of them have gone through," you know.

I still don't think I'm totally safe. I still think he could come after me. Just like this, through this whole custody thing, it was pretty tense. Everybody kept telling me: "Don't let your guard down—always look behind your back." And I still, I still don't think I'm totally safe from him yet. I don't know if I'll ever feel totally safe, but I think I have come a long ways. I got my degree and I worked hard and I like who I am. When I look in the mirror, I like who I see. Yes, I have faults, like we all have faults, but I think my kids are very well behaved. I think I'm very lucky considering everything that they have gone through that I don't have some troublemakers and they are all three Christians, and they all—even though I don't see Bobbie very much, when he comes home, he's very loving. At first he's standoffish but, boy, once he gets used to being back here he just totally just wants to sit on my lap the entire time, you know.

To me it feels like another lifetime. It doesn't even feel it's me that has gone through that. Because now I can sit back and see just how far I've come. It used to be just the mention of his name would just freak me out. I'm getting better at that. But you know, I really just can't stand him, and I struggle with that because being a Christian, I am supposed to forgive. But with him—[grimaces]—really, it would be so much better if he wasn't around. But Bobbie seems to be doing really well.

Teresa's Story

[Q: THINK ABOUT WHERE your first memories are and start from the very beginning. What was it like growing up? What do you remember?]

That's easy. Growing up in my house—I came from a dysfunctional family, very abusive, my dad and my mom fought morning, noon, night, and day. He was a farmer. I grew up with four other brothers and sisters. We weren't what you would call today a tight-knit family. What went on in our family—not only was he abusive toward my mom—it was also towards the kids as well. My dad was the kind of person that it didn't matter what reasoning it was, whether it was right or wrong, it was his own, so you were punished for things—such as what he thought was important is not putting something, you know, right back into place, but even if you put that item back, you know, where you found it, it was either always a half an inch off—he was a perfectionist type of person. And that, later on in my life, you know, came to be, as with almost anybody, a good factor or a bad. And I still find today, years later, trying to break away from that because I didn't realize until, you know, which most of us don't when we're little kids, that, being a perfectionist, to me it's more of a hazard than it is, you know, as far as being good. Because, for my sense of being a perfectionist, people don't tend to, like, want to be around you as much sometimes because, you know, it's different from being a perfectionist and finding a little spot for everything, but that was hard for me because I always—I became afraid of a lot and that's where the abuse was a lot, too. We knew that—it was a mind game, I guess you could say. We were always constantly thinking how he did it, how would he do it. Because we knew if we didn't do it his way we were going to be punished. I was never abused so bad that I could—bled or nothing like that from him—but did witness other abusive behaviors.

One in particular, he was a farmer back then and I can remember one time him coming home, and he had a herd of cattle, just truckloads of cattle, that he was getting ready to unload and, at the time my brother was in high school, and they were helping him unload these cattle and it was cold. Just really cold. And he, for some reason as always, the perfectionist he was, sadistic as well, wanted, they were out in the barn doing it, and the next minute we're hearing this very abusive verbal language as well as he did as a lot of that as well, he came running into the house and he was telling them, you know, you need to

194

get your butts downstairs and I was like, well, what's up with that? This is one of those times that I can remember as though, even though it didn't happen to me, that I will never forget about my dad and why I think I've grown up just to hate him and hate him more and more because I had to witness this particular time. He had taken my brothers downstairs and made them remove their clothes as far as their pants and we had horse hitching rings and he tied my brothers to a pole and began to whip the two of them with these metal hitching rings. And my oldest brother was always the one that whenever my mom and dad would fight would always say, you know, might go out there, you know, and make sure Mom's alright. And he always would—he always was the one that had to be the mediator and was always punished for that as well. But my dad beat these two boys so severely that when they went to take showers at school, the high school coach asked them what had happened. Out of fear, they didn't say anything.

Everybody knew, in our town, because I grew up in a small town of three hundred people and less, what our family was like. I had friends at school but that was where it stayed. There was no communication. He had gotten us a phone at one time but we were never allowed to talk on it. As a child, I always played by myself. That was why, now, I believe, I'm still isolated, because I don't know how to relate to other people sometimes. My sister and the rest of my family, we're still not close. That's for a lot of reasons, too. With him, only that because he ended up developing lung cancer and died at our house when I was fourteen. And the day he died, the night before, I didn't sleep with an ear infection, the night before he died was the nicest day he had ever been to me because I can *never* remember this man saying anything nice to any of us. There are so many episodes, it would take me forever to tell you all the things. One example would be, he would get, if he was sitting at a table, which we, you know, if that was what you want to call normal, what normal people do at nighttime to eat—but in a sense it was never normal because always when you sit down to eat what you might say or think as a normal family dinner—it would end up in a dispute of him throwing tea or him throwing dishes. It was always something over anything and everything. So, it was just like you came to the table and you never knew how to act. I think that's part of my problem today, and I don't know who I am because I never had the chance to know who I was. We were just—we were like puppets; we did what we were told to do and if you asked questions about, you know, because, you know, you're curious. You're a little kid and you're curious and you want to know, well, "What's that for?"—it got to the point where you knew if you asked, you were going to get, you know, a whipping, so therefore you don't do anything.

So you just—you tend to be in your own little world. I imagined a lot and pretended a lot. I, you know, didn't have a lot of toys. If we had one toy at

Christmastime we were lucky with that and I was really good about taking care of things because I knew it would be a long time before—if ever—I got another toy like that.

I can't say that we weren't taken care of well, but my mom worked, okay, full time, and I never understood why she put up with what he did to her. Never. I always—I'd lay at night and, even though I never felt close to my mom, she took very good care of us kids. She worked a full-time job and he, I guess, he claimed worked as a farmer, but now I know, as I grew up and I've talked to her since—you know, we're still not close—I've learned a lot of things about him. During the time that I grew up I didn't really know anything about him. I would always want him to be gone because I knew if he was there the shit was going to start, so I never wanted him to be around. I hated him. I hated him from the time I knew, even as a little kid, probably back, I'd say eight or nine, maybe ten, at the oldest, of what he was capable of doing. I knew it wasn't right. Because I would go out, even to school, because we weren't allowed to go anywhere else, okay, we didn't function like a family. What I would hear and watch on T.V., people saying "I love you," okay, our family wasn't like that.

Still to this day, if I hug my mom or tell my mom that I love her, she's like, "Why are you doing that?" you know; she can't relate to that, okay, and I often wonder if it was because she was abused, how she grew up, or just for the simple fact that he took that away from her. I believe it's all of it. You know, a lot of it, I believe from going through it, experiencing it in my life, that he drove that out of her. She's a very cold woman. She does feel that—she tends to hide those feelings, you know, she doesn't want anybody expressing to her, or she has a hard time expressing her feelings even to her own children. Her way of taking care of stress in her family is basically showing okay, that's the thing. But that abuse went on—he died when I was fourteen and I was glad.

And I'll never forget the day he died; my sister was running around the house trying to save him, and I can remember that day so vividly. It was almost like he waited till my mom left for work and he started having a breathing spell because he was in and out of the hospital full time and he went to have a breathing spell and the last thing that I remember was us running around, had no telephone again, and she got his truck keys and was like going to go to the corner to use a phone to call an ambulance. But I was like, "For what, to save him? Don't you realize that if he dies . . . ?" And I know I still have a hard time dealing with this and God, because they say the only way out of this past is to learn to forgive him. I never will forgive him for what he did. I don't care. I may die and go to hell, but it doesn't haunt me because I don't think about him, that I'm all full time because I acknowledge his presence not as my father but as a human being, okay? As a title, okay? And I acknowledge him twice a year, on his birthday and the anniversary of his death, which was a couple days ago; he died June 22, 1976, so he's been dead twenty-some years. But the day that he died, like I said, again, I was just in the focus mind of: "Let him die. Why are you running around? Why should we save him? What has he saved us from? Don't you understand that if he dies everything will end?"

And during that time I was pissed at my mom, actually for, because, well, one of the times she tried to get away from the abuse and we had five kids just spread out everywhere through families and—I'll never forget. We were away from my father then and that was when I was in eighth grade, I'd say, for three months. And so, for three months, I actually had a chance to be a teenager. I actually was allowed to go places, I was actually allowed to have friends. I was actually starting to feel like a human being. And she would write us letters and during those times, you know, even then I can remember, her saying she loved us. And the day she came back and told us that we were going back, I was like, "You don't love us, because if you loved us you'd keep us away from that abuse." I didn't want to go back. Okay?

And so me and my brother—my brother, I'll remember this, too, for a long time: He went and hid in the church; he wanted to pray because that's how afraid he was to go back to the violence. And he was the favorite. He never, ever went through any abuse. He was daddy's little boy. Nobody ever got a lot for Christmas, but boy, Bobby did. He was the baby. Bobby got everything. He was his little buddy. So Bobby went and hid so that tells me—Bobby and I were close—that told me Bobby does not like him. Bobby had feelings. He went to a church—that's where we found him, praying in a church because he was afraid for the safety of his family. And, you know, it kind of blew all of us away because, you know, we never thought that any of us would have feelings like that, you know, I know I didn't. I never prayed to God, you know. The only thing I ever thought was, "I'm free. I'll never have to go back to this shit again."

But we went back and I asked her, "Why are we going back? Why? Give me one reason why you want to go back to any of that. You know, there's days that you—you have worked your tail off. Seven days a week. You cook for seven people, frying seven or eight chickens, you know, working clear up till ten or eleven o'clock at night. To what? Go back to his abuse? When is your free time? This is your freedom. Now. Go." And she went back.

But from that time on, I grew hatred toward my mom. Because I couldn't understand—now, this, of course, too, is all before he died. Okay, I'd say this is months before he died; I could not understand: "Why are you doing this—not to us but to yourself?" You know, and then years later, I would ask her, I'd be like, "So, okay why *did* you go back?" And she'd still say, "Because of the kids." And I'm like, "I can't buy that because, you know, none of us want to be around him."

We don't—I don't consider him my dad. My dad's . . . "I don't have a dad." That's what I would tell people. "Well, where's your dad?" "I don't have one." I would lie. I would *lie*. I would lie because I was so embarrassed and ashamed of what he was. I'm like—I guess I used to sit back and think, "How could I have been put—or any of us—in this kind of situation? Why?" So that's when the fantasies and the pretense of what small times we got to play, protecting my life, you know, it was an escape, I know now, just to get the hell away from anything. But that never lasted very long, you know, because if he even was in the other room he would either say, "What are you doing in there?" to where he would bother you so much that you couldn't play, or he would purposely come in and see that you were doing playing and he would disrupt it. "Okay, it's time to go pull weeds." He *always* had that control, always. He was sadistic. But, finally, I have—I am working on that process. Like I said, I don't know if I'll ever forgive him.

You know, I will say this. I don't hate him anymore for what he did, because I just came to the conclusion what, you know, people told me he couldn't help that. Well, I don't buy that, either. I just believe that possibly he was abused. I don't know, you know. I have tried to find out a lot of things and I didn't find that out. But anyways, I went from that and then, in my life with me and my mom, it was just the two of us. My sister, she had already moved out and had a baby. Everyone was doing their own thing. Bobby, before my dad had died, my mom had sent him off to a Catholic school so he was away from the abuse so he—he was pretty much doing his thing. Everybody was just doing their own thing. That's when—life was starting to get good, okay? I was probably a sophomore or junior in high school. I had two jobs. I had a car. I was popular in high school then. I was in cheerleading. My high school years were the best years of my life. If I had one wish on this earth, it would be to go back to high school because my mom used to tell me to "enjoy your high school years," because once you get out, you know, it will be a rough life, and she's right.

I thought I had problems then, but man that was like the heaven of it, you know, because you had school, you had friends, you really had no worries; you had none. Compared to what I've learned, you know, twenty years later. And, I enjoyed school; I, you know, often thought I'd go to college, but that, you know, never worked out. I got into what we all get into: drugs; I got pregnant when I was seventeen.

My daughter is now nineteen, getting ready to give me my first grandbaby. But that too is another issue. I won't go into great detail, but with that pregnancy, because my mom had raised us Catholic, abortion as a method of birth control [snicker] we were not even taught of. I'm not going to say that I had sex to find out, because for many years I never even enjoyed sex, because

I didn't know what it was. Because sex—how could you know what sex is, or even love, or any of that, if you're not shown it in your home? You know, I never saw my mom and dad kiss, I didn't know any of that. But, I knew one thing: that the guy that I hanged with, I was attracted to him just as a human being. He made me feel good as a human being. He was the first person that ever showed any kind of care towards me and we had a yearlong relationship. When I got pregnant, he offered to marry me. And I told him no, so he went ahead and went off to school because I knew that yeah, he cared about me, but deep down the kind of person I was, that would just be a marriage out of convenience so that he could take care of me.

Well, my mom didn't know, so I decided I'm going to keep this baby. So, I ended up secretly having this baby. I delivered this baby all by myself at my house around 5:30 in the morning. With my mom, she was there, and then, like I said, its details, umm, it's been a long road as far as working on that, because people don't understand; they're like, "How did you do that?" But, that's just where my head was, you know; I got people telling me that I'm crazy—today I'm not crazy. I know I'm not right still at times, but I know I did the right thing now. I love my daughter very much. I would not have changed anything about that. And that's how much I valued her life, okay? I value—I finally knew I was going to be able to have something that nobody could [crying] ever take away from me—[fiercely]—nobody! Nobody could *ever* take that bond away. Nobody. Nobody could take that away. And Suzie and I are very close. *Very* close. Very close.

So, I guess after that, well, I met my first husband; I've been married twice. He was abusive. He was a mama's boy. And we were married for a year and a half. So, I'm not going to go into great detail about that. Basically I took care of Suzie as much as I could. And then I got married for the second time. It was years after that. And that relationship wasn't abusive, but I guess in one aspect it was, because he ended up cheating on me. And I never have quite figured that out. But we had a happy relationship. We did. And, I guess, sometimes I wonder what's wrong with me, because my daughter says, "Why don't you wonder about that?" I had another daughter that's ten, and she is with my mom. He divorced me, he got custody, and she has been with my mother ever since.

I had legal problems, trouble with the law a lot, because one time I got drunk and I got a DWI and I lost my license; I went to court. I was supposed to get it back, but I didn't. So, I was in a bad deal because I was trying to raise two kids, but I couldn't do it on welfare. I had no child support. So, I was not going to—I refused to sit and be a welfare queen. So I had to drive. And every time I drove, they caught me; I went to jail. I went to jail for ninety days in a federal and state withholding facility. Did time with criminals—all conspiracy of murder, grand theft auto. Three months of my life with my kids [given up] for not having a picture I.D.

I got out; first day, I started looking for work. Because I think the justice system is wrong. You know, I think it's been real trying sometimes—they're always messing with people that are trying. And that's one time that I feel like the justice system failed me. When I got divorced, he got everything. I got nothing. Okay? And, in a way, he really even got—he didn't get—well, yeah, he did, he got custody rights of Diana. And, Diana and I, we have a relationship, that's basically like trying to get on my feet in case anything happens to my mom. But it's still not the same. And that part hurts me because, I had to leave her when she was like, three. We're not close. And I know that's my fault. But it's not to the point where she—she always knows and calls me mom. But it's just not like it is with me and Suzie. I'll be honest. I don't find myself, well, I do think about her on a daily routine basis. But I don't know how to describe it; I don't sometimes understand why I don't think about her more.

Other than the fact that there are a couple—few reasons—I'm kind of like the black sheep of the family. They seem to think that I'm a cop-out. You know, I take full responsibility. There were times when I hadn't, but they seem to think that—they don't understand abuse. None of it. Okay, like now. My mom—not because I've told her I'm here [at the shelter], but because my daughter told her—she hasn't called, she hasn't written, and she won't. So, you know, it's hard. It really is. I mean, people, I haven't even had a chance to really focus on my abuse. Okay? I really haven't. Here and there, but I have so many other problems now because my daughter is getting ready to have a baby, I'm getting ready to go away. It's just—I don't know, you know? I . . . if I, if I focus on things like Diana, you know, then I'd be kind of depressed. You know? And I have been diagnosed as manic-depressive. I am bipolar. I am being treated for it. They just now started the process even though that's been ongoing all my life, you know.

I cried a lot as a kid, you know, people would tell me—I could be at school and just start crying. People don't understand mental illness. And, I'm just now starting to understand it. I do a lot of research on it, I do as much reading as possible. But once, once you have told anybody that you're manic or bipolar, you're automatically considered a nut. Nobody wants to be around you, therefore, what's your chances of having any sort of life or friends, so I'm a loner anymore. You know, I am the complete [getting upset] total opposite of what or who I could possibly be [crying], I know. And that scares me; I tried to commit suicide a million times. But, I don't know. You know, I mean, a lot of people in my family always tell me I just want sympathy. You know, I am a very outgoing person, and I know I can be that person, I just have so much shit inside of me that I believe it will take a lot of time to heal. I don't think I'll ever be all over it, so I don't even try at times. [Crying; then long sigh] I get lost in all that. Where am I at right now? Where am I at right now?

Okay, well, how I ended up coming here. Okay, throughout all this crap when my husband divorced me, my second one, because that's the last time I got married, that was such a shock to me that I got really involved in drinking, okay? I mean, I—I was to the point where that's all I did, so heavy duty that I was actually going into what they call "the [final?] stages." I was there. I was drinking anywhere from up to a fifth, drinking all day and all night, not getting any sleep, to where I was hearing things, seeing things, I was losing my mind. I was literally losing my mind. And, I knew I needed help. And so, I—before I came here, I did thirty days at the center in Concordia. I knew if I got out and didn't get further treatment, that I would never make it. And I wanted to stay clean that bad. So I—from there, I came here. Right next door, I did ninety days at the center. Had an excellent therapist, Louise. Actually when the abuse started with my last fiancé, I had tried to get into counseling with her, and could not, so that wasn't an option. But I didn't—backing up to the Concordia deal, I did ninety days, and from there, got me a job, and stayed clean. During that time, I was seeing somebody in treatment. He ended up cheating and all that. So that's when I shot the bottle. I was like, all right, how could I possibly go back? I know it's a matter of control, so I'm not copping out on that again. But it was a situation once again where I was blown away. I can't [understand it]—I still, and I don't think I'll ever have the answer to "why me?" Because I know, I understand he was abusive in the end and that's why I quit seeing him. But, basically, why?

And I'll be so honest because the Lord upstairs knows I have trouble with faith. Because it seems like every time I get on a mission to do right, I don't understand why they get as destructive as they do. I know why they get destructive if I choose to let them be destructive, but I have a hard time understanding the "why me's" of abuse and why—like is it stamped here [motions to her forehead], I mean is it stamped here, you know, "abuse me"? I mean, why can't people just leave me alone, you know? I want to know why I keep doing the repeats all the time, you know. Is it me? Do I do these things to cause it? Sometimes I think, yeah, I do. And that's what I'm dealing with right now, because what landed me here, I, once again, got into a relationship. But this time it was different. Because I still have feelings for this person, and that's why, too, I'm leaving for Tennessee, because I don't want to go back, and that's a daily, daily issue of dealing. Okay, and I am going to go to therapy for my manic with that once I get located. I've already had a counselor here, but I want to start something and I'll be able to transfer everything at the clinic down there. I need that help, I know. If I don't get that help I know it's a fight daily—there's just times that I want to hear his [my latest boyfriend's] voice, because I still, in my sick mind, believe that it could be different.

But when I met this man, this was like walking into heaven and—[long pause; crying]—he was the most kind and considerate and very loving person I ever could have begun to imagine. It was *me*. I got to be involved in this. [Sobbing] And we had a good relationship for a long time, but he took advantage of that relationship; I once again made a mistake in telling my past, okay? Just things that I guess some people call standards, okay? Like this time, I thought, I'm not going to make this mistake again. But as we grew closer together, I started to tell him more and more. He was the only man that knew that my daughter was born the way she was. He was the only man that knew that I had problems with alcohol and drugs. He was the only man that knew about my dad. He was the only man that ever knew I was sexually molested by my brothers. He knew everything about me [sobbing]. Just as if he was God. And I was absolutely trusting of him, that's how much I loved him, so I knew this was love, because, in my mind, I always thought—well, I didn't know really what love was.

I just knew, you know, it had to be the most wonderfulist thing imaginable. It had to be so secret that you would be willing to do anything or tell anything, that you would want this person, it would be so special that you would do anything for this person if he was that person. As I said, the more I told, in the end, it became [hurtful], and that's still stuff that I know is all scrambled, that I'm trying to figure out exactly what kind of person he was, because when we were able to go out and socially drink, he was very good to me. He was just, like I said, he was what you would call a prince, okay? He was a fairy tale that was going to close the doors to the madness that I grew up with. [Crying] He was going to be my hero and I would live happily ever after with this man. And that never happens, either, so that's why [I know], okay, that's my lost hope, so that's never going to happen. And I believe it's not. That fairy tale's gone. [Crying] But he had a way of making me want it everyday. I—what few friends I did make—I forsaked it all. He didn't want me to see them, [so] I didn't like that person: "Okay, consider it done." That was manipulation. I believe it started [because] he was a heavyset man. People would look at me like, "Teresa, you're a pretty girl." Well, you know, I just think I'm okay, you know. I just wanted someone to love me and halfway feel [crying] the way I feel inside, the way, you know, I don't even know. I'm totally confused because the way I looked wasn't right, either. I got my ass whipped for that.

But he had a way of tearing apart everything as far as the way I looked. And it wasn't because he didn't want me to look nice. He would tell me I was beautiful, and I'd be like, "Eeeeh, you know, no, you're crazy." He goes,

"No, you're not only beautiful on the inside, but you don't need to get up and put makeup . . ." He was the first man I ever had been with [crying] that you could actually wake up with and . . . [slowly] feel the way I felt when I was with him. He made me feel that way. And I knew he loved me. I knew there was something there. So we got engaged to be married and [then there were more things] I was starting to see things about him, okay.

I'd be like, okay, you know, you didn't want me to work. Well, he made good money. He was a construction worker. He had his own business. Made, like, thirty dollars an hour. And I was like, "This can't be happening to me. There is *no way*. I'm set. This man loves me." Yeah, he may be heavyset, but I was that kind of person. I don't look for what's on the outside. I go on the inside and he was—he was what I've . . . [slowly] always wanted and everything I ever dreamed of, because it was like he—[crying]—he had just connected so much to my heart. He was unreal. I knew that this was where, not only that I finally wanted to be with my life, but yet, at times that I deserved. Finally, I finally am going to get what I deserved in my life. Because, see, I thought I was being punished all those years during my childhood.

You know, I still don't know with all that, too. I'm so confused that I don't even know, like I said, there's not enough time left in my life, so I don't even want to mess with it at times. I'm like, okay, it happened. And it's done. Gotta move on. Okay? So, therefore, it's more pain to go back there and grab all those things, and I don't know if I want to go that route at times. You know, they say it helps, but, for me, it's only a constant reminder that it'll always be there. Always. You know, that I'll always end up crying. I'll always have to refeel all those feelings, you know.

And what's so weird is I read all those [books]—about the incest and the abuse. The only real abuse that I'm ever able to go back to, that I will spend one half of a second to remember, is not my dad's, it's not my brother's with the molestation, and it's not even now, okay? There's been others, you know. Every relationship except my second husband has been abusive. I had knives pulled on me. I've been hit. I've had teeth knocked out. I've had black eyes. Ribs cracked. I've had all that done to me. I've been suffocated, choked, had my hair pulled, thrown in the wall, but the only abuse that I'm focusing on now was why I'm here. *His*. Because there's still some sick part of me that can't let go. [Crying] And I try hard, okay. I miss him. And I know—I miss what we had. You know, I would give anything, like they always say, to go back, because I feel like I'm responsible in some parts, I guess probably I am, you know, because when he started taking away from me and not wanting me to work, I felt trapped. Like, okay, "I've gave everything. I cook for you. When you come home I take your shoes off, I rub your feet [crying], I wash your hair, because I'm that kind of woman."

And he told me, he would tell me, I'd be like, we'd be kidding, and I'd be like, "You better hang tight and not take advantage of me, because I'm a good woman, and a good woman's hard to find." That's how I was raised. My mom, you know, most people would look at me, and I'm a pretty good cook, and would think, "You're a good cook—your mom was." Well, my mom didn't teach me nothing about cooking. I learned because I wanted so hard to be accepted and that's all I want in my life. Most people, if you ask them, "What would make you happiest in life?"—I just want to be loved, you know, to be loved or to be happy with myself. And I'm almost forty; I'll be, not forty, but thirty-seven in August and it's never going to happen. I'm to the point where I've been through so many relationships that I don't care if another man ever looks at me. But yet, that's a loss, man, that's a loss of your life. [Crying]

It's hard. Some days when you wake up, when you lay down—I don't want to be alone. So, you know, there's so many reasons why women become the way they become. Why they drink. Why they abuse. Why do you overeat? I've seen all of them because they're all so tempting at times, you know. But that's the one thing I know—I'm on a mission now. I, with what he put me through [pause], I just feel like, at times, I gave so much [crying], starting over is just—like how many more times, you know, am I going to have to start over? Well, you know, I'm afraid—well, if you get with a man, you know, so you prepare for that. I'm just so afraid of what's going to happen, you know. That's where my faith kicks in and I think, you know, "What is your plan?"

So now I'm like grasping for areas; I have different talents. I know I can do anything, because I've had to—not as far as walking streets and things like that—I'm a hard worker and I know I could make it. It's just that it's going to be hard and I'm not asking for anything to be handed to me. But it's been very hard because I'm without a car now. What jobs I did work, I worked a management position at like the mall, as a manager, seasonal during Christmas and at Easter; I took photos for the kids with Santa and the Easter Bunny and, you know, not making real good money, but the bonuses were nice.

He's the type of person that was very materialistic, but he was very giving, as well. And I was like, it was just like being in paradise. I never thought this would ever happen to me. But when it ended, it ended like it always does. It's like starting something and being so blown away because you don't want to be spun around on a carousel over and over and over again. Same old shit. It's a repeat. It's a pattern. And I guess I have it. We all have it. What is it? We like abuse; I've been told that. You like it; that's why you stay in it. You're crazy because you suffer from depression. With him, I just now started to learn how to wear makeup again. He stripped me of my identity when, which I didn't know who I was for all these years to begin with.

I don't even know who I could have been. I'm like a bed that was just there that never really even got the blankets or the sheets. I never even got to that point of being made. Nobody wanted to take—nobody wanted that bed. Nobody wanted to be near that bed. It was that bad, you know. I think I'm a bad person sometimes. I know I can be, because I just can't figure out why. If I can get used to the whys of some of the shit, I guess we'd all know, wouldn't we? But the deal with Bud, I—you know—it's so overpowering because I have still so much love for this man. But I know—it's not even a matter of going back.

Well [pause], I know I can't go back, okay? It's not because I can't just pick up a phone. Anyone could do that. And most of their abusers take them back. I don't—I don't believe that that would ever happen but in the same aspect, I'm trying—I'm beginning to listen to other people. See, normal people would think, "Just think about the abuse." I try to do that. I try so hard. Go back to the night when he cracked your ribs. Go back to the night when he took your head and hit his head so hard it busted your nose open and left you with two black eyes, to where you couldn't even walk for three months. You were in a bed. Go back to that. And like, I can, but it—it's like okay, yeah, he did all that and I stayed with him then. It's like I think I could change it. But then, I wonder, well, why haven't you made that call. What are you so afraid of? Are you afraid of rejection? That he won't want you [crying], because I think then why did he do what he did to me to begin with? He said he loved me. I guess, you know, I believe he did. He was good to me. He took care of me. He gave me nice things. But yet, why . . . could he do that to me? He couldn't believe that a woman like me could love him as much as I did. [Crying] And I got abused anyway. I got beat because he was too what? Weak? To believe that someone simple like me didn't deserve ways to love. And that's the biggest thing that I have to deal with right now.

I realize this now, unless I think about it. He threw me out Memorial Day with no underwear, wouldn't even let me wait for my daughter to pick me up, not a dime to my name. For the first time in a long time, I was scared. [Pause; sobbing] My whole life changed again within an hour's time. So here I am. And I tried to make better goals now. That's why this Tennessee thing is coming up. I'm scared about that. Fear—fear is something that you would think that if you go through as much shit like what I've just told you that you either think, God, something would tell you inside to know the warnings, like why don't I know any of this? Why, when I go upstairs, it's not like I'm dumb, you know. And I guess that's what people say I have a repeater pattern because with him when I started seeing the first signs of anger and temper, I thought, whoa!—but yet I used it as an excuse: "Well, he's just been drinking; he'll never do that again."

But he did. He did it quite often. And even near the end, he'd only told me he was sorry the first time because he cried and I thought well, he's really got to be sorry because he did this. He's crying; it's not normal for a man to cry because that shows that they're weak. But I never heard—from the time that it continued to be a repeated episode of the abuse—and if I did hear "I'm sorry," I always knew—even though I didn't say it—"No, you're not, because if you were sorry—" From the first time, I knew, because I tripped on it for the longest. I mean, I just did. Everyday that I was with him, I'd be like, God, I cannot believe he did this. But it would be—that would be where it would just end. I'd be like, "Oh, he'll never do it again. He was just drinking."

I never thought the possibility of me ever ending up here or on my own was ever there. Because we always made up and the abuse would just run its course, but it was always abuse, you know, I would try—back then it wasn't abuse when we was fighting and it was verbal. He would call me a bitch or useless or all the dirty things that he would say, they were vulgar. He would make me feel so bad about myself when I knew I hadn't done anything wrong. That I purposely do things because I was so angry at what he was trying to do because he was trying to change me. He loved me, but he was trying to change me, and he did change me. I went from that outgoing person to not wanting to wear makeup. Sometimes not taking baths for a couple of days. Not caring about myself to not even wanting to leave the house. I totally isolated myself. I did not want to be around anyone, but I feared him because I was like I didn't even care. He could do what he wanted to do but I'm not going, you know.

But the greatest fear of all was when I had to realize towards near the end that, yes, this is a repeat, this is a pattern. But for the first time ever in my life, I'm seeing my father. [Pause] So . . . from that point on, I really believe a part of me grew to hate him. [Pause]

And now I'm sitting here, sometimes wondering, "Well, did you love him?" I don't even know. I mean, I don't know anymore. I'm totally confused, because how am I supposed to say what really love is, you know, what is it, you know. I don't know, you know, what really love is. I thought I had that and I, you know, apparently not, so I don't really know, you know. I don't have—if somebody threw it in my face, I really wouldn't know because it's never been anything compared to what they say it is and I don't know—does anybody really know what love is? You know, do they? To me, I mean the only thing I can say that real love is [is] unconditional love for another person. Through thick and thin, and that's how I know I can honestly say I loved him, because any woman that will let a man deteriorate their inner being, I guess that's love. You have to have some great amount of feeling for that person and then a part of you wants to say, well, it's a batterer—is it that you just don't want to be alone? Or that you can't do any better? But I know, you know, that I could do better. But I don't, I don't know, it's a roller-coaster ride.

So my life today is boring, you know; like I told you, I get up at 4:30 to walk down to the ghetto, which is scary because of people possibly, men especially, and I'm not prejudiced, constantly stopping to want to mess with you, so I worry about my life. I'm like, okay, I'm walking down here in the early morning when it's still dark, risking my life, not even knowing if I'm going to get a job for that day.

And my life's changed a lot. [Pause] It messes with your head after a while. You begin to wonder if this is all there will ever be; where am I going to end up? I understand why people become street bums. I mean, I understand a lot because, when you're there, you're pretty much—you can't always escape it. There's always going to be a point in time when you're going to have to face it. I mean, the only way you're not going to face it is with suicide. I've been through that since I've been here, too. I actually went to the psychiatric hospital. I had to. I felt like I was coming unglued, I mean, I just went nuts. I broke. Zapped. And here I'm thinking all this will pass, you know—they'll tell me, "This is because of your abuse." That's not even what's wrong. It's manic depression, you know. So now I'm really freaking out, thinking, okay, now I'm responsible for this.

Because it was my moods—my moods—I could have stopped this. My moods, I could have done something to help the situation. So, then I start thinking, "Okay, if I tell him that I'm on medication, 'cause we discussed that, go to counseling, that everything will return to Day One." I can have this again, but I have to do the footwork. In the back of my mind, I swear, it's just lately it's been changing in my mind, and I think a lot is because I'm getting ready to go to Tennessee, a part of me just—I want to know—and I don't know why.

Either that, or, as I've talked to one other person about it, maybe a part of me wants him to just suffer, you know, if he is hurting. Maybe I want him to hurt like I hurt. And I know he's not going to, you know. And that hurts me—real bad. Because they take so much out of you with the abuse; that really depresses me a lot to think how they can sleep at night. When we're here crying because a lot of what we had and then, I guess I want to get just to the point with him where I get so sick that I just want to vomit when I think about him [crying] and I can't. Because I don't know how else I'm going get over it. Because I loved him so deeply.

I'm not saying I didn't make mistakes, but that was after, you know, I learned on trial and error, you know. An example of that was, he'd come home, I'd be in a good mood. Not in a depressed mood. First thing through his mouth when he come through the door: "Why you in such a good mood? Been drinkin' today?" To where I became a closet drinker. It was like, alright, I'm being accused of this and I haven't been drinking, so I started drinking, you know? So, there, that's when I said okay, I caused the abuse because if I hadn't been drinking—I do blame myself for that. I do blame myself so, yeah, I guess, most women would say, no, I didn't deserve to get hit. It's a control thing. It's a mind game. He was a mind-game player. He refused to believe that and he had a temper to begin with, you know, even after or before you said anything about the mind games, you know. He had a temper, and that's what I told him.

Then I thought, well, maybe we're so much alike, but, no, he was a very, very, I believe, inner-anger type of person because of his weight. He was so insecure about who he was. Then I felt like I always had to take the punishments for that. [Crying]

And I will never understand why, because in the beginning, I swear, so help me, God, he knows and I know it wasn't until the end. It wasn't really till he cracked my ribs [sniff] and threw me into three walls. That night, from that time on, it was like, whatever I do, and if I keep putting up with the abuse as far as the questioning. It was like, "Well, I have the right to question you." I'm like [slowly]: "Not every day." And I said, "It's how you say it." And I go, "You go on and on and on and you remind me of my dad. Okay? That's how he did my mom. Okay? That is not normal, Bud. You do not sit and just constantly pick at somebody. Especially . . ." like, he would call me at lunch and I would think everything was fine. Okay, you know. Cool.

And this is where, again, once the role playing of me becoming a closet drinker set in because I would think everything's fine and would want to start getting feelings back, even after he had done the abuse and stuff. I would think, "Well, maybe I'll take a shower tonight and I'll fix my hair." But as soon as I started to feel that way I would [snaps her fingers] snap back quick and go, no, I'd be on pins and needles because I knew that if I fixed my hair or put makeup on, it was because I was screwing somebody in our own home during the day. So, I didn't possibly even care. I was like, you don't have to worry about me, whatever it is, and that inner beauty, because I don't feel it anymore.

He had qualities like no man had ever had, and I really don't believe it was a natural knack of just being conned and charmed. I believe he was very capable of feeling that way and I believe he had a lot of inner problems that I knew nothing about. I firmly believe that. Now I don't understand why he had such good communication. I know that's why I have a hard time. That—I don't know—I know it sounds confusing, because it's very confusing. I don't know what happened.

I guess just time and two people learning a real part of each other; and I'm not proud of the closet drinking and, you know, and I acted like, no, and if I was drinking, it would be like, no, it was my revenge then, of like, "See? How's it feel, okay? How's it feel to be abused, okay? How's it feel for you to hurt 'cause you don't know what's going on," okay? It was my way to get back at all the times he had struck out and lashed and done all the things he did. He had hurt me so much that I didn't care. I was like, "See how it feels this time." And I kept doing it. Every time we'd get in a fight, I'd do it. Like, "I'll show you. I'll do this again." And, I mean, it wasn't the fact I never was home. It was the fact that what was the big deal about having a cocktail, okay? The only reason I abused it was because he went on and on and on and on: "Why," you know, "are you going to have a drink in the afternoon?" Well, maybe I deserved it. Maybe that was my leisure time after cleaning the house all day long and doing your dirty laundry and having dinner ready and I want to sit down to a movie and relax. It's only okay if I do it. He wouldn't even have to say that. He wanted everything and I believe firmly that he wanted a woman that thought like he did, too. And I'm like, he'll never find her anywhere, 'cause no two people are uniquely the same. If you do, you know, good luck, but, I don't know. So that's where I am with it.

[Q: Is this the first time you've been in a shelter?]

Yes.

[Q: One night I was sitting next to you in group, and I could tell from the way you were sitting that you were going to say something, and I didn't know what it was going to be, and then you just spoke out and you were so strong and powerful, and I was just like, whoa! I could just feel the power around you and I wondered—I got a sense that night that being in a shelter has been empowering in some way. You mention that you've learned stuff. I wonder, has it been good to be with other women? Are you coming away feeling a little bit stronger, or not? And you're going away with somebody?]

Right.

[Q: Is that new? Is this something a little new for you?]

Ahh, this strength so far, that's telling me, I know, within myself. They gave me strength here, too. It's a comfort zone. It's not because I'm afraid. For a long time when I first came here I was very paranoid, and it wasn't because, well, the day he kicked me out he told me—I had no choice—he told me that he would kill me. And I believed him—that's all I had to do was hear it and I was gone. You know, I came here, like I said, with no underwear, not a stitch of clothing. Walking down, one of the neighbors saw me, I mean just totally humiliated. Had nothing. Okay? Again, I didn't shed a tear, okay? Could not even cry for the son of a bitch, okay? 'Cause I'm like, this is unreal. I guess I—at that time—could not accept it and it wasn't even a part of me while I was in the process but [sigh] it took me the biggest portion of the time being here, isolating. That's why I didn't go outside; I was paranoid from my experience of being so isolated, the fears, the paranoias, people, just any people, that's why I hid in my room a lot, slept a lot, I was just—

I didn't want to be around other people. I don't trust people. That's still a factor, too.

But I'm starting to focus on some different things. Even though I'm going with this person that I don't know a lot about, most people would say it's a big challenge and maybe crazy, as well, I am going to another shelter. I'm being transferred, like I said before. I have a goal. I have a couple of goals. I've been spending a lot of time—this decision was kind of on a whim, but I told the reasons why I'm doing that. They're not very justifiable, I know that as well. But I didn't just make that decision knowing that if that didn't work I couldn't come back here. I know that I can come back. This shelter is here if I need to. I'll transfer back. Like I said, one of my goals is to get a vehicle. I haven't had a vehicle for a while, so I know I can attain that. I'm already in the process of some cash being saved. But, like I said, you know the deal with that. It would take three times as long with the process I have here. I need a vehicle as well, because my grandbaby is getting ready to be born.

But I'm in limbo with a lot of those things because I don't know what I'm going to do down there. I mean, I'm willing to do anything. The good Lord knows I've done it up here. I'm that kind of person. I will survive; I will survive. I've survived so much in my life, you know, that this is just a minute transaction. It's going to take time because, like I said, I have so many things to work on. Things that I didn't ever even think that I'd have to mess with.

But I think that for my peace there are going to be things that I'm going to have to focus on. The more I read, the more research I do on a few things that we've talked about that I'm going to have to do, you know, and the one thing above all that I know I have to do, is research myself. I have got to spend the time to know—I can't even say that—not to know [pause] but to look inside this person and see all the many options that there probably already has been, see what's available to me. I'm just like a job working on the inside just dying to get out. And there's, like I said, so much searching inside of me to do something because sometimes when I say things, I don't know how to feel them. But I want to learn how to feel those things [pause] because I think that's the key to me succeeding [crying] 100 percent.

And I always say that I'm going to fight this time, but I always seem to get sidetracked. But I'm doing things a little bit different, since I came to the shelter, than I've ever done before. I started to make goals for myself instead of getting here and maybe going out and doing crazy things, you know what I'm saying, because you're depressed. So that is a peace and serenity in my life—[strongly]—I do feel that when I talk about it. That's one thing that has changed my life. So when I feel that, that peace and serenity, I know it's faith. He's right here now, 'cause I feel it. And that's how I can safely say that maybe, if I felt this way all the time, that the best will come—but I have to learn what the best could possibly be for me. I have to learn how to feel, but I don't always go with that feeling. I mean I really am on a mission: I'm on a mission so powerful within myself that if I ever get there, if I live long enough to get there, it should be pretty good. I hope that, in time, that as some friends have said—one especially; she's gone—if you're up there, Tammy [her eyes lift up]—it will be an explosion. What you used to tell me. If I ever get to where I need to be, it will be dynamite! [Laughing]

Cathy's Story

MY EARLIEST MEMORIES ARE of an uncle that I had who, I guess, spent a lot of time with our family, although I don't know why. He was actually abusive. To the best of my knowledge, that started about the time I was three or before, but that is the first memory that I have of it.

And I can remember when it used to happen, thinking, even as little as I was, that he can hurt my body but he can't hurt me, and I always had this sense of kind of being outside of myself watching what was going on. And I don't know if he threatened me. I don't know why that I had to cover this up or hide it, but I do know that when I was sort of outside of myself watching what was going on, I would think things like, "Oh, that is going to leave a bruise. I'll have to cover that up. I can't let Mom see that"—those kinds of things.

And I really believe that has caused a lot of dysfunction in my life. I have tried over the years to put that sexual abuse into its perspective in my life. It went on until I was about probably thirteen or fourteen years old, sporadically. It wasn't constant—but it was at least probably three or four times a year. It was more often when I was younger because we lived closer to them, and then we moved farther away, so it didn't happen as often. Also there was a friend of our family who sexually abused me when I was about, oh, I think I was ten, and that was a male friend of our family.

And—as a little child I always felt—unwanted—I was the youngest of five children; only four of us lived with my parents; my half-sister lived with her mother in a different place. My mom told me, when I was about eight years old, that when she found out that she was pregnant with me, that she wanted to have an abortion, because they already had so many children, and they couldn't afford children. But abortion wasn't legal in 1957, so she went to find out how much it would cost her to have an illegal abortion, and it was going to be seventy-five dollars, and she said it might as well have been a thousand, and so she went to my grandmother and asked my grandmother for the money, and my grandmother wouldn't give it to her, and, otherwise, I suppose I would have been aborted at that time. So I've always had really strong feelings about abortion for that reason, because I'm kind of glad I'm here in spite of everything.

But I always had a feeling growing up that I really wasn't wanted. My mom was the kind of person who always took good care of me in the sense that I always had all of my physical needs met as far as, you know, clothes and food and, you know, being watched. She watched after me, she didn't abandon me. I was lucky in that sense. She took good care of my clothes. It was more like: She would dress me up, show me off, and then send me to my room. You know, I just always really felt that I wasn't wanted and wasn't loved. My mom was a very critical person. She criticized and criticized. And it made me very withdrawn. I was a very withdrawn child, and my dad, he worked shiftwork, like rotating shifts, and so he was always either not home or sleeping, and so I really never saw my dad much. He wasn't much—he wasn't part of my life except as a disciplinarian. When my mom couldn't deal with something, then she called my dad in, and he would take over the discipline and, I don't know, I've often wondered if maybe that was where I got the idea that the man is in control and the man is in charge.

My mom was a very controlling person. I know growing up I had no privacy in the sense that I wasn't allowed to lock my door to my room. I wasn't allowed to have that privacy. My mom would go through my drawers even as I got older, and go through my purses. She would go through everything all the time and find things to get upset about. And it was like, no matter how hard I tried, there was just no pleasing my mom. And so I guess I became a real perfectionist because of that. I was always, always, always trying to be perfect. When I got older, I can remember my family would just cringe when my mom was coming to visit because I would spend days cleaning my house, from top to bottom, inside closets, and they were like, "She's not going to look inside in there," but if she does, you know! I drove myself really hard for a lot of years because of that.

And—I started looking outside of my family, for I was six years younger than my nearest sibling. My half-sister's fifteen years older than me, my oldest sister is thirteen years older than me, and my oldest brother is eleven years older than me. My youngest brother is six years older than me. So I was pretty young when I remember them being around, and I don't remember them being people that I could go to to talk. When he was sixteen, which would mean that I was ten, my youngest brother was in a car accident and had his neck broken, and he was in a hospital for about three months in traction and they finally did surgery on his neck, replaced some of his vertebrae with bone from his hip, and after that he became very, very abusive to me. Anytime that we were alone, he would—it was like he would just find a reason to get angry with me and he would strangle me. He would put his hand over my mouth and hold my nose until I passed out. One time he put me down the laundry chute that went from the main floor to the basement, when my mom was gone and he was left to babysit for me for the day, and he put me down the laundry chute and wouldn't let me out, because downstairs, it opened (of course) from the outside, and so I couldn't get it open and I was in there all day and was terrified. And so he was very abusive to me. I don't remember there being anyone in my immediate family that I could ever go with to talk to or to feel that I was safe with.

My dad's mother, my grandmother, was a very gentle, kind human being. And her sister, who was my aunt Ginny, she was my great aunt, she was a very kind, gentle person, and she had had a very difficult life. She grew up in Denmark and she became pregnant before she was married, which, in that day, was absolutely scandalous, and the family pretty much banished her from the family, would have nothing to do with her except for her sister, my grandmother, and they were very close and I loved these two women a lot. They were a great influence in my life and I used to spend a lot of time talking to them, but I always felt like there was so much about myself and about my experiences in life that I just couldn't talk about. And I think they probably would have accepted it, but, at the time, my feeling was just that "I can't talk about this."

And so I guess I was thirteen when I had my first boyfriend, and he was seventeen at the time. So my parents were not very pleased that I had a boyfriend and they wouldn't allow me to date or anything like that, but he used to come to our house a lot and sometimes he would bring his friends over. He had one particular friend, Eddie Smith was his name, who used to come over with him every now and then. And Eddie was like nineteen.

But one day I was at home by myself and my parents were at work, and apparently it must have been summertime, because I wasn't in school but there were tornado warnings out. A storm had come up pretty sudden and there was a lot of wind, hail, lightning. It was really bad. And a knock came at the door. And I went to the door and it was Eddie Smith. And he was standing there with a suitcase in his hand and he said, "I was on my way to the bus station and this storm came up. Can I come in until it stops raining?" Well, I didn't even think twice about it. I opened the door and I let him in because I would have done that probably for anyone, short of Jack the Ripper or something.

So, anyway, of course that was against the rules; I wasn't supposed to have boys in the house when my parents were gone, or anyone in the house for that matter, but I let him in and he asked me if he could have a glass of water and I said yes and I went to the kitchen to get him a glass of water, and I heard this sound, and before I could react to it he brought a switchblade around in front of me holding it to my throat. And I dropped the glass of water in the sink and I was like, "What is this about?" And he let me know he wanted to have sex with me and I wasn't in a position to fight with him. He was holding a knife to my throat and so he basically pulled me, holding a knife to my throat, down the hallway to my parents' bedroom, and he nicked me several times in the process because I was trying to walk backwards and so was he and it was kind of a clumsy thing. And he nicked my neck several times with the blade and we got back to the room and I was just pleading with him the whole time, "Please don't do this. Please don't do this. If you just leave now I won't say anything" and whatever, but it seemed to just make him angry.

So when we got to the bedroom he told me to take off my clothes and I was crying and pleading for him not to do this and he took the knife and swiped at me with it and he didn't cut me badly but he did catch my throat and cut it a little bit and I was very afraid. So I took off my clothes and he then proceeded to—he didn't remove his clothes—he just undid his pants and he then proceeded to have sex with me. While he was doing that, he was on top of me and he had his arm across my throat holding the knife next to my throat and so he nicked me several more times. He never did cut me badly; they were just nicks. And then when he was finished with what he wanted to do, he got up, and just about the time that he was getting ready to walk out of the room—I was just curled up on the bed crying—I heard a sound and I knew it was the car door, that my dad was home from work, and I was just terrified.

And I guess it was the instincts from what had been happening with my uncle for all those years or whatever to try to hide or cover up what had just happened. And I told him, I said, "Oh, my God, that's my dad. He's home from work." And he took off—he had been in our house enough that he pretty much knew our house—and he took off running down the basement stairs and out the basement door and just about the time the basement door slammed my dad walked into the living room. The way our house was laid out the basement stairs were next to an outside wall that was by the driveway.

So when my dad came in, he said, "Who was in here?"

And I said, "Nobody. Why?" Because I knew I'd get in trouble for having someone in the house. And I was still shaking and I was just, you know, kind of in shock and very frightened. And I said, "Nobody. Why?"

And he said, "I heard somebody running down the steps when I got out of the car." And he took off out the front door, looking, I guess, for whoever had been in the house, and he didn't find anyone, and so he came back in and said, "I know I heard somebody."

I said, "Dad, I was downstairs. I came upstairs."

He said, "I thought I heard the back door close."

I said, "No, I was coming up the stairs."

And he said, "Okay." And he let it go at that.

But my mom came home from work probably an hour or so later, and I had been in the bathroom trying to—I had wiped the blood off my neck before my dad got home because there wasn't a lot of blood, just little drops and you really couldn't see the nicks too much. But by this time they were starting to show. They had turned red and whatever and I was trying to find my dad's styptic pencil, because I knew he used that when he shaved if he nicked himself. And I was trying to find it because they would still ooze, these little drops of blood, and I wanted them to stop bleeding. So I was in the bathroom trying to find that when my mom came home. Might not have even been an hour later.

But one thing I guess I had forgotten to do was straighten up the bed. My dad hadn't been in the bedroom yet, and the first thing my mom always did when she came in the house was put her purse in the bedroom and take her shoes off. So she walked straight to the bedroom, which was directly across the hall from the bathroom, where I was, and she called out to my dad and she said, "Were you—did you lay down when you got home from work?"

And he said, "No. Why?"

And she said, "Well, the bedspread's all messed up on the bed." And then she got to looking at it. It was a white chenille bedspread and there were drops of blood on the bedspread. And so she immediately called for me. And I went in there and she was very visibly upset and she wanted to know what that was about. And I broke down and started crying and told her what happened. Well, I hadn't really thought of it, but Eddie left without his suitcase, and so my parents found his suitcase stashed behind the living room couch. So I wonder, since he hid it behind the couch, if he actually came to our house for the purpose of raping me. I guess I'll never know the answer to that question.

But what ultimately happened was my parents made me—Eddie was nineteen years old, and I was only thirteen—and my parents called his parents and they came over to our house. And his parents basically had the attitude that, well, I should know better than to let people into the house when I'm there by myself. And, ultimately, I ended up having to apologize to his parents for having let him in the house and that kind of thing. There was never anything done about him raping me. My parents were very angry with me for having let him in the house and brought this embarrassment onto our family. And so I apologized to his parents for what I had done and that was that.

At that moment I felt so much humiliation that, for probably the only time in my life, I wished him dead. And I always had a deep guilt complex about wishing people dead, like the boy who did this to me. I should say man: He was nineteen years old; he was an adult. But I wished him dead. And two weeks later he was decapitated in a car accident, and for a lot of years I felt like that was my fault, that I somehow caused that to happen. It took me a long time to realize that just because I wished he were dead didn't mean that that's why he died in a car accident. It was just a struggle for me. But in a way, I almost felt justified, too.

When I was nine years old, my mom called me a "whore" one day, and I had no clue what the word meant. And so I got a dictionary and a flashlight and hid in my bedroom closet and I was looking up the word. And I just was looking under *h*, trying to find the word *whore*, and I couldn't find it anywhere, and, being a halfway intelligent child, I thought, "Maybe it starts with *w*," you know. So I looked it up and I read the definition. I don't remember what the definition said, but what I remember was this horrible sense of shock that came over me that this was the reason that my uncle had done these things to me all my life, that basically men treated me the way that they did, because somehow I was born that way, that it was a condition you were born with and that's what was wrong with me. And I internalized that very much, I guess because my mother said it to me.

I don't even remember why [she called me a whore]. She was just mad at me. When she would get angry she would say all kinds of things, but that was the first time I had ever heard that word or at least heard it from out of my mom's mouth, the first time I remember hearing it. And, at the time, she was very angry with me and had knocked me down in the kitchen. I was between the kitchen cabinets and the stove. There was a space there where the trash can usually was and for some reason the trash can wasn't there that day. She had knocked me down on the floor and she took off her shoe and raised it up to hit me with it and that was when she said—when she called me "a little whore."

And that's why I needed to look up the word. I guess I was about six or seven when my mom told me I was too big to sit on my dad's lap anymore. My mom was sexually abused by her father, who was an alcoholic when she was growing up, which I didn't know until many years later. But I was very confused about being too big to sit on my dad's lap, you know. And then when I was about maybe eleven or twelve, she told me I was too big to run to him and hug his neck, you know, all that kind of stuff when he came home from work, so I wasn't allowed to be affectionate with my dad at all, and I guess my mom just has a lot of unfinished business as far as things like that go.

But anyway, when I was fourteen I decided that I didn't want to be there anymore—that I always had this sense that, even though I felt like there was something wrong with me that I was always being treated this way, something deeper in me always said, "It's not me; it's them," you know, because I know me, and I know that I'm a good person, and I know that I didn't do anything wrong. But why does everyone else think that I'm this bad person and whatever? And so when I was fourteen I just finally decided that it was time for me to prove to myself that I was the person that I believed that I was, not the person everyone—everyone meaning my family—was telling me that I was. And I ran away from home. They didn't have a clue, and I was found within a few days.

So, my parents committed me to—at the time it was called the Girls' Housing Center in Conrad, across from the hospital. It was affiliated, I guess, with the hospital. And they committed me to there and I was promptly assigned a therapist and I could not stand her. After I talked to her twice, I just could not stand her. I did not like her at all and I just would not go to my counseling sessions with her. And they worked on a merit system there, and so I didn't get my merits and get the privileges that I should have got. I didn't even go to school for a long time because I didn't go to my therapy sessions.

But one of the therapists who was there, who happened to be the assistant to the director, sort of took me under his wing and talked to me—impromptu therapy sessions—and he talked to me in great detail about things people had never asked me about before. And that was the first time that I ever told anyone about the sexual abuse, but I didn't really come all the way clean with it, but I, I don't remember exactly how I did it, but I just sort of let him know that it had been going on and I guess he sensed that it wasn't really something that I was ready or could talk about at the time so he didn't pressure me about it. Basically, he took me to see the director, and they put me through a lot of different tests, and their consensus was that I didn't belong in there. This particular therapist, the assistant to the director, also conducted group therapy sessions with the kids and their families and so knew my parents and had talked to my parents a lot. And their consensus was that I didn't belong there and that I would be okay. Actually, what he told me was that I would be okay, but the only way it was ever going to happen was if I found a legal way to get away from my parents and from that household, because my household was extremely dysfunctional. And so I spent my fifteenth birthday in that place, but what they did was basically push me through the stages where I got all my merits, and all these passes that I really hadn't earned, and they got me out because my parents wouldn't sign me out. You know, they had signed me in and they were just basically going to keep me there. And so anyway they got me to the point where I could get out but they told me, "You've got to find a legal way to get away from that household."

And I said, "Okay." And so, what I did was—there was, when I went home, there was a guy that I had known most of my life just as an acquaintance, you know, not really even a friend, but I knew him and the kind of person he was, and I went to him and I told him what was going on and I said, "I have to find a legal way to get out of the house." I said, "Will you marry me?"

And he said, "Sure." He was in the Seabees and he was stationed on the West Coast, and he happened to be home on leave when I came home. And he said, "Sure. I can do that."

And I said, "Good." So we went to my parents, asked them—told them we were madly in love and asked them if we could get married.

They said, "If that's what you really want to do."

So, at fifteen, I married him and went to California and legally got away from home. And, he wasn't under any delusions. I didn't love him and I don't think he loved me, either, but it was just a convenience thing. But we were young—he was nineteen, I was fifteen—but we were young and we made the most of it. We stayed together for a year and a half and we were good friends and we had a good time and, you know, we respected each other a lot. And we got a divorce a year and a half later. He moved on and I no longer needed to get away from home, so, but it was a good thing. He was good to me. He treated me well. I can't say he made a good husband, because we really weren't husband and wife. You know, in name only, you know. And so, he went out and he drank some with his friends and that kind of thing. But, I did my thing, too, you know, and we didn't fight about it and anything I ever asked of him, he was more than accommodating and, you know.

So, he treated me very well. He was a very good person and I'll always respect him and appreciate him for that. And, at the time, being fifteen, I couldn't get a job. I wasn't old enough to get a job, and so he supported and took care of me. And I will always respect and appreciate him for that. So then I was seventeen when I met my boys' dad. And we did fall madly in love and I thought the sun rose and set in him.

And, when we were dating, at one point in time I worked at Wal-Mart and there were some people there from—they sell organs—they come to Wal-Mart and set up all these organs—not human organs, you know, instrument organs. So one of the salesmen—they stayed in a motel locally—and one of the salesmen asked me when I was getting off work. He said, "Can you give me a ride to the motel?" He said, "I called a cab and they're not here." By the time I was off work and closed up, he had been waiting for an hour.

I said, "Sure. I'll give you a ride." So I was giving him a ride to the motel. And my boyfriend, who ultimately I married, happened to be at the four-way stop and I was at the four-way stop in this little bitty town that I lived in and he was very, very, very angry that I had this other person in the car with me and he pulled me over, and I told him, I said, "I'm just taking him to the hotel. I'll be right back."

And he said, "I will be here waiting for you to come right back here." So I did. And he was so extremely angry that he got out of his car, jumped out of it, started kicking the hood of his car, dented the hood of his car, punching the windshield, and I laughed hysterically because I had never seen anyone in all of my life act like that. It was hilarious. A lot of it was nervousness, too, I mean, it scared me, made me nervous, plus I thought it was hilarious. I wondered what was wrong with him, you know. But it was just—well, he explained it to me that he just loved me so much and he could not stand to see another man around me. That it just drove him crazy, because if anybody ever hurt me . . . because I had already told him, you know, pretty much my history—the things that had happened as I was growing up—and he was just so terrified that someone would hurt me or whatever and that explained it away.

So it was all good. He basically put me up on a pedestal and treated me like a queen. One time he actually had to break a date because he had to work and he sent me two dozen—not one—but two dozen long-stemmed red roses to my work. We just—I don't know—we had this sort of fairytale thing going on and three months later we got married. And we were married for twenty years and I really did love him. And I think he really did love me. At least in the beginning.

We had two sons, our first one was born nine months and two weeks after we got married. And I'm quite sure he was late, because I had morning sickness on our honeymoon—but we did not know that I was pregnant when we got married. And then our oldest son was twenty-six months old when the second one was born. And their dad always told me that our second son was my child because he wasn't ready to have another child yet. Well, I wasn't exactly ready, either, but, it, you know, I wasn't in total control of that, but anyway, he was always very neglectful and abusive to our younger son much more than to our older son. And I guess I tried to compensate for that.

He joined the navy right after we got married, while I was still pregnant with our first son, so he was gone a lot—their dad was, he was gone out to sea and off to schools a lot, six to nine months out of the year most of the time. And, of course, when he would come home it was kind of like a whole honeymoon thing and, you know, Daddy was the hero. He brought all the presents and all that stuff and Mom was the one who stayed home and carried out the discipline, daily routine, and put up with all the whatever, but—I enjoyed it.

I love my kids. I built my life around my kids. They were my life and, you know, now looking back, I have two very fine sons and, for so many years, I put up with so much verbal abuse from their dad, and after we had been married for about twelve years, it became physical and he started getting physically violent with me. Before that he had run his fist through walls and things like that when he would get angry, but it sort of progressed from that to where he would punch the wall right next to my head or something very intimidating, and I've often thought, in retrospect, that I think maybe that's the reason or the way that abuse progresses. Originally when he would yell and scream and pound his fist on the table, that would intimidate me so badly I would back down. And then I sort of became immune to that and he would yell and scream and pound his fist on the table and I still didn't back down, and so it took something more to intimidate me. And I've thought about it a lot but I think that's how it progresses.

If I'd always got intimidated when he'd yell and scream and pound his fist on the table, maybe he would never have hit me, or maybe he would. I don't know. But I know that after twelve years, he started getting physically violent with me. And never in front of the kids, never in front of anyone. Because they'd hear it, but never did they see him do that. But he was abusive toward our kids. He didn't beat them up, hit them with his fists, things like that, but he was very liberal with a belt when they misbehaved and always, always, always more so with our younger son than with the older son. A lot of times that, especially earlier, that's where our fights began. Was he would be so abusive toward Nathan and I would just go ballistic. I couldn't stand it. And [quietly pausing] let's see. I got kinda lost. [Pause] I never reported any of the abuse until we had been married about fourteen years, I guess. [At this point, her tone of voice changes, perhaps just a little bit louder, definitely a lower pitch. She also sounds much more "involved"; there are more fluctuations—and more animation—in her voice.]

And one night—I have no idea why—but I was in bed asleep and, I don't recall whether he was gone somewhere, or whether he had just been in the other room—why I was in bed asleep and he wasn't there—I don't remember, but I do know that what I woke up to was him pulling me by the hair out of bed onto the floor and kicking me and just kicking me and kicking me. And I never experienced anything like that before and I was just in so much shock I couldn't believe what was happening to me, and when it first happened it was dark and I thought someone had broken into our house and was attacking me, because I was sound asleep. And I realized it was him and he was screaming and yelling but it was unintelligible—I have no idea—and I've had a lot of people say, "Did he drink?" No. He didn't drink. He was just mean. That was the first time I ever reported it. I called the police. I got an ex parte order.

He wasn't allowed to even go to school to pick up our children; he had to stay away from them and stay away from me. That's one thing I'll say about this county, we lived in the county at the time—and I've heard a lot of people say that this county is not very cooperative about those kinds of things—but they sure were with me that night. They came there immediately. They helped me fill out the ex parte order—the police helped me fill out the ex parte order there at my house. They took him out of the house. They told [him], "Do not come back here or you will go to jail." I mean they were very helpful to me, because I had no clue. I'd never done anything like that before in my life, and, of course, he immediately started calling me, which I did not know was a violation of the ex parte. I didn't realize that. And he immediately started calling me and [saying], "How dare you have me thrown out of my house and propose to take my kids away from me. I'll see you in court, bitch," and whatever, whatever—[he said] he was going to do everything to me except draw and quarter me. He wore me down to the point where I dropped the ex parte. And at the time when I went to do it, I was asked if I was coerced into dropping it. Of course, I said, "No," because I knew they wouldn't drop it if I said yes. So, you know, duh: I said, "No," and so they dropped it, and he gave me to understand that [slowly, in low voice] *if I ever* got him thrown out of his house ever again that *there would be hell to pay;* he would kill me.

So, as the pattern developed, it was about once every six months that he actually got physically violent with me, and the second time that it happened, my mom happened to be at our house and she was downstairs and we had our basement fixed up and there was a guest room down there. And that's where she was when the argument broke out because he had spent money that I put in the bank for our kid's school clothes when he went to [the bank]—at this time he was out of the navy and he was working for a place here, where he still works—and he had taken money out of the bank when he went to pay for a prostitute, and I became aggravated about that and we had a big argument. My older son still remembers the time Dad spent his school clothes money on a hooker. [Laughs]

Yeah, I can laugh about it now, but at the time it was not funny. And we were arguing and I was so angry with him and told him that I didn't want to be with him anymore. And he picked up a dining room chair and threw it at me. We were only about four feet from each other so it hit me pretty hard and whatever. And my mom heard a noise and she came flying up the stairs. "What's going on up here?" And, sort of while she was coming up the stairs, he was looking at me going like this, you know [makes a gesture across her throat], motioning for me not to say anything, not to say anything because he could hear her and I said, "He just threw this chair at me." I said, "Mom, call the police."

And he was like, "Don't you dare call the police!"

I said, "Mom, call the police." And she went downstairs and used the phone downstairs and called the police. And so that was the second time I had him thrown out of his house. He went to bed as soon as my mom went back downstairs. He thought everything was okay. And I wasn't sure if she called the police or not. I was just sort of sitting there on pins and needles wondering what was going to happen next. And he went to bed.

And it was about maybe five minutes later and we did live way out in the county so actually they responded quickly. The police came to the house and actually they went back and got him out of bed and took him out, and that was the second ex parte order that I had. This time he didn't start calling me and all that—I was now aware that calling me on the telephone and harassing me was a violation of the ex parte order, so they informed him of that. And we were separated for about two months, I guess, that time. And I started missing him and, like I said, we had been married almost fifteen years at that time, and I started missing him, and he was my boys' dad, and blah, blah, blah. So I was the one who ultimately—he wouldn't accept my phone calls because he said, "You're just trying to get me thrown in jail." And so, ultimately, I went to his work and just walked right in and said, "I want to talk to you. I want to end this foolishness. I went today and dropped the ex parte," you know, blah, blah, blah.

So we got back together and shortly thereafter we bought a home in a small town near here, twenty-one acres, gentleman's farm with a three-acre lake, thirty-one hundred square-foot home. For the first time in my life, I was in the country, where I wanted to be, and I loved it. That place—that place—I put everything, my heart and soul into that place. I had a garden of about an acre that I kept all the time. I grew everything—you name it. I canned our food. He hunted deer, I butchered our deer and I raised Dorset sheep, which originally started out being our youngest son's FFA project. I inherited the sheep but I loved it. The sheep were so cool. I just loved it. Plus we didn't have to brushhog around the pond. We just fenced it in and the sheep kept it all nice. But I loved the sheep and the garden. I put in an orchard of dwarf fruit trees. I put in grapevines, blackberries, blueberries. I mean, I just loved that place. It was my heart and soul.

And I was—my husband and I were getting along pretty well [pause] and then one day—[much quieter, sounding very sad] I don't really know—he just went ballistic. We were arguing but I don't remember about what. And we had in our possession—we had hunting rifles and that sort of thing, and our kids had been taught how to use them properly and not to play with them. They were very responsible about the guns. But I had in a bedroom drawer a .38 special that had belonged to my dad, and my mom had given it to me several years before, because Rob was gone so much and I was there alone. She said, "I know you'll probably never use it. Don't keep the bullets in the same drawer because of the kids, but I want you to have it because you are so often in places alone where you know no one and there's no one with you and the kids."

So this night we were arguing. What prompted him to do it, I don't know, but we had a breakfast nook in our house that was like a booth, you know, a table with a booth against the wall. And he had thrown me down in the booth and he had the gun in his pocket and I didn't know this. And he pulled it out of his pocket and laid it on the table, and the way I was laying it was right in front of my face, and he got the bullets out and he stood there and loaded it, and he said, "I'm going to kill you." And he held it to my head and cocked it.

And I was terrified and I said, "Ron, think of the boys." I said, "They're upstairs. They'll hear it." I said, "When they come downstairs, what are they going to think?" I said, "What is that going to do to them if they hear?" I mean,

I was desperate. I was searching for anything and—I wasn't this calm, believe me—I said, "What is that going to do to them if they come downstairs and find their dad's in here with a gun having blown their mom's brains out? Come on. You don't want to do that."

But he was getting more and more agitated, and he said, "I might as well kill them and you and myself, too. I've ruined everybody's life." And he just went off and I was so terrified. I believed he was going to kill me. And I grabbed for the telephone. I thought it might be my last act but I grabbed for the phone to try to call the police. It was at the corner of the breakfast booth and he grabbed it from my hand and starting hitting me in the face with it. Finally I just managed to get underneath the table and he left the room. And I got up—my mouth was bleeding—he had hit my mouth several times with the receiver and my eye had already swollen up so where it was like nearly shut tight, but I was going toward the entryway—I was going to leave the house and I was completely hysterical. And I got to the entryway and I just collapsed. When I came to, he was standing over me screaming and yelling and just crazy, crazy, and telling me that I wasn't going anywhere, that I would die before I left the house and whatever.

So he went to bed and we had a guest bedroom and I went to that bed and laid down to go to sleep and, *for the first time in my life,* this overwhelming feeling came over me that I should just get the gun and kill myself and get it over with. And it was almost like it wasn't coming from me. It was almost like some kind of outside thing driving me to do it. And I became so terrified because it was almost like something was possessing me to do it—almost—I don't know—almost forcing me or pushing me to do that and it terrified me. And I went and woke him up, knowing that he probably wasn't going to be happy but hoping that when I told him what was happening to me that he would listen. I was terrified. I needed something to stop me. And I went and woke him up and told him what was happening. And he just started screaming and yelling at me—like why did I just want to keep on fighting. He said I wasn't going to let it die. Goddamn it, why did I keep doing this? And he just started yelling and—[she does not finish this sentence, but the next paragraph indicates that he beat her badly here].

So the next day, he went to work, and I called the family counseling center, which was close to where we lived. And I asked to talk to someone and the lady that I talked to was very compassionate and made us an appointment to come and see her. It was for both of us or for just me if I couldn't get him to come. And I called him at work and told him not to come home, that I had changed the locks on the doors—which was a lie—I hadn't, but I told him I had changed the locks on the doors, that the police were watching for his truck, that I was getting an ex parte order, and not to come home. None of that was true, of course, but I just didn't want him to come home.

And it was the first time that my kids ever saw—to my knowledge—that they ever saw my injuries. Always before, if I had bruises on my arms and legs, I covered them up. But this was the first time he had ever beaten me in the face and I had a split lip and my eye was—there was no way to hide it. And they knew—I knew the boys always knew that their dad was abusive, but we never really talked about it. Actually, that's not true. My oldest son—he's a very straightforward young man—he would say to me sometimes, "Mom, why do you even stay with Dad? He's such an asshole. We know what he does to you." And many times my younger son, when we would be fighting in the night, my younger son would get up and go get in bed with his brother and so, you know, these kinds of things went on, but it was just never really sat down and discussed. And so my oldest son, that day, said, "This is going to stop. You can't keep letting Dad do this to you. It's getting worse."

And I said, "I know. But what am I going to do? I have no job skills, no training. I dropped out of school when I was fifteen. The only thing I know is to be a wife and raise kids"—which I did well, but you can't really get a job doing that. And I said, "I have nothing, and you know if I leave he'll take everything."

And he said, "You can get a lawyer."

And I said, "Not without money, I can't." And my kids understood. Usually what happened in these situations was my older son would talk to me, and then my younger son would talk to him. My younger son never really talked to me about it; they would talk to each other. My older son was just kind of like his brother's support system, I guess. And so they understood my frustration at not wanting to stay and not wanting to leave—not being able to leave. There was nothing that was mine, because he was the one who worked and he was the one who made the money. There was nothing that was mine; I had nothing. And I had left him a couple of times for a couple of days and, you know, all the threats that he was taking the kids away from me, I was unfit, blah, blah, blah, and so, anyway, I always told myself, I will stay here and get my kids through school, because at least they have a nice home, they have good clothes, they have good food, all of that. And that was pretty much my reasoning behind it. I still loved their dad [pause]—but that love was dying. And I was hurting a lot—to see it die—because I had loved him for a long time [crying]. And their dad was the love of my life, and he always will be. It was really tough living through—

When I see—when I think about it—at that time the kids were, you know, when we bought that house, the kids were in high school and I was to the point where I was like, okay, you know, I was going to go back to school, I had gotten my GED over the years, taken a few college courses, and I decided I was going to go back to school and, you know, I was looking forward to the future—when we first moved there we were getting along really well. Things were going much better for us. We had been to some counseling, whatever. And I was looking forward to the time when the kids would be grown because we had our first son, boom, right after we got married, and I was looking forward to this time when he and I would have this time to get to know each other again and maybe rekindle some of the stuff that had died, and grow old together. And the kids would grow up and get married and have their children and bring them there to that really cool place where they had lots of room to run—I just had all these dreams about what the future was going to be like and, actually, in the long run, that hurt me a lot worse than the act of losing him. And that's the truth because there was so much of me in that place.

But, anyway, I told him not to come home and he didn't, but he still kept calling me because he had found out that I didn't have an ex parte order. But he did move in with a guy that he had worked with and he would call me and talk to me. And he wasn't begging to come home. He was talking about being sorry and all that, but he wasn't begging to come home yet. And so, finally one night, I guess he had been gone for about two weeks, I guess, and he called me and he said, "Would you mind if I came up there so we could talk?" He was staying with his friend here and it was a long distance call. And he said, we were talking every night and it was long distance, whatever, and he said, "Would you mind if I came up there to talk?"

And I said, "All right, but you're not going to stay." I said, "Know that before you come here."

And he said, "All right." And he came up there and basically started begging me to let him come home. And I told him that he could come home on one condition, and that was that he go to counseling—keep this appointment that I had made and that he do something about his problem. He cried, begged, pleaded, promised, you know, he'd pull the moon down out of the sky and give it to me on a silver platter, whatever it took. But I took that with a grain of salt because I had heard it so many times, you know. And so he did go to counseling.

Unfortunately, though, before our appointment—I think it was something like three weeks or something before they could get us in, there was a space of time before they could get us in—unfortunately, he lost his temper once again before our counseling session, actually the night before. And I had this big "Footprints" poster, a framed "Footprints" poster my mother had given me, because she knew I loved the footprints in the sand. And he took it off the wall and broke it over my head, pushed me down our basement stairs, and then drug me back up by the hair. Chunks of my hair came out on the way, so he kept having to grab different spots. And, basically, he got me in our main floor bathroom and had me up against the wall. The towel bar was in my back. And he had me by the throat up against the wall and he brought his fist back and he said, "I'm gonna bash your face in, you bitch."

And I closed my eyes because I knew what was coming and then—everything that I'm going to tell you happened in a split second—all of a sudden, every Oprah Winfrey show, every magazine and newspaper article that I had read, everything that I had ever heard about domestic violence all just came rushing back to me. I saw myself being carried out of the house in a body bag and the thought went through my mind—and I don't think it originated with me, I don't know where it came from, but the thought went through my mind: "Does he have to kill you before you realize that this man is dangerous?" And for the first time, I saw the day that he jumped on top of his car and kicked it, and all of that right up to that moment, as one big picture instead of a bunch of little isolated segments. It was one big picture. It was this big [gestures widely with both arms], you know, and it was progressing and it was going to kill me. And it was the first time I ever saw that. And all that happened like this fast [snaps fingers] because he had brought his fist back and said, "I'm gonna bash your face in, bitch." And he meant it; he was going to. I know this for an absolute fact.

And the next thing I heard was our oldest son's voice saying, "Oh, no, you don't, Dad." And I opened my eyes, and for the first time my son had his dad by the wrists, and he had his fist brought back and he said, "You will not hit my mom again."

And his dad turned around, pushed his sleeve up, and raised his fist to our son, and I jumped between them. I said [slowly, enunciating each word], "You will not hit my son." And he backed off.

And I just turned around and I said, "Matt, go in the other room."

And he said, "No, Mom, I'm not going to let him do anything else to you."

And I said, "He's not going to do anything else to me. Go in the other room."

And he [Ron] looked at me and said, "I love the way you've turned our kids against me. I left them with you to nurture them and mother them and you turned them against me like this." And Matt hollered at his dad, "Mom didn't do it, Dad. *You* turned us against you."

And he turned around and grabbed me and just literally threw me into the bathtub and walked out.

So the next day was our counseling session. And he went to work—our appointment wasn't until like 6:30 or something, because I knew he would be working or whatever, so I made it at a time that was convenient for him—and so we went to this counseling session. We sat down. At first there were two ladies there. And the first thing that—you might know her?—the first thing the main therapist said was, "Okay, what would you consider to be your most immediate problem?"

And I thought, "Oh, wow!" And I deferred. I looked at my husband and I said, "What would you say is our most immediate problem?" Because this was my way of testing the waters, thinking, "Are you here because you want to be here, because you want to work this out, or are you here just to appease me until I'm finished being mad at you again?" So I said, "What would you say was our most immediate problem?" And he said, "Oh, I don't know. You go ahead. What do you think it is?"

So, in a very bold move, I stood up, raised my shirt up, undid my pants, showed them all my bruises, and said, "As far as I'm concerned, this is my most immediate problem."

He went ballistic. He jumped up, turned over the coffee table, said, "You're just trying to get me arrested, you bitch." I guess it didn't cross his mind—if I wanted to get him arrested, I would have done it while he was at work that day. I would have gone and reported it. But anyway, these two women both jumped back frightened that he turned over this table and walked out and slammed the door and there was glass in the door and I just knew it was going to break. I was just like, oh, no—but it didn't. And they tried desperately to get me to go to a shelter that night. And I wouldn't do it, because my kids were at home; even though they were a sophomore and a junior, I mean, sophomore and senior in high school, I still would not let him go home like that to them. And I was terrified of what he was going to do to them.

And so they let me go out and look and he was just sitting in the car out front. So they talk with me, we talked a little bit. They basically wanted to know how this happened, what happened, and I told them. And they wanted me to wait there until he came back in. They said eventually he'll either leave or he'll come back in. And they said, "Before we let you go with him, we want him to promise us that he will not hurt you." And so he did—he came back up there and they were asking me if I felt safe and I said, "I guess I feel as safe as I ever do with him." And they talked to him, and he was by that time crying and apologizing and whatever, and they basically made him promise that if I went with him—they told him that I could go to a shelter, that I had that option, that I was aware of that, and that I didn't want to, because our children were at home, but they could send a police officer with me and get the kids and go to a shelter and that it was basically his choice and whatever and, you know, could he promise that he would not abuse me or the children. And he said, "Yes." Of course he wasn't going to say no. And so I got in the car and went home with him and he just didn't speak to me—for days, he didn't speak to me.

But, shortly after we got home, the director at that time of the counseling center down the street, he's no longer their director but he was at the time, called me within half an hour after we got home and introduced himself over the phone and said that he would like to see us. And so I asked Ron if he would go and do that and he said, "No, I don't see any point in it." And it was like, okay. So I told him [the director]. He said, "Okay."

But I got myself a job and found an apartment, paid a deposit on it, and started collecting boxes because I was going to move out. I didn't have in mind that I was going to divorce Ron but that I was going to move out and he was either—if I stayed married to him for the rest of my life that was one thing, but, you know, he was either going to get some help, or he was never going to live with me again.

And I just made up my mind and it was terrifying. I was absolutely terrified. I had gotten away from Ron a couple of times before, and I was at the old shelter here one time and he found me when I was waiting at the bus stop across from the school. I was waiting at the bus stop and he found me and pulled a knife on me and made me go home with him. And I was really terrified to get away from him, but I was going to die if I stayed there so I might as well die trying to get away, you know.

And he—it was a very small town—and somehow or other found out that I had put a deposit down on an apartment and saw the boxes in the basement, didn't buy my story about packing up my winter things, and he left. I came home from work one day and there was a note on the kitchen counter that said, "I don't want to be married to you anymore." And his wedding ring was laying there. He had left me several times before, but he had never left his wedding ring behind, so I took him seriously. And it was a huge relief on one hand, but on the other hand I knew exactly what he was going to do, and that's exactly what he did. He immediately filed for divorce. He took everything. When I got home he had taken our computers. He had taken everything that was worth anything. And he had a pickup truck and he had taken everything that was worth anything—all my jewelry—over the years, I had quite a jewelry collection because those apologies got bigger and bigger and bigger, and I had some nice jewelry, had some furs, basically a pretty privileged life, and he took it all. And that's when I realized it was never really mine; it was just on loan to me for as long as I put up with his crap.

Anyway, the upshot of it was the judge never really ruled for him to have to pay my attorney's fees or anything. We ended up having to sell the house. I got fifty dollars a month maintenance and he got everything. And that was four years ago. And the county sheriff's department was not cooperative with me at all as far as keeping him away from me, honoring the ex parte orders. He came back about two months after he had left, came in his mom's car, because he knew they were watching for his truck. He came in his mom's car because I wouldn't let him in the house, knocked me down in the driveway, gave me a concussion, fractured my collarbone, broke two of my ribs, and then proceeded to try to run over me with his mother's car. And I rolled out of the way, which I was hardly capable of doing; I couldn't breathe very well at the time. And I went to the doctor the next day. He told me everything that was wrong with me was because of domestic violence, and I went to the prosecuting attorney of the county—well, I went to the police station, to file charges and then went to talk to the prosecuting attorney.

He said, "I'm not going to file these charges."

And I said, "Why not?"

And he said: "Because it's just your word against his—you don't have any witnesses or anything."

I said, "Excuse me! I'm the one with the injuries. Okay? That kind of supports my story a little more than it would support his saying he didn't know anything about it. How's he going to explain his whereabouts during the time?"

And he was like, "Uh, I'm not going to file that!"

I do believe, though, that he will eventually come after me. He will try to kill me, but—and I watch over my shoulder everywhere I go and everything I do, because I know. I don't go out alone after dark, you know, if I'm ever going home and there's a car that's been behind me or three or four cars behind me or a block away from me for quite a while, I won't go home. I drive around and drive around. Where I am now is pretty centrally located, but it's also kind of secluded. You probably have to know where it is at, and I'm not leading anybody there.

I feel good about coming here [the shelter]. After divorcing my boys' dad, this is the best thing I've ever done for myself. I'm clueless, you know, but I'm just trying to figure it out as I go. That's all I can do. Actually, I was talking in counseling about it the other day. She was talking about, you know, like in twenty years, where do you see yourself? I'm like, I can't even look at that. And the job that I have, the reason that I'm working that job, is that I want to go back to college. There are some things that I want to do. The reason that I'm working that job right now is because it's like no stress. They have a very lenient attendance policy. If I get overwhelmed at work, I go home.

My boss is—she's been an angel through this whole thing. I was off work for a month, and I went back to talk to her, and she was just like, "If you still want to come back, your job's here." She was in an abusive relationship for seven years, and she barely escaped with her life. Beautiful! She's twenty-four years old and she's beautiful. She was just so good, just beautiful, and still is. I went to tell her that he went to jail Friday and all that. And she was like [yelling]: "*Yes!*" and she was jumping up and down. She said, "Don't you back down"; she said, "write everything down when you go to court, because I got up there, I didn't even know what happened. I knew what happened to me, but my mind just went blank. I couldn't remember anything. Write it down; take it with you. Remember every detail you can remember. Write it down." I mean, she's just been really good.

I'm working this job, which is kind of, I guess—I don't want to sound conceited—but I guess it's kind of like beneath my skills, you know, my abilities. But, right now, that's what I need, it's the thing to do. Because there's so much of my energy that has just been drained. And, even though I've gotten stronger since Ron and I split, this situation has held me back tremendously. I learned a lot over the last four years about myself. And [long pause]—I kind of agree with the sign in the office that says, "She who waits for a knight in shining armor gets to clean up after the horse." I'm pretty cynical now—well, maybe I'm not cynical, I'm just defensive. I'm pretty defensive. But I know that I'm never going to let anybody walk on me like that again. And, so, you know, I just don't know how long it's going to take. You know, the counselors I've talked to say I'll probably never be completely over it; I mean, it will always be there. But, I know it will get better, it'll get a little bit easier, I'll get stronger. But until I am, I'm just not going to put a hell of a lot of pressure on myself. I'm going to give myself permission to kind of take it easy, and I'll take it easy on myself, because as hard as the men in my life have been on me, I've been ten times harder on myself. And—that's what I was talking about in group tonight—just learning how to take it easy on myself and giving myself permission to be me, hurt and wounded, but free.

And my roommate, I love her to death, and you know, she is like, the best therapy for me. And we sit and we talk and we just, like—I don't know if you've ever heard her talk about it, but there are so many parallels in our lives that it's unbelievable. I mean, it can't be coincidences, and, that's really strange. I never would have thought just meeting her that we would have anything in common. But we do. And, I think we're really good for each other and we really affirm each other a lot. And there is no "Why did you do this; why didn't you do that?" You know, we just get along. It's just like there's a kind of symbiosis there between us, you know, it's just great.

[Q: What time is it? You've got to go to work in the morning, right? So, give me your last words.]

That's my story and I'm sticking to it.

Notes

INTRODUCTION: GATHERING STORIES

1. Ruth Behar, *The Vulnerable Observer: Anthropology That Breaks Your Heart;* see especially chapter 6, "Anthropology that Breaks Your Heart," 161–77.

2. Ibid., 27.

3. Nelle Morton, *The Journey Is Home.*

4. Mary P. Koss, et al., *No Safe Haven: Male Violence against Women at Home, at Work, and in the Community,* 79; these results were garnered from studies done in the 1980s and 1990s.

5. Diane E. Russell, *The Secret Trauma: Incest in the Lives of Girls and Women,* 138.

6. Koss, *No Safe Haven,* 78.

7. Judith Rich Harris, *The Nurture Assumption: Why Children Turn Out the Way They Do.*

8. L. H. Bowker, *Ending the Violence: A Guidebook Based on the Experiences of 1,000 Battered Women,* 56.

9. See Lenore E. Walker, *The Battered Woman,* and *The Battered Woman Syndrome;* and Suzanne K. Steinmetz, *The Cycle of Violence: Assertive, Aggressive, and Abusive Family Interaction.*

10. For discussions of the "master narrative" in literary and historical arenas, see Jean François Lyotard, *The Postmodern Condition: A Report on Knowledge;* and Jeffrey Fox and Shelton Stromquist, *Contesting the Master Narrative: Essays in Social History.*

11. M. Houston and C. Kramarae, "Speaking from Silence: Methods of Silencing and of Resistance," 427.

12. Gayle Greene, *Changing the Story: Feminist Fiction and the Tradition,* 7; Ursula K. Le Guin, *Dancing at the Edge of the World: Thoughts on Words, Women, Places,* 159–60.

13. Martha C. Nussbaum, *Cultivating Humanity: A Classical Defense of Reform in Liberal Education,* 88.

14. Guy A. M. Widdershoven, "The Story of Life: Hermeneutic Perspectives on the Relationship between Narrative and Life History," 2, 7.

15. Amos Funkenstein, "The Incomprehensible Catastrophe: Memory and Narrative," 23 (emphasis mine). Compare Roy Schafer, *Retelling a Life: Narration and Dialogue in Psychoanalysis,* whose Freudian analysis seems to support a phallocentric narrative that leaves women in the passive/victim roles.

16. Sue Monk Kidd, *Dance of the Dissident Daughter,* 198, 199.

17. Jerome Bruner, *In Search of Mind: Essays in Autobiography,* 293.

18. Sally Robinson, *Engendering the Subject: Gender and Self-Representation in Contemporary Women's Fiction,* 190.

19. Ibid. Compare Leigh Gilmore, *Autobiographics: A Feminist Theory of Women's Self-Representation.*

20. Over the years, I made fifty-seven taped interviews of life stories. Some of these ran only one or two hours, but several ran three to four hours. I have transcribed most of the tapes, yielding hundreds of pages of typed copy. My work at the shelter enabled me to hear many more stories that were never taped but which, nevertheless, helped to shape this work.

2. POWERFUL WORDS

1. J. L. Austin, *How to Do Things with Words.*

2. See Jill McLean Taylor, Carol Gilligan, and Amy M. Sullivan, *Between Voice and Silence: Women and Girls, Race and Relationship,* about women's voice and silences.

3. See David A. Ford, "Conducting Family Violence Research: Thoughts on Guiding Principles."

4. These figures change depending upon who is quoting them. In fact, they are quite unverifiable, as we cannot actually know how many women are beaten and killed; we only know of those incidents that are reported. For some recent statistics and general domestic violence information, see Kathleen Daly and Lisa Maher, *Criminology at the Crossroads: Feminist Readings in Crime and Justice;* and Ann Jones, *Next Time She'll Be Dead: Battering and How to Stop It.*

5. See Ford, "Conducting Family Violence Research"; Barbara Hart, "Coordinated Community Approaches to Domestic Violence"; and Jones, *Next Time She'll Be Dead.*

6. See Bowker, *Ending the Violence;* R. E. Dobash and R. Dobash, *Violence against Wives: A Case against the Patriarchy;* Marsali Hanson, Michele Harway, and Nancyann Cervantes, "Therapists' Perceptions of Severity in Cases of Family Violence"; G. NiCarthy, *Getting Free: A Handbook for Women in Abusive Relationships;* M. D. Pagelow, *Family Violence;* and S. Schechter, *Women and Male Violence: The Visions and Struggles of the Battered Women's Movement.*

7. See C. P. Ewing, *Battered Women Who Kill: Psychological Self-Defense as Legal Justification;* G. Goolkasian, *Confronting Domestic Violence: A Guide for Criminal Justice Agencies;* Ngaire Naffine, *Feminism and Criminology* (Naffine's bibliography in this work is an excellent introduction to the area of women and crime); Russell, *Secret Trauma;* D. J. Sonkin, ed., *Domestic Violence on Trial: Psychological and Legal Dimensions of Family Violence;* and Cheribeth Tan, Joanne Basta, Chris M. Sullivan, and William S. Davidson II, "The Role of Social Support in the Lives of Women Exiting Domestic Violence Shelters: An Experimental Study."

8. See especially K. Yllo and M. Bograd, eds., *Feminist Perspectives on Wife Abuse.* Compare C. Gillespie, *Justifiable Homicide;* and E. Goodman, "Curtains for 'The Bitch-Deserved-It' Defense."

9. Elisabeth Schüssler Fiorenza and M. Shawn Copeland, eds., *Violence against Women;* and Phyllis Trible, *Texts of Terror: Literary-Feminist Readings of Biblical Narratives.*

10. See Fiorenza and Copeland, *Violence against Women,* and J. M. K. Bussert, *Battered Women: From a Theology of Suffering to an Ethic of Empowerment.*

11. See Audre Lorde, "The Master's Tools Will Never Dismantle the Master's House," 101.

12. Compare L. H. Bowker, ed., *Masculinities and Violence.*

13. Roger Langley and Richard C. Levy, *Wife Beating: The Silent Crisis.*

14. Lorde, "Master's Tools."

15. Wendy S. Hesford, "Reading *Rape Stories:* Material Rhetoric and the Trauma of Representation."

16. Alice Walker, *In Search of Our Mothers' Gardens: Womanist Prose.*

17. Henry Glassie, *Passing the Time in Ballymenone: Culture and History of an Ulster Community,* xiv.

3. DESCRIBING THE UNSPEAKABLE

1. See Maurice Blanchot, *The Writing of the Disaster.*

2. Ibid., 2.

3. Ibid., 7.

4. Michael Bernard-Donals, "History and the Disaster: The (Im)possibility of Writing the Holocaust," 10 (emphasis mine), 51.

5. Walter Benjamin, *Illuminations;* see especially his essay, "Theses on the Philosophy of History," 253–64.

6. Elaine Scarry, *The Body in Pain: The Making and Unmaking of the World,* 3, 4.

7. Ibid., 27.

8. Janice Haaken, *Pillar of Salt: Gender, Memory, and the Perils of Looking Back,* 11.

9. Jill Ker Conway, *When Memory Speaks: Reflections on Autobiography,* 88; Blanchot, *Writing of the Disaster,* 2.

10. Conway, *When Memory Speaks,* 109–14.

11. Ibid., 176.

12. Haaken, *Pillar of Salt,* 5, 11, 14, 15.

4. HEARING SILENCE

1. Mary Pipher, *Reviving Ophelia: Saving the Selves of Adolescent Girls,* 2, 26, 24.

2. Mary Field Belenky, Blythe M. Clinchy, Nancy R. Goldberger, and Jill M. Tarule, *Women's Ways of Knowing: The Development of Self, Voice, and Mind,* 23.

3. Deirdre Lashgari, "To Speak the Unspeakable: Implications of Gender, 'Race,' Class, and Culture," 1, 2.

4. Toni Morrison, "Unspeakable Things Unspoken: The Afro-American Presence in American Literature," 210.

5. Judith Herman, *Father-Daughter Incest,* 70.

6. Elisabeth Fiorenza, preface to Fiorenza and Copeland, *Violence against Women,* xvii.

7. Russell, *Secret Trauma,* 128, 33–35.

8. Taylor, Gilligan, and Sullivan, *Between Voice and Silence,* 1, 3; Fiorenza, preface to Fiorenza and Copeland, *Violence against Women,* xiv.

9. Taylor, Gilligan, and Sullivan, *Between Voice and Silence,* 4.

10. Anne B. Dalton, "The Devil and the Virgin: Writing Sexual Abuse in *Incidents in the Life of a Slave Girl,*" 39; see Judith Herman, *Trauma and Recovery: The Aftermath of Violence—from Domestic Abuse to Political Terror.*

11. Taylor, Gilligan, and Sullivan, *Between Voice and Silence,* 24, 29.

12. George B. Handley, " 'It's an Unbelievable Story': Testimony and Truth in the Work of Rosario Ferre and Rigoberta Menchu," 69; Belenky et al., *Women's Ways of Knowing,* 39.

13. Matthew McKay and Patrick Fanning, *Self-Esteem,* 1.

5. LOOKING BACK

1. A good introduction to American feminist thinking is Linda S. Kauffman, ed., *American Feminist Thought at Century's End: A Reader.* For introductions to French feminist writing, see Elaine Marks and Isabelle de Courtivron, eds., *New French Feminisms: An Anthology;* and Toril Moi, ed., *French Feminist Thought: A Reader.*

2. Scarry, *Body in Pain,* 27.

3. Ibid., 33.

4. Ibid.

5. Maxine Hong Kingston, "No Name Woman," 3–16.
6. Haaken, *Pillar of Salt.*

6. TURNING POINTS

1. Scarry, *Body in Pain,* 33.

CONCLUSION: COMING HOME TO SHELTER

1. Haaken, *Pillar of Salt,* 14, 15 (emphasis mine).
2. Sandra Cisneros, *Woman Hollering Creek,* 56.
3. See the title essay in Walker, *In Search of Our Mothers' Gardens;* and Virginia Woolf, *A Room of One's Own.*

Bibliography

Agronick, Gail, and Ravenna Helson. "Who Benefits from an Examined Life? Corre-lates of Influence Attributed to Participation in a Longitudinal Study." In *Ethics and Process in the Narrative Study of Lives,* vol. 4 of *Narrative Study of Lives,* ed. Ruthellen Josselson and Amia Lieblich, 80–93. Thousand Oaks, Calif.: Sage, 1996.

Apgar, Sonia C. "Fighting Back on Paper and in Real Life: Sexual Abuse Narratives and the Creation of Safe Space." In *Creating Safe Space: Violence and Women's Writing,* ed. Tomoko Kuribayashi and Julie Tharp, 47–58. New York: State University of New York Press, 1998.

Armstrong, Nancy, and Leonard Tennenhouse, eds. *The Violence of Representation: Literature and the History of Violence.* London: Routledge, 1989.

Austin, J. L. *How to Do Things with Words.* Oxford: Oxford University Press, 1962.

Barnett, Ola W., and Alyce D. LaViolette. *It Could Happen to Anyone: Why Battered Women Stay.* Newbury Park, Calif.: Sage, 1993.

Bart, Pauline B., and Eileen Geil Moran. *Violence against Women: The Bloody Foot-prints.* Newbury Park, Calif.: Sage, 1993.

Bass, Ellen, and Laura Davis. *The Courage to Heal: A Guide for Women Survivors of Child Sexual Abuse.* 3d ed. New York: HarperPerennial, 1994.

Bass, Ellen, and Laura Davis, eds. *I Never Told Anyone.* New York: HarperCollins, 1983.

Behar, Ruth. *The Vulnerable Observer: Anthropology That Breaks Your Heart.* Boston: Beacon, 1996.

Behar, Ruth, and Deborah Gordon. *Women Writing Culture.* Berkeley and Los Angeles: University of California Press, 1995.

Belenky, Mary Field, Blythe M. Clinchy, Nancy R. Goldberger, and Jill M. Tarule. *Women's Ways of Knowing: The Development of Self, Voice, and Mind.* New York: Basic Books, 1986.

Benjamin, Walter. *Illuminations.* Ed. Hannah Arendt; trans. Harry Zohn. New York: Schocken, 1969.

Bernard-Donals, Michael. "History and the Disaster: The (Im)possibility of Writing the Holocaust." Manuscript delivered to English Department Colloquium. University of Missouri–Columbia, September 1998.

Blanchot, Maurice. *The Writing of the Disaster.* Trans. Ann Smock. Lincoln: University of Nebraska Press, 1995.

Blixseth, Edra D. *Uncharged Battery.* New York: Warner Books, 1987.

Bowker, L. H. *Ending the Violence: A Guidebook Based on the Experiences of 1,000 Battered Women.* Holmes Beach, Fla.: Learning Publications, 1986.

Bowker, L. H., ed. *Masculinities and Violence.* Thousand Oaks, Calif.: Sage, 1998.

Brettell, Caroline B. "Blurred Genres and Blended Voices: Life History, Biography, Autobiography, and the Auto/Ethnography of Women's Lives." In *Auto/Ethnography: Rewriting the Self and the Social,* ed. Deborah E. Reed-Danahay, 223–46. Oxford: Berg, 1997.

Brettell, Caroline B., ed. *When They Read What We Write: The Politics of Ethnography.* Westport, Conn.: Bergin and Garvey, 1993.

Brock, Rita Nakashima, and Susan Brooks Thistlethwaite. *Casting Stones: Prostitution and Liberation in Asia and the United States.* Minneapolis: Fortress, 1996.

Brown, Lyn Mikel, and Carol Gilligan. *Meeting at the Crossroads: Women's Psychology and Girls' Development.* New York: Ballantine, 1992.

Bruner, Jerome. *In Search of Mind: Essays in Autobiography.* New York: Harper and Row, 1983.

Bussert, J. M. K. *Battered Women: From a Theology of Suffering to an Ethic of Empowerment.* New York: Lutheran Church in America, 1986.

Butler, Sandra. *Conspiracy of Silence: The Trauma of Incest.* San Francisco: New Glide, 1978.

Caruth, Cathy. *Trauma: Explorations in Memory.* Baltimore: Johns Hopkins University Press, 1995.

Cisneros, Sandra. *Woman Hollering Creek.* New York: Vintage, 1992.

Conley, Verena Andermatt. *Helene Cixous: Writing the Feminine.* Expanded ed. Lincoln: University of Nebraska Press, 1984.

Conway, Jill Ker. *When Memory Speaks: Reflections on Autobiography.* New York: Knopf, 1998.

Dalton, Anne B. "The Devil and the Virgin: Writing Sexual Abuse in *Incidents in the Life of a Slave Girl.*" In *Violence, Silence, and Anger: Women's Writing as Transgression,* ed. Deidre Lashgari, 38–61. Charlottesville: University Press of Virginia, 1995.

Daly, Kathleen, and Lisa Maher. *Criminology at the Crossroads: Feminist Readings in Crime and Justice.* New York: Oxford University Press, 1998.

Daniels, Cynthia R. *Feminists Negotiate the State: The Politics of Domestic Violence.* New York: University Press of America, 1997.

De Lauretis, Teresa. "The Violence of Rhetoric." In *Technologies of Gender: Essays on Theory, Film, and Fiction.* Bloomington: Indiana University Press, 1987. Reprint, in *The Violence of Representation,* ed. Nancy Armstrong and Leonard Tennenhouse, London: Routledge, 1989.

De Rivera, Joseph, and Theodore R. Sarbin. *Believed-In Imaginings: The Narrative Construction of Reality.* Washington D.C.: American Psychological Association, 1998.

Dobash, R. E., and R. Dobash. *Violence against Wives: A Case against the Patriarchy.* New York: Free Press, 1979.

Ewing, C. P. *Battered Women Who Kill: Psychological Self-Defense as Legal Justification.* Lexington, Mass.: Lexington Books, 1987.

Felman, Shoshana, and Dori Laub. *Testimony: Crisis of Witnessing in Literature, Psychoanalysis, and History.* New York: Routledge, 1992.

Fiorenza, Elisabeth Schüssler, and M. Shawn Copeland, eds. *Violence against Women.* London: SCM Press, 1994.

Fleckenstein, Kristie S. "Writing Bodies." *College English* 61, no. 3 (1999): 281–306.

Ford, David A. "Conducting Family Violence Research: Thoughts on Guiding Principles." Paper delivered at the Violence against Women Research Strategic Planning Workshop, sponsored by the National Institute of Justice and the Department of Health and Human Services, Washington. D.C., 1995.

Foss, Karen A., and Sonja K. Foss. *Women Speak: The Eloquence of Women's Lives.* Prospect Heights, Ill.: Waveland, 1991.

Fox, Jeffrey, and Shelton Stromquist. *Contesting the Master Narrative: Essays in Social History.* Iowa City: University of Iowa Press, 1998.

Funkenstein, Amos. "The Incomprehensible Catastrophe: Memory and Narrative." In *The Narrative Study of Lives,* vol. 1 of *Narrative Study of Lives,* ed. Ruthellen Josselson and Amia Lieblich, 21–29. Newbury Park, Calif.: Sage, 1993.

Gillespie, C. *Justifiable Homicide.* Columbus: Ohio State University Press, 1989.

Gilligan, Carol. *In a Different Voice: Psychological Theory and Women's Development.* Cambridge: Harvard University Press, 1982.

Gilmore, Leigh. *Autobiographics: A Feminist Theory of Women's Self-Representation.* Ithaca: Cornell University Press, 1994.

Glassie, Henry. *Passing the Time in Ballymenone: Culture and History of an Ulster Community.* Philadelphia: University of Pennsylvania Press, 1982.

Godino, Victoria. "Accommodation Strategies and the Cultural Transformation of a Social Movement: A Case Study of Two Shelters for Battered Women." Ph.D. diss., University of Missouri–Columbia, 1992.

Goetting, Ann. *Getting Out: Life Stories of Women Who Left Abusive Men.* New York: Columbia University Press, 1999.

Goodman, E. "Curtains for 'The Bitch-Deserved-It' Defense." *Boston Globe,* May 23, 1989.

Goolkasian, G. *Confronting Domestic Violence: A Guide for Criminal Justice Agencies.* Washington, D.C.: Office of Justice Programs, National Institute of Justice, 1986.

Gordon, Linda. "Women's Agency, Social Control, and the Construction of 'Rights' by Battered Women." In *Negotiating at the Margins: The Gendered Discourses of Power and Resistance,* ed. Sue Fisher and Kathy Davis, 122–44. New Brunswick: Rutgers University Press, 1993.

Gregg, Gary S. *Self-Representation: Life Narrative Studies in Identity and Ideology.* New York: Greenwood Press, 1991.

Greene, Gayle. *Changing the Story: Feminist Fiction and the Tradition.* Bloomington: Indiana University Press, 1991.

Haaken, Janice. *Pillar of Salt: Gender, Memory, and the Perils of Looking Back.* New Brunswick: Rutgers University Press, 1998.

Handley, George B. " 'It's an Unbelievable Story': Testimony and Truth in the Work of Rosario Ferre and Rigoberta Menchu." In *Violence, Silence, and Anger: Women's Writing as Transgression,* ed. Deirdre Lashgari, 62–79. Charlottesville: University Press of Virginia, 1995.

Hanson, Marsali, Michele Harway, and Nancyann Cervantes. "Therapists' Perceptions of Severity in Cases of Family Violence." *Violence and Victims* 6, no. 3 (1991): 225–35.

Harris, Judith Rich. *The Nurture Assumption: Why Children Turn Out the Way They Do.* New York: Free Press, 1998.

Hart, Barbara. "Coordinated Community Approaches to Domestic Violence." Paper delivered at the Violence against Women Research Strategic Planning Workshop, sponsored by the National Institute of Justice and the Department of Health and Human Services, Washington, D.C., 1995.

Hedges, Elaine, and Shelley Fisher Fishkin. *Listening to Silences: New Essays in Feminist Criticism.* New York: Oxford University Press, 1994.

Heilbrun, Carolyn G. *Writing a Woman's Life.* New York: Ballantine Books, 1989.

Hennessy, Rosemary. *Materialist Feminism and the Politics of Discourse.* New York: Routledge, 1993.

Herman, Judith. *Father-Daughter Incest.* Cambridge: Harvard University Press, 1981.

———. *Trauma and Recovery: The Aftermath of Violence—from Domestic Abuse to Political Terror.* New York: Basic Books, 1992.

Hesford, Wendy S. "Reading *Rape Stories:* Material Rhetoric and the Trauma of Representation." *College English* 62, no. 2 (1999): 192–221.

hooks, bell. *Wounds of Passion: A Writing Life.* New York: Henry Holt, 1997.

Horowitz, Sara R. *Voicing the Void: Muteness and Memory in Holocaust Fiction.* Albany: State University of New York Press, 1997.

Houston, M., and C. Kramarae. "Speaking from Silence: Methods of Silencing and of Resistance." *Discourse and Society* 2, no. 4 (1991): 425–37.

Jones, Ann. *Next Time She'll Be Dead: Battering and How to Stop It.* Boston: Beacon, 1994.

Jones, Ann, and Susan Schechter. *When Love Goes Wrong: What to Do When You Can't Do Anything Right.* New York: HarperCollins, 1993.

Josselson, Ruthellen. *Finding Herself: Pathways to Identity Development in Women.* San Francisco: Jossey-Bass, 1987.

———. "Imagining the Real: Empathy, Narrative, and the Dialogic Self." In *Interpreting Experience,* vol. 3 of *Narrative Study of Lives,* ed. Ruthellen Josselson and Amia Lieblich, 27–44. Newbury Park, Calif.: Sage, 1995.

Josselson, Ruthellen, and Amia Lieblich, eds. *Ethics and Process in the Narrative Study of Lives.* Vol. 4 of *Narrative Study of Lives.* Thousand Oaks, Calif.: Sage, 1996.

———. *Exploring Identity and Gender.* Vol. 2 of *Narrative Study of Lives.* Thousand Oaks, Calif.: Sage, 1994.

———. *Interpreting Experience.* Vol. 3 of *Narrative Study of Lives.* Newbury Park, Calif.: Sage, 1995.

———. *The Narrative Study of Lives.* Vol. 1 of *Narrative Study of Lives.* Newbury Park, Calif.: Sage, 1993.

Kauffman, Linda S., ed. *American Feminist Thought at Century's End: A Reader.* Cambridge, Mass.: Blackwell, 1993.

Kidd, Sue Monk. *The Dance of the Dissident Daughter.* San Francisco: HarperCollins, 1996.

Kingston, Maxine Hong. "No Name Woman." In *The Woman Warrior: Memoirs of a Girlhood among Ghosts,* 3–16. New York: Vintage, 1975.

Kolbenschlag, Madonna. *Kiss Sleeping Beauty Good-Bye: Breaking the Spell of Feminine Myths and Models.* San Francisco: Harper and Row, 1979.

Koss, Mary P., et al. *No Safe Haven: Male Violence against Women at Home, at Work, and in the Community.* Washington, D.C.: American Psychological Association, 1994.

Kristeva, Julia. *Revolution in Poetic Language.* Trans. Margaret Waller. New York: Columbia University Press, 1984.

Kuribayashi, Tomoko, and Julie Tharp, ed. *Creating Safe Space: Violence and Women's Writing.* New York: State University of New York Press, 1998.

Langley, Roger, and Richard C. Levy. *Wife Beating: The Silent Crisis.* New York: E. P. Dutton, 1977.

Lashgari, Deirdre. "Disrupting the Deadly Stillness: Janice Mirikitani's Poetics of Violence." In *Violence, Silence, and Anger: Women's Writing as Transgression,* ed. Deidre Lashgari, 291–304. Charlottesville: University Press of Virginia, 1995.

———. "To Speak the Unspeakable: Implications of Gender, 'Race,' Class, and Culture." Introduction to *Violence, Silence, and Anger: Women's Writing as Transgression,* ed. Deidre Lashgari, 1–21. Charlottesville: University Press of Virginia, 1995.

Lashgari, Deirdre, ed. *Violence, Silence, and Anger: Women's Writing as Transgression.* Charlottesville: University Press of Virginia, 1995.

Lather, Patti, and Chris Smithies. *Troubling the Angels: Women Living with HIV/AIDS.* Boulder, Colo.: Westview Press, 1997.

Lawless, Elaine J. *Holy Women, Wholly Women: Sharing Ministries of Wholeness through Life Stories and Reciprocal Ethnography.* Philadelphia: University of Pennsylvania Press, 1993.

———. *Women Preaching Re-volution: Calling for Connection in a Disconnected Time.* Philadelphia: University of Pennsylvania Press, 1996.

Le Guin, Ursula K. *Dancing at the Edge of the World: Thoughts on Words, Women, Places.* New York: Harper and Row, 1989.

Liebow, Elliot. *Tell Them Who I Am: The Lives of Homeless Women.* New York: Free Press, 1993.

Linde, Charlotte. *Life-Stories: The Creation of Coherence.* New York: Oxford University Press, 1993.

Lorde, Audre. "The Master's Tools Will Never Dismantle the Master's House." In *This Bridge Called My Back: Writings by Radical Women of Color,* ed. Cherrie Moranga and Gloria Anzuldua, 98–101. New York: Kitchen Table Women of Color Press, 1981.

Lyotard, Jean François. *The Postmodern Condition: A Report on Knowledge.* Minneapolis: University of Minnesota Press, 1985.

Maracek, Mary. *Breaking Free from Partner Abuse: Voices of Battered Women Caught in the Cycle of Domestic Violence.* Buena Park, Calif.: Morning Glory Press, 1993.

Marcus, Sharon. "Fighting Bodies, Fighting Words: A Theory and Politics of Rape Prevention." In *Feminists Theorize the Political,* ed. Judith Butler and Joan W. Scott, 385–403. New York: Routledge, 1992.

Marks, Elaine, and Isabelle de Courtivron, eds. *New French Feminisms: An Anthology.* Amherst: University of Massachusetts Press, 1980.

McKay, Matthew, and Patrick Fanning. *Self-Esteem.* 2d ed. Oakland, Calif.: New Harbinger, 1992.

Miller, Alice. *For Your Own Good: Hidden Cruelty in Child-Rearing and the Roots of Violence.* Trans. Hildegarde Hannum and Hunter Hannum. New York: Farrar Straus Giroux, 1983.

Mirikitani, Janice. *Shedding Silence.* Berkeley, Calif.: Celestial Arts, 1987.

Moi, Toril, ed. *French Feminist Thought: A Reader.* Oxford: Basil Blackwell, 1987.

Morrison, Toni. "The Site of Memory." In *Inventing the Truth: The Art and Craft of Memoir,* ed. William Zinsser, 101–24. Boston: Houghton Mifflin, 1987.

———. "Unspeakable Things Unspoken: The Afro-American Presence in American Literature." In *Toni Morrison,* ed. Harold Bloom, 201–30. New York: Chelsea, 1990.

Morton, Nelle. *The Journey Is Home.* Boston: Beacon, 1985.

Naffine, Ngaire. *Feminism and Criminology.* Philadelphia: Temple University Press, 1996.

NiCarthy, G. *Getting Free: A Handbook for Women in Abusive Relationships.* Seattle: Seal Press, 1982.

Nussbaum, Martha C. *Cultivating Humanity: A Classical Defense of Reform in Liberal Education.* Cambridge: Harvard University Press, 1997.

Nye, Andrea. *Words of Power: A Feminist Reading in the History of Logic.* New York: Routledge, 1990.

Olney, James. *Memory and Narrative: The Weave of Life-Writing.* Chicago: University of Chicago Press, 1999.

Olsen, Tillie. *Silences.* New York: Delacorte Press/Seymour Lawrence, 1978.

Orenstein, Peggy. *Schoolgirls: Young Women, Self-Esteem, and the Confidence Gap.* New York: Doubleday, 1994.

Ostriker, Alice. *Writing Like a Woman.* Ann Arbor: University of Michigan Press, 1983.

Pagelow, M. D. *Family Violence.* New York: Praeger, 1984.

Penelope, Julia. *Speaking Freely: Unlearning the Lies of the Father's Tongues.* New York: Pergamon Press, 1990.

Piercy, Marge. "Unlearning to Not Speak." In *Circles on the Water.* New York: Alfred Knopf, 1989.

Pipher, Mary. *Reviving Ophelia: Saving the Selves of Adolescent Girls.* New York: Ballantine, 1994.

Radner, Joan N., and Susan S. Lanser. "Strategies of Coding in Women's Cultures." In *Feminist Messages: Coding in Women's Folk Culture,* ed. Joan Newlon Radner, 1–30. Urbana: University of Illinois Press, 1993.

Reed-Danahay, Deborah E., ed. *Auto/Ethnography: Rewriting the Self and the Social.* Oxford: Berg, 1997.

Reineke, Martha J. *Sacrificed Lives: Kristeva on Women and Violence.* Bloomington: Indiana University Press, 1997.

Reuman, Ann E. " 'Wild Tongues Can't Be Tamed': Gloria Anzaldua's (R)evolution of Voice." In *Violence, Silence, and Anger: Women's Writing as Transgression,* ed. Deirdre Lashgari, 305–22. Charlottesville: University Press of Virginia, 1995.

Robinson, Sally. *Engendering the Subject: Gender and Self-Representation in Contemporary Women's Fiction.* Albany: State University of New York Press, 1991.

Russ, Joanna. *To Write Like a Woman.* Bloomington: Indiana University Press, 1995.

Russell, Diane E. *The Secret Trauma: Incest in the Lives of Girls and Women.* New York: Basic Books, 1986.

Sarbin, Theodore R. *Believed-In Imaginings: The Narrative Construction of Reality.* Washington, D.C.: American Psychological Association, 1998.

Saxton, Ruth O. "Dead Angels: Are We Killing the Mother in the House?" In *Violence, Silence, and Anger: Women's Writing as Transgression,* ed. Deirdre Lashgari, 135–45. Charlottesville: University Press of Virginia, 1995.

Scarry, Elaine. *The Body in Pain: The Making and Unmaking of the World.* New York: Oxford University Press, 1985.

Schafer, Roy. *Retelling a Life: Narration and Dialogue in Psychoanalysis.* New York: Basic Books, 1992.

Schechter, S. *Women and Male Violence: The Visions and Struggles of the Battered Women's Movement.* Boston: South End Press, 1982.

Sipe, Beth, and Evelyn J. Hall. *I Am Not Your Victim: Anatomy of Domestic Violence.* Thousand Oaks, Calif.: Sage, 1996.

Smiley, Pamela. "The Unspeakable: Mary Gordon and the Angry Mother's Voices." In *Violence, Silence, and Anger: Women's Writing as Transgression,* ed. Deirdre Lashgari, 124–34. Charlottesville: University Press of Virginia, 1995.

Sonkin, D. J., ed. *Domestic Violence on Trial: Psychological and Legal Dimensions of Family Violence.* New York: Springer, 1987.

Steinmetz, Suzanne K. *The Cycle of Violence: Assertive, Aggressive, and Abusive Family Interaction.* New York: Praeger, 1977.

Stout, Karen D., and Beverly McPhail. *Confronting Sexism and Violence against Women: A Challenge for Social Work.* New York: Longman, 1998.

Straus, M. A., R. J. Gelles, and S. Steinmetz. *Behind Closed Doors: Violence in the American Family.* New York: Anchor Press, 1980. [Includes an excellent, although somewhat dated, 56-page bibliography on violence in the family and in the workplace.]

Tan, Cheribeth, Joanne Basta, Chris M. Sullivan, and William S. Davidson II. "The Role of Social Support in the Lives of Women Exiting Domestic Violence Shelters: An Experimental Study." *Journal of Interpersonal Violence* 10, no. 4 (1995): 437–51.

Tanner, Laura E. *Intimate Violence: Reading Rape and Torture in Twentieth-Century Fiction.* Bloomington: Indiana University Press, 1994.

Taylor, Jill McLean, Carol Gilligan, and Amy M. Sullivan. *Between Voice and Silence: Women and Girls, Race and Relationship.* Cambridge: Harvard University Press, 1995.

Tomkins, Jane. *A Life in School: What the Teacher Learned.* Reading, Mass.: Perseus Press, 1997.

Trible, Phyllis. *Texts of Terror: Literary-Feminist Readings of Biblical Narratives.* Philadelphia: Fortress Press, 1984.

Walker, Alice. *In Search of Our Mothers' Gardens: Womanist Prose.* San Diego: Harcourt Brace Jovanovich, 1983.

Walker, Lenore E. *The Battered Woman.* New York: Harper and Row, 1979.

———. *The Battered Woman Syndrome.* New York: Springer, 1984.

Watson, Martha. *Lives of Their Own: Rhetorical Dimensions in Autobiographies of Women Activists.* Columbia: University of South Carolina Press, 1999.

Wayne, Linda D. "Silence and Violence: The Woman behind the Wall." In *Women and Language* 19, no. 2 (1996): 1–7.

Widdershoven, Guy A. M. "The Story of Life: Hermeneutic Perspectives on the Relationship between Narrative and Life History." In *The Narrative Study of Lives,* vol. 1 of *Narrative Study of Lives,* ed. Ruthellen Josselson and Amia Lieblich, 1–20. Newbury Park, Calif.: Sage, 1993.

Woolf, Virginia. *A Room of One's Own.* 1929. Reprinted in *The Norton Anthology of Literature by Women: The Tradition in English,* ed. Sandra M. Gilbert and Susan Gubar, 1376–83. New York: Norton, 1985.

Yllo, K., and M. Bograd, eds. *Feminist Perspectives on Wife Abuse.* Newbury Park, Calif.: Sage, 1988.

Index

Abuse, 7, 8, 9; assumption that men will abuse women, 11–12, 14, 45; author's own experiences with, 2, 159; from childhood to marriage, 9, 103; development of in relationships, 124; early abuse, 9–10, 14, 36, 84–87; embedded stories of, 59; examples from shelter, xxi; exposing of, 119; guilt of revealing, 82; in home, 37; hot-line questions about, 39; marriage and, 2; occurrence of, 39; scholarship on, 43; and silencing, 75; spousal, 35; and violent rape, 41, 106–13; of young women, 73–98. *See also* Cycle of abuse; Rape; Sexual abuse

Abusers: bonding out of jail, xix; characteristics of, 12–13; exposing of, 119; interacting with, 5; prosecuting, 5, 41, 50–51

Adolescence, 73–98 *passim*

Advocate, xx. *See also* Shelter workers

AFDC (Aid to Families with Dependent Children), xix, xxi

Austin, John, 38

Bass, Ellen, 82

Battered women, 8, 9, 37, 44; critique of term, 45–46; experiences of, 9; moving beyond position of, 123; prosecuted for fighting back, 12, 22

Batterers, 44. *See also* Abusers

Beauty, societal notions of, 73, 74

Behar, Ruth, 2, 7

Belenky, Mary, 79, 85

Benjamin, Walter, 61–63, 71

Bernard-Donals, Mike, 59–61

Betrayal of trust by authority figures, 82, 89–90

Blanchot, Maurice, 157; contrast with Elaine Scarry, 64; contrast with Jill Kerr Conway, 66–67; critique of, 61–63, 64, 71; and Holocaust memories, 62; Mike

Bernard-Donals on, 59–60; and the unspeakable, 61; *Writing the Disaster,* 60

Brunner, Jerome, 19

Child custody, xix, 5, 31–32, 139

Child Order of Protection, 23–24

Children: abduction of, 36; parents' responsibility for, 11; at shelter, xxi, 22–24, 26, 27, 32, 33, 36

Christianity. *See* Religion

Cisneros, Sandra, 157–58, 159

Conway, Jill Ker, 66, 68

Counselors, xx, 5, 25, 40. *See also* Shelter workers

Court advocate: and court hearings, xx; and ex partes, 52. *See also* Shelter workers

Court clerk, and ex partes, 52

Court system, xv, 5, 11

Crisis calls, 50; and police, 51; potentially harmful, 38–39; and shelter, xvii–xviii, 22, 35–36

Culturally shaped responses, 79

Cycle of abuse, 12–13, 140; as narrative, 12–13, 155, 156; telling stories breaks, 10–11

Cycle of violence. *See* Cycle of abuse

Dalton, Anne, 84

Davis, Laura, 82

Deaf, as shelter clients, 25

De Rivera, Joseph, 85

"Disaster," the, 57–58, 59; essence of, 16, 63; skirting, 61; unspeakability of, 63; and what is "glimpsed," 71; witnessing, 70

Disempowerment through words, 38

Domestic violence, 1, 8, 44; bureau-cracy/business of, 11, 42, 43; critique of term, 45; feminists on, 44; movement, 11; prosecution of and recidivism, 11; research and statistics on, 10, 11, 42, 43, 234; "wife beating," 45. *See also* Abuse; Violence

About the Author

ELAINE J. LAWLESS is Professor of English and Women's Studies at the University of Missouri–Columbia. She is the author of several books, including *Women Preaching Revolution: Calling for Connection in a Disconnected Time.* Lawless is also the new Editor of the *Journal of American Folklore.*